Advanced Information and Knowledge Processing

Series Editors
Professor Lakhmi C. Jain
lakhmi.jain@unisa.edu.au

Professor Xindong Wu
xwu@cems.uvm.edu

For further volumes:
www.springer.com/series/4738

Georg Peters · Pawan Lingras · Dominik Ślęzak ·
Yiyu Yao

Editors

Rough Sets:
Selected Methods
and Applications
in Management
and Engineering

 Springer

Editors
Georg Peters
Munich University of Applied Sciences
Munich, Germany

Pawan Lingras
Department of Mathematics and
Computer Science
St. Mary's University
Halifax, Canada

Dominik Ślęzak
University of Warsaw
Warsaw, Poland

Yiyu Yao
Department of Computer Science
University of Regina
Regina, Canada

ISSN 1610-3947   Advanced Information and Knowledge Processing
ISBN 978-1-4471-2759-8   e-ISBN 978-1-4471-2760-4
DOI 10.1007/978-1-4471-2760-4
Springer London Dordrecht Heidelberg New York

British Library Cataloguing in Publication Data
A catalogue record for this book is available from the British Library

Library of Congress Control Number: 2012932960

Printed on acid-free paper

Springer is part of Springer Science+Business Media (www.springer.com)

Preface

Rough Set Theory was introduced by Pawlak in the early 1980's. In the last quarter century it has become an important part of soft computing and has proved its relevance in many real-world applications.

While initially most of the articles on Rough Sets had been centered on theory, currently the focus of the research has shifted to practical usage of mathematical advances. A state of the art survey on Rough Sets from an application perspective is highly desirable but still missing.

The book is written for business and industry professionals who would like to evaluate the potential of Rough Sets. The intended readership includes (1) managers looking for methods to improve their businesses, (2) researchers in industrial laboratories and think tanks who are investigating new methods to enhance efficiency of their solutions, (3) researchers at universities who want to use Rough Sets to solve real-world problems and seek for guidance on how to describe their ideas in a way understandable for the industry readers.

The approach to Rough Sets presented in the following chapters differs from the most of articles in other publications on this subject. This book focuses on practical use cases backed by sound theory, in contrast to the presentation of a theory applied to a problem. Furthermore, it provides a unified view and easily accessible description of applications.

The book covers methods in data analysis, decision support, as well as management and engineering in order to show the great potential of Rough Sets in almost any domain. The number of real-world applications of Rough Sets has increased significantly and goes probably into hundreds. Hence the book can only give a sample of the selected practically relevant case studies.

The editors of the book would like to acknowledge the authors of all chapters for their excellent contributions. Special thanks go to Mr. Sebastian Widz for his great help with revising and indexing the materials.

Munich, Germany	Georg Peters
Halifax, Canada	Pawan Lingras
Warsaw, Poland	Dominik Ślęzak
Regina, Canada	Yiyu Yao

Contents

Contributors

Haider Banka Department of Computer Science and Engineering, Indian School of Mines, Dhanbad, Jharkhand, India

Parag Bhalchandra School of Computational Sciences, Swami Ramanand Teerth Marathwada University, Nanded, India

Cory Butz Department of Computer Science, University of Regina, Regina, Saskatchewan, Canada

Fernando Crespo Industrial Engineering School, Universidad de Valparaíso, Santiago, Chile

M. Gordon Hunter Faculty of Management, University of Lethbridge, Lethbridge, Alberta, Canada

Pawan Lingras Department of Mathematics and Computer Science, Saint Mary's University, Halifax, Canada; School of Computational Sciences, Swami Ramanand Teerth Marathwada University, Nanded, India

Sushmita Mitra Machine Intelligence Unit, Indian Statistical Institute, Kolkata, India

Georg Peters Department of Computer Science and Mathematics, Munich University of Applied Sciences, Munich, Germany

James F. Peters Computational Intelligence Laboratory, Department of Electrical and Computer Engineering, University of Manitoba, Winnipeg, MB, Canada

Sheela Ramanna Department of Applied Computer Science, University of Winnipeg, Winnipeg, MB, Canada; Computational Intelligence Laboratory, Department of Electrical and Computer Engineering, University of Manitoba, Winnipeg, MB, Canada

Beata Sikora Institute of Mathematics, Silesian University of Technology, Gliwice, Poland

Marek Sikora Institute of Innovative Technologies EMAG, Katowice, Poland; Institute of Informatics, Silesian University of Technology, Gliwice, Poland

Dominik Ślęzak Institute of Mathematics, University of Warsaw, Warsaw, Poland; Infobright Inc., Poland, Warsaw, Poland

Roger Tagg School of Computer and Information Science, University of South Australia, Adelaide, Australia

Richard Weber Department of Industrial Engineering, Universidad de Chile, Santiago, Chile

Sebastian Widz Systems Research Institute, Polish Academy of Sciences, Warsaw, Poland; XPLUS SA, Warsaw, Poland

Yiyu Yao Department of Computer Science, University of Regina, Regina, Saskatchewan, Canada

Part I
Foundations of Rough Sets

An Introduction to Rough Sets

Yiyu Yao and Dominik Ślęzak

Abstract Fundamental philosophy, concepts and notions of rough set theory (RST) are reviewed. Emphasis is on a constructive formulation and interpretation of rough set approximations. We restrict our discussions to classical RST introduced by Pawlak, with some brief references to the existing extensions. Whenever possible, we provide multiple equivalent definitions of fundamental RST notions in order to better illustrate their usefulness. We also refer to principles of RST based data analysis that can be used to mine data gathered in information tables.

1 Introduction

Rough set theory (RST) provides a mathematical formalism and means for representing and analyzing data [1–4]. Several unique features of the theory make it attractive to practitioners. RST is simple, elegant and, at the same time, flexible. It has been successfully applied in many areas, including those described in this book [5–10], as well as many others [11–14].

It is also worth mentioning that quite a few RST based data analysis software packages have been developed, including LERS,[1] ROSETTA,[2] RSES[3]/RSES-lib[4]

---

[1]http://lightning.eecs.ku.edu/LERS.html.

[2]http://www.lcb.uu.se/tools/rosetta/.

[3]http://logic.mimuw.edu.pl/~rses/.

[4]http://rseslib.mimuw.edu.pl/.

Y. Yao (✉)
Department of Computer Science, University of Regina, Regina, Saskatchewan, Canada S4S 0A2
e-mail: yyao@cs.uregina.ca

D. Ślęzak
Institute of Mathematics, University of Warsaw, Banacha 2, 02-097 Warsaw, Poland
e-mail: slezak@mimuw.edu.pl

D. Ślęzak
Infobright Inc., Poland, Krzywickiego 34 pok. 219, 02-078 Warsaw, Poland
e-mail: slezak@infobright.com

G. Peters et al. (eds.), *Rough Sets: Selected Methods and Applications in Management and Engineering*, Advanced Information and Knowledge Processing,
DOI 10.1007/978-1-4471-2760-4_1, © Springer-Verlag London Limited 2012

and RoughICE.[5] One can apply them to mine data sets in a tabular form, which can be easily extracted from a relational database or derived using some extraction and transformation techniques.

RST leads toward a unique methodology of intelligent knowledge discovery. It may be useful in, for instance, categorization, approximation, concept formation and inductive learning [15–18]. In this chapter, we focus on the following aspects related to the foundations of RST:

- Description of concepts using a decision logic language.
- Discernibility of objects based on equivalence relations.
- Rough set approximations of sets and concepts.
- Dependencies between subsets of attributes.

We demonstrate basic notions and ideas through examples. A reader interested in more details is referred to the seminal book by Pawlak [2].

2 Objects and Concepts

RST uses a simple knowledge and data representation scheme called an information table (or an information system [19]). Two important notions related to the analysis of data gathered in information tables are the decision logic language and the indiscernibility of objects.

2.1 Information Tables

It is usually assumed that an information table contains a finite set of objects described by using a finite set of attributes.

Definition 1 An information table is a tuple:

$$M = (U, At, \{V_a | a \in At\}, \{I_a | a \in At\}), \tag{1}$$

where U is a finite nonempty set of objects, At is a finite nonempty set of attributes, V_a is a nonempty set of values for an attribute $a \in At$, and $I_a : U \longrightarrow V_a$ is an information function, which maps objects in U into values in V_a.

The value of an object $x \in U$ on an attribute $a \in At$ is denoted by $I_a(x)$. In general, for a subset of attributes $A \subseteq At$, we use $I_A(x)$ to denote the vector of values of x on A.

The notion of an information table can be extended in many ways. As an example of such extension, consider the notion of a decision table (or a classification table) as

---

[5]http://www.mimuw.edu.pl/~bazan/roughice/?sLang=en.

Table 1 An information
table

	a	b	c	d
o_1	0	0	1	+
o_2	0	0	1	+
o_3	0	1	0	−
o_4	1	0	0	+
o_5	1	0	1	+
o_6	1	1	2	+
o_7	1	2	1	−
o_8	1	2	1	−
o_9	1	2	1	−

a special information table in which the set of attributes is divided into two disjoint subsets called condition attributes C and decision (or classification) attributes D, namely, $At = C \cup D$ and $C \cap D = \emptyset$.

Example 1 Consider an information table illustrated by Table 1, in which rows represent objects and columns represent attributes. The set of objects is given by $U = \{o_1, o_2, \ldots, o_9\}$, the set of attributes by $At = \{a, b, c, d\}$, and the sets of attribute values are $V_a = \{0, 1\}$, $V_b = \{0, 1, 2\}$, $V_c = \{0, 1, 2\}$ and $V_d = \{-, +\}$. Each cell in the information table is a value of an object on an attribute. For instance, we have $I_a(o_1) = 0$, $I_d(o_3) = -$, and so on. We have also $I_{\{a,b\}}(o_1) = (0, 0)$, $I_{\{b,c,d\}}(o_2) = (0, 1, +)$ and so on. We can divide the set of attributes into two disjoint sets $C = \{a, b, c\}$ and $D = \{d\}$ to produce a decision table, where C is the set of three condition attributes and D is the set containing a single decision attribute.

Another possible aspect of extending the original notion of an information table relates to the values of attributes. If the information function I_a is a partial function, i.e., it is not defined or missing for certain objects, we obtain an incomplete information table [20]. If I_a maps an object to a subset of attribute values, we obtain a set-valued information table [21]. Some authors go even further and, for example, combine the set-valued and interval-valued attributes within the framework of incomplete information databases [22]. In this chapter, for the sake of clarity, we only consider the simplest case of complete information tables. However, various extensions may be useful for specific applications, without sacrificing the important advantage of clarity of RST.

2.2 Decision Logic Language

One of the key aspects of RST relates to the notion of a concept. There are many ways of interpreting concepts [4]. We adopt the view of representing a concept jointly by a pair of intension and extension [23]. The intension (also called the description) is an intrinsic property of a concept, based on which one can determine if an object is an instance of the concept. The extension (also called the support) is the set of instances of a concept. Orłowska [24] and Pawlak [2] use a decision logic language $\mathcal{L}$ in order to define concepts in information tables. The intension and extension of a concept can be precisely defined as a formula in $\mathcal{L}$ and the meaning of this formula, respectively [17].

Definition 2 A decision logic language $\mathcal{L}$ in an information table can be defined as follows. An atomic formula is given by a descriptor $(a = v)$, where $a \in At$ and $v \in V_a$. Additional formulas of $\mathcal{L}$ are constructed recursively. If ϕ and ψ are in $\mathcal{L}$, then $\neg(\phi)$, $(\phi \wedge \psi)$, $(\phi \vee \psi)$, $(\phi \rightarrow \psi)$, and $(\phi \leftrightarrow \psi)$ are in $\mathcal{L}$.

In some applications, it is enough to use only a subset of logic operators. For example, one may use the set of operators $\{\wedge, \vee\}$ or $\{\wedge\}$. In general, usage of the decision logic language while formulating knowledge derived from data puts RST based data analysis into a wider category of symbolic machine learning techniques aimed at describing things in a user friendly fashion [1, 25].

One may also consider different forms of descriptors, depending on the types of attributes. For instance, in case of the set-valued and interval-valued attributes (see Sect. 2.1), it might be reasonable to consider inclusion or overlap instead of equality in $(a = v)$. Other examples may include descriptors with inequality operators for attributes with ordered domains of values [26, 27] or descriptors based on degrees of similarity and closeness [18, 28]. In this chapter, we restrict ourselves to the simplest equality based descriptors.

Formulas in $\mathcal{L}$ are interpreted based on the notion of satisfiability. For a formula ϕ, by $x \models \phi$ we denote that the object x satisfies ϕ.

Definition 3 The satisfiability of any formula is defined recursively as follows:

(0). $x \models (a = v)$ iff $I_a(x) = v$,
(1). $x \models \neg(\phi)$ iff not $x \models \phi$,
(2). $x \models (\phi \wedge \psi)$ iff $x \models \phi$ and $x \models \psi$,
(3). $x \models (\phi \vee \psi)$ iff $x \models \phi$ or $x \models \psi$,
(4). $x \models (\phi \rightarrow \psi)$ iff $x \models \neg\phi \vee \psi$,
(5). $x \models (\phi \leftrightarrow \psi)$ iff $x \models \phi \rightarrow \psi$ and $x \models \psi \rightarrow \phi$.

Definition 4 If ϕ is a formula, the set $m(\phi)$ defined by:

$$m(\phi) = \{x \in U \mid x \models \phi\}, \tag{2}$$

is called the meaning of the formula ϕ in an information table.

The meaning of a formula ϕ is indeed a set of all objects having the properties expressed by the formula ϕ. This way, a connection between formulas and subsets of U is established. The meanings of formulas can be computed recursively as well, by drawing a correspondence between the logic and set operators.

The decision logic language $\mathcal{L}$ provides a formal description of concepts. A concept in an information table is represented as a pair $(\phi, m(\phi))$, where $\phi \in \mathcal{L}$ and $m(\phi) \subseteq U$. The formula ϕ is a description of $m(\phi)$ in M, i.e., the intension of concept $(\phi, m(\phi))$, and $m(\phi)$ is the set of objects satisfying ϕ, namely, the extension of $(\phi, m(\phi))$. The outcomes of RST based learning processes can be precisely formulated based on formal representation of concepts.

Example 2 Consider the information table given in Table 1. Consider the following formulas: $a = 0$, $a = 1$, $b = 1$, $a = 0 \wedge b = 1$, $a = 0 \vee b = 1$, and $a = 1 \wedge \neg(b = 1)$. Their meaning sets are as follows:

$$m(a = 0) = \{o_1, o_2, o_3\},$$

$$m(b = 1) = \{o_3, o_6\},$$

$$m(a = 0 \wedge b = 1) = m(a = 0) \cap m(b = 1) = \{o_3\},$$

$$m(a = 1) = \{o_4, o_5, o_6, o_7, o_8, o_9\},$$

$$m(a = 0 \vee b = 1) = m(a = 0) \cup m(b = 1) = \{o_1, o_2, o_3, o_6\},$$

$$m(a = 1 \wedge \neg(b = 1)) = m(a = 1) \cap (m(b = 1))^c = \{o_4, o_5, o_7, o_8, o_9\}.$$

They define the following concepts in the information table:

$$(a = 0, \{o_1, o_2, o_3\}),$$

$$(b = 1, \{o_3, o_6\}),$$

$$(a = 0 \wedge b = 1, \{o_3\}),$$

$$(a = 1, \{o_4, o_5, o_6, o_7, o_8, o_9\}),$$

$$(a = 0 \vee b = 1, \{o_1, o_2, o_3, o_6\}),$$

$$(a = 1 \wedge \neg(b = 1), \{o_4, o_5, o_7, o_8, o_9\}).$$

The explicit expression of a concept as a pair of a formula and a set of objects, enables us to analyze an information table in both logic and set-theoretic terms. For example, we can refer to the concept $(a = 0, \{o_1, o_2, o_3\})$ by either the formula $a = 0$ or the set of objects $\{o_1, o_2, o_3\}$. Of course the same set of objects can be obtained using many formulas.

In RST based data analysis, one often considers only a subset of attributes $A \subseteq At$, i.e., only attributes from A are used in forming formulas of the logic language. We use $\mathcal{L}(A)$ to denote the language defined using only attributes from A. All notions introduced so far for $\mathcal{L}$ can be reformulated for $\mathcal{L}(A)$.

2.3 Indiscernibility Relations

Indiscernibility is another fundamental notion or RST. By the indiscernibility of objects, one can granulate the universe into subsets of objects.

Definition 5 For a subset of attributes $A \subseteq At$, we can define an indiscernibility relation $IND(A)$ as follows:

$$x\,IND(A)y \iff \forall_{a \in A}(I_a(x) = I_a(y))$$
$$\iff I_A(x) = I_A(y). \tag{3}$$

Two objects are indiscernible with respect to a subset of attributes A if they have the same values on every $a \in A$. It can be verified that $IND(A)$ is reflexive, symmetric, and transitive, namely, $IND(A)$ is an equivalence relation on U. $IND(A)$ induces a partition of U, denoted by $U/IND(A)$ or U/A. Let

$$[x]_{IND(A)} = [x]_A = \{y \in U \mid x\,IND(A)y\} \tag{4}$$

denote the equivalence class of $IND(A)$ that contains x. The partition is given by $U/A = U/IND(A) = \{[x]_A \mid x \in U\}$.

The notion of indiscernibility can be extended in many ways. Extensions may be required to address the need of dealing with non-standard values (see Sect. 2.1) and non-standard descriptors (see Sect. 2.2) that are supposed to correspond to indiscernibility classes. We refer a reader to some tolerance based and fuzzy based generalizations considered in, e.g. [29, 30].

Let us focus on the simplest type of indiscernibility. The set inclusion of equivalence relations defines a partial order on the set of all partitions.

Definition 6 A partial order called refinement-coarsening relation on the set of all partitions of U is defined according to set inclusion of the corresponding equivalence relations as follows: for two relations E and E' on U,

$$U/E \preceq U/E' \iff E \subseteq E', \tag{5}$$

i.e., each block of U/E' is the union of some blocks of U/E. Thus, U/E is called a refinement of U/E' and U/E' is called a coarsening of U/E.

Different subsets of attributes may define different equivalence relations. Equivalence relations defined by single attributes play an important role, as they can be used to construct equivalence relations defined by any subset of attributes. For a subset of attributes $A \subseteq At$ and $x \in U$, we have:

$$IND(A) = \bigcap_{a \in A} IND(\{a\}), \qquad [x]_A = \bigcap_{a \in A} [x]_{\{a\}}. \tag{6}$$

For two subsets of attributes $A, A' \subseteq At$ and $x \in U$, we have:

$$\mathrm{IND}(A \cup A') = \mathrm{IND}(A) \cap \mathrm{IND}(A'), \qquad [x]_{A \cup A'} = [x]_A \cap [x]_{A'}. \qquad (7)$$

The partial order $\preceq$ on partitions defined by subsets of attributes is related to set-inclusion of attributes, that is, for $A, A' \subseteq At$ and $x \in U$, we have:

$$A \subseteq A' \implies U/A' \preceq U/A \wedge [x]_{A'} \subseteq [x]_A. \qquad (8)$$

That is, the refinement-coarsening relation $\preceq$ is monotonic with respect to set inclusion of subsets of attributes.

Example 3 Consider again Table 1. The partitions induced by subsets of attributes $\{a\}, \{b\}, \{c\}, \{a, b\}$ and $\{a, b, c\}$ are given by:

$$U/\{a\} = \{\{o_1, o_2, o_3\}, \{o_4, o_5, o_6, o_7, o_8, o_9\}\},$$

$$U/\{b\} = \{\{o_1, o_2, o_4, o_5\}, \{o_3, o_6\}, \{o_7, o_8, o_9\}\},$$

$$U/\{c\} = \{\{o_1, o_2, o_5, o_7, o_8, o_9\}, \{o_3, o_4\}, \{o_6\}\},$$

$$U/\{a, b\} = \{\{o_1, o_2\}, \{o_3\}, \{o_4, o_5\}, \{o_6\}, \{o_7, o_8, o_9\}\},$$

$$U/\{a, b, c\} = \{\{o_1, o_2\}, \{o_3\}, \{o_4\}, \{o_5\}, \{o_6\}, \{o_7, o_8, o_9\}\}.$$

It can be verified that $U/\{a, b, c\} \preceq U/\{a, b\} \preceq U/\{a\}$. For example, for object o_1, we have:

$$[o_1]_{\{a,b,c\}} = [o_1]_{\{a\}} \cap [o_1]_{\{b\}} \cap [o_1]_{\{c\}}$$

$$= \{o_1, o_2, o_3\} \cap \{o_1, o_2, o_4, o_5\} \cap \{o_1, o_2, o_5, o_7, o_8, o_9\}$$

$$= \{o_1, o_2\}.$$

2.4 Definable Sets

For a given formula, one can obtain a unique subset of U as its meaning set. In contrast, one may not find a formula that produces a given subset of U. As already mentioned, it may also happen that some subsets of U have multiple representations in $\mathcal{L}$.

Example 4 In Table 1, the subset of objects $\{o_1, o_2, o_3\}$ is the meaning set of several formulas, such as: $a = 0$, $a = 0 \wedge b = 0 \vee a = 0 \wedge b = 1$, and $a = 0 \wedge c = 1 \vee b = 1 \wedge c = 0$. That is, the set of objects $\{o_1, o_2, o_3\}$ has multiple representations in terms of logic formulas. On the other hand, it is impossible to find a formula whose meaning set is $\{o_2, o_3\}$.

Definition 7 A subset $X \subseteq U$ is called a definable set in an information table if there exists a formula ϕ in the logic language $\mathcal{L}$ such that $m(\phi) = X$; otherwise, X is undefinable. A subset $X \subseteq U$ is called a conditionally definable set with respect to a subset of attributes $A \subseteq At$ if there exists ϕ in the logic language $\mathcal{L}(A)$ such that $m(\phi) = X$; otherwise, X is conditionally undefinable.

A definable set may be viewed as a conditionally definable set with respect to the entire set of attributes, i.e., $A = At$. Let

$$\mathrm{DEF}_A(U) = \{m(\phi) \mid \phi \in \mathcal{L}(A)\} \tag{9}$$

denote the set of all definable sets with respect to attributes $A \subseteq At$. It is important to study the structure of $\mathrm{DEF}_A(U)$. Consider the empty set $\emptyset$. By the definition of an information table, we have $m(a = v \wedge \neg(a = v)) = \emptyset$. Hence $\emptyset \in \mathrm{DEF}_A(U)$. Consider the equivalence class $[x]_A$, $x \in U$. We have $m(\bigwedge_{a \in A} a = I_a(x)) = [x]_A$. Thus, $[x]_A \in \mathrm{DEF}_A(U)$. In fact, $[x]_A$ is a minimal nonempty definable set in $\mathrm{DEF}_A(U)$. $\mathrm{DEF}_A(U)$ is also closed under set complement, intersection and union. In summary, $(\mathrm{DEF}_A(U), ^c, \cap, \cup, \emptyset, U)$ is an atomic Boolean algebra with the minimum element $\emptyset$, the maximum element U, and the set of atoms corresponding to U/A.

One may say that a decision logic language and the indiscernibility relation provide two ways for characterizing subsets of a universe, through definable sets in the former and indiscernibility classes in the latter. The families of all definable sets and all indiscernibility classes form the basic ingredients of RST based data analysis. Let us note that definable sets can be equivalently expressed as unions of some subsets of U/A, that is:

$$\mathrm{DEF}_A(U) = \left\{ \bigcup F \mid F \subseteq U/A \right\}. \tag{10}$$

It may be useful to operate exchangeably with formulations (9) and (10) while considering both foundations and applications of RST.

Example 5 Consider the set of attributes $A = \{a, b\}$ in Table 1. The atoms of the Boolean algebra $(\mathrm{DEF}_A(U), ^c, \cap, \cup, \emptyset, U)$ are as follows:

$$U/\{a, b\} = \{\{o_1, o_2\}, \{o_3\}, \{o_4, o_5\}, \{o_6\}, \{o_7, o_8, o_9\}\}.$$

Equivalence class $[o_1]_A = [o_2]_A = \{o_1, o_2\}$ is defined by a formula $a = 0 \wedge b = 0$, equivalence class $[o_3]_A = \{o_3\}$ is defined by a formula $a = 0 \wedge b = 1$, equivalence class $[o_4]_A = [o_5]_A = \{o_4, o_5\}$ is defined by a formula $a = 1 \wedge b = 0$, and so on. The family of all definable sets takes the following form:

$\mathrm{DEF}_A(U) = \{\emptyset,$

// 1 atom $\{o_1, o_2\}, \{o_3\}, \{o_4, o_5\}, \{o_6\}, \{o_7, o_8, o_9\},$

// 2 atoms $\{o_1, o_2, o_3\}, \{o_1, o_2, o_4, o_5\}, \{o_1, o_2, o_6\}, \{o_1, o_2, o_7, o_8, o_9\},$
            $\{o_3, o_4, o_5\}, \{o_3, o_6\}, \{o_3, o_7, o_8, o_9\}, \{o_4, o_5, o_6\},$
            $\{o_4, o_5, o_7, o_8, o_9\}, \{o_6, o_7, o_8, o_9\},$

// 3 atoms $\{o_1, o_2, o_3, o_4, o_5\}, \{o_1, o_2, o_3, o_6\}, \{o_1, o_2, o_3, o_7, o_8, o_9\},$
            $\{o_1, o_2, o_4, o_5, o_6\}, \{o_1, o_2, o_4, o_5, o_7, o_8, o_9\},$
            $\{o_1, o_2, o_6, o_7, o_8, o_9\}, \{o_3, o_4, o_5, o_6\}, \{o_3, o_4, o_5, o_7, o_8, o_9\},$
            $\{o_3, o_6, o_7, o_8, o_9\}, \{o_4, o_5, o_6, o_7, o_8, o_9\},$

// 4 atoms $\{o_1, o_2, o_3, o_4, o_5, o_6\}, \{o_1, o_2, o_3, o_4, o_5, o_7, o_8, o_9\},$
            $\{o_1, o_2, o_3, o_6, o_7, o_8, o_9\}, \{o_1, o_2, o_4, o_5, o_6, o_7, o_8, o_9\},$
            $\{o_3, o_4, o_5, o_6, o_7, o_8, o_9\},$

// 5 atoms $U\}.$

Each definable set can be expressed as a union of some equivalence classes. For example, $\{o_1, o_2, o_3, o_4, o_5\} = \{o_1, o_2\} \cup \{o_3\} \cup \{o_4, o_5\}$ is described by a formula $(a = 0 \wedge b = 1) \vee (a = 0 \wedge b = 1) \vee (a = 1 \wedge b = 0)$, which is a disjunction of formulas defining three equivalence classes $\{o_1, o_2\}$, $\{o_3\}$ and $\{o_4, o_5\}$. In contrast, an undefinable set cannot be expressed this way.

3 Rough Set Approximations

Approximations of sets are the fundamental construct that distinguishes RST from other approaches. They are very important for applications developed within the standard RST based data analysis [31], as well as for other examples of employing RST, such as rough clustering [32], granular database engines [33] and complex pattern learning based on domain knowledge [15].

3.1 Approximations of a Single Set

Each definable set can be represented by a logic formula and hence we can make inference about definable sets. On the other hand, we cannot find a formula to represent an undefinable set. In order to make inference about undefinable sets, RST considers an approximation of an undefinable set by definable sets. More specifically, one can approximate the undefinable set from the below and the above by using two definable sets. By properties of the set of all definable sets, such approximations are unique.

With respect to a subset of attributes $A \subseteq At$, one can either define a logic language or an equivalence relation. As already mentioned, both of them produce the same definable sets in an information table. Thus, it is reasonable to apply atomic definable sets corresponding to the elements of U/A to approximate other sets. This idea can be formalized using the notion of an approximation space $apr_A = (U, \mathrm{IND}(A))$ (or $apr_A = (U, \mathrm{DEF}_A(U)))$ [1, 2].

Below, if a subset of attributes A is understood, we may drop it by simply writing $apr = (U, \mathrm{IND})$ or $apr = (U, \mathrm{DEF})$.

Definition 8 In an approximation space $apr = (U, \mathrm{IND})$, a pair of lower and upper approximations of a subset $X \subseteq U$ is defined by

$$\underline{apr}(X) = \text{the largest definable set in } \mathrm{DEF}(U) \text{ that is contained by } X,$$
$$\overline{apr}(X) = \text{the smallest definable set in } \mathrm{DEF}(U) \text{ that contains } X. \tag{11}$$

Example 6 Consider Table 1. The set of decision attribute $D = \{d\}$ produces a partition $U/D = \{X_1 = m(d = +) = \{o_1, o_2, o_4, o_5, o_6\}, X_2 = m(d = -) = \{o_3, o_7, o_8, o_9\}\}$. The set of attributes $\{a, b\}$ gives rise to an approximation space $apr_{\{a,c\}}$. The approximations of the two sets X_1 and X_2 are given by:

$$\underline{apr}_{\{a,c\}}(X_1) = \{o_1, o_2, o_4, o_6\}, \qquad \underline{apr}_{\{a,c\}}(X_2) = \{o_3\},$$
$$\overline{apr}_{\{a,c\}}(X_1) = \{o_1, o_2, o_4, o_5, o_6, o_7, o_8, o_9\},$$
$$\overline{apr}_{\{a,c\}}(X_2) = \{o_3, o_5, o_7, o_8, o_9\}.$$

Lower and upper approximations may be expressed also in other forms [34], which are convenient when seeking for analogies between RST and other approaches to data analysis and knowledge representation.

Definition 9 In an approximation space $apr = (U, \mathrm{IND})$, approximations can be expressed in one of the following three equivalent ways:

– Element based definition

$$\underline{apr}(X) = \{x \mid x \in U, [x]_{\mathrm{IND}} \subseteq X\}$$
$$= \{x \mid x \in U, \forall y \in U (x \, \mathrm{IND} \, y \Longrightarrow y \in X)\},$$
$$\overline{apr}(X) = \{x \mid x \in U, [x]_{\mathrm{IND}} \cap X \neq \emptyset\}$$
$$= \{x \mid x \in U, \exists y \in U (x \, \mathrm{IND} \, y, y \in X)\}; \tag{12}$$

– Granule based definition

$$\underline{apr}(X) = \bigcup \{[x]_{\mathrm{IND}} \mid [x]_{\mathrm{IND}} \in U/\mathrm{IND}, [x]_{\mathrm{IND}} \subseteq X\},$$
$$\overline{apr}(X) = \bigcup \{[x]_{\mathrm{IND}} \mid [x]_{\mathrm{IND}} \in U/\mathrm{IND}, [x]_{\mathrm{IND}} \cap A \neq \emptyset\}; \tag{13}$$

– Subsystem based definition

$$\underline{apr}(X) = \bigcup \{Y \mid Y \in \mathrm{DEF}(U), Y \subseteq X\},$$
$$\overline{apr}(X) = \bigcap \{Y \mid X \in \mathrm{DEF}(U), X \subseteq Y\}. \tag{14}$$

It is convenient to operate with the above three formalizations exchangeably when applying and extending the original notions of RST. For instance, different definitions of approximations provide different means for handling information tables with missing values [35]. For the case of complete information tables, lower and upper approximations satisfy the following properties:

(L0)	$\underline{apr}(X) \in \text{DEF}(U)$	(U0)	$\overline{apr}(X) \in \text{DEF}(U)$
(L1)	$X \in \text{DEF}(U) \Longrightarrow \underline{apr}(X) = X$	(U1)	$X \in \text{DEF}(U) \Longrightarrow \overline{apr}(X) = X$
(L2)	$\underline{apr}(X) \subseteq X$	(U2)	$X \subseteq \overline{apr}(X)$
(L3)	$\underline{apr}(X) = (\overline{apr}(X^c))^c$	(U3)	$\overline{apr}(X) = (\underline{apr}(X^c))^c$
(L4)	$\underline{apr}(X \cap Y) = \underline{apr}(X) \cap \underline{apr}(Y)$	(U4)	$\overline{apr}(X \cup Y) = \overline{apr}(X) \cup \overline{apr}(Y)$
(L5)	$\underline{apr}(X \cup Y) \supseteq \underline{apr}(X) \cup \underline{apr}(Y)$	(U5)	$\overline{apr}(X \cap Y) \subseteq \overline{apr}(X) \cap \overline{apr}(Y)$
(L6)	$X \subseteq Y \Longrightarrow \underline{apr}(X) \subseteq \underline{apr}(Y)$	(U6)	$X \subseteq Y \Longrightarrow \overline{apr}(X) \subseteq \overline{apr}(Y)$
(L7)	$\underline{apr}(X) = \underline{apr}(\underline{apr}(X))$	(U7)	$\overline{apr}(\overline{apr}(X)) = \overline{apr}(X)$
(L8)	$\overline{apr}(X) = \underline{apr}(\overline{apr}(X))$	(U8)	$\overline{apr}(\underline{apr}(X)) = \underline{apr}(X)$

Properties (L0) and (U0) state that approximations of a set are definable sets. They imply properties (L1) and (U1), namely, the approximations of a definable set are the set itself. In general, according to Properties (L2) and (U2), a set falls within its lower and upper approximations, namely, $\underline{apr}(X) \subseteq X \subseteq \overline{apr}(X)$. Properties (L3) and (U3) state that lower and upper approximations are a pair of dual operators $\underline{apr}, \overline{apr} : 2^U \longrightarrow 2^U$ [36]. Hence, properties labeled by the same number may be interpreted as dual ones. The remaining properties formalize other important aspects of RST such as, for instance, monotonicity of approximation operators with respect to set inclusion or stability of outcomes of chains of successive approximations.

3.2 Rough Set Regions for a Single Set

Rough set approximations are often rephrased in terms of positive, negative and boundary regions, which gather objects (or rather some classes or granules of objects) that, respectively, certainly satisfy, certainly do not satisfy, and maybe (do not) satisfy the concepts represented by subsets of universe. Such regions are very useful in RST based decision making [37] and many other rough set applications, such as already mentioned granular database architecture [33], where, in a sense, only boundary related blocks of data need to be accessed to execute some common types of analytic SQL statements.

Definition 10 Based on lower and upper approximations, one can divide the universe U into the following positive, boundary and negative regions:

$$\text{POS}(X) = \underline{apr}(X),$$
$$\text{BND}(X) = \overline{apr}(X) - \underline{apr}(X), \qquad (15)$$
$$\text{NEG}(X) = (\overline{apr}(X))^c.$$

It is worth remembering that the above representations may not be equivalent any longer for some extensions of standard RST notions briefly mentioned in Sect. 2. However, in both of above cases, $\{POS(X), BND(X), NEG(X)\}$ forms a partition of the universe U.

Example 7 Let us continue Example 6. For the set of decision attributes $D = \{d\}$ and its corresponding partition classes X_1 and X_2, the set of attributes $\{a, b\}$ induces the following regions:

$$POS_{\{a,c\}}(X_1) = \{o_1, o_2, o_4, o_6\}, \qquad POS_{\{a,c\}}(X_2) = \{o_3\},$$
$$BND_{\{a,c\}}(X_1) = \{o_5, o_7, o_8, o_9\}, \qquad BND_{\{a,c\}}(X_2) = \{o_5, o_7, o_8, o_9\},$$
$$NEG_{\{a,c\}}(X_1) = \{o_3\}, \qquad NEG_{\{a,c\}}(X_2) = \{o_1, o_2, o_4, o_6\}.$$

One can notice a kind of duality of regions in the case of two sets that are complementary to each other. The situation gets more complicated when the number of classes increases. In such cases one may consider using, for example, generalized decision functions introduced into RST for the purpose of dealing simultaneously with larger collections of sets to be approximated [3].

The above-introduced regions can be employed to build the following representations of the approximated sets, which—although mathematically equivalent—support different intuitions of reasoning about data:

(i) $(POS(X), BND(X), NEG(X))$
(ii) $(POS(X), POS(X) \cup BND(X))$
(iii) $(POS(X), BND(X))$
(iv) $(POS(X), NEG(X))$

Representation (ii) is the pair of rough set approximations. Representations (iii) and (iv) emphasize the roles of boundary and negative regions, respectively. It is also worth mentioning about some useful extensions of regions and approximations based on combination of standard rough set methodology with, for instance, probability calculus [38, 39] and fuzzy sets [30, 40].

3.3 Approximations and Regions of a Partition

The approximation of a set can be easily extended to the approximation of a partition, also called a classification [2].

Definition 11 Let $\pi = \{X_1, \ldots, X_n\}$ be a partition of the universe U. Its approximations can be defined as the families of approximations of particular partition classes:

$$\underline{apr}(\pi) = \{\underline{apr}(X_1), \ldots, \underline{apr}(X_n)\},$$
$$\overline{apr}(\pi) = \{\overline{apr}(X_1), \ldots, \overline{apr}(X_n)\}.$$
(16)

It can be easily verified that $\underline{apr}(X_i) \cap \overline{apr}(X_j) = \emptyset$, $i \neq j$.

Definition 12 Positive, boundary and negative regions can be extended using the following formulas:

$$\text{POS}(\pi) = \bigcup\{\underline{apr}(X_i)\} = \bigcup\{\text{POS}(X_i)\},$$

$$\text{BND}(\pi) = \bigcup\{\overline{apr}(X_i) - \underline{apr}(X_i)\} = \bigcup\{\text{BND}(X_i)\}, \qquad (17)$$

$$\text{NEG}(\pi) = \left(\bigcup\{\overline{apr}(X_i)\}\right)^c = (\text{POS}(\pi) \cup \text{BND}(\pi))^c = \emptyset.$$

We have $\text{POS}(\pi) \cap \text{BND}(\pi) = \emptyset$ and $\text{POS}(\pi) \cup \text{BND}(\pi) = U$. That is, the positive region and boundary region form another partition of the universe.

In practice, as one could see in previous examples, we are usually interested in approximations and regions of partitions $\pi = U/D$ corresponding to decision attributes. It is related to applications of RST in supervised learning of classification models [16] and optimizing decision support systems [41].

Example 8 Continued with Examples 6 and 7, the approximations of the partition U/D in the approximation space $apr_{\{a,c\}}$ are given by:

$$\underline{apr}_{\{a,c\}}(U/D) = \{\{o_1, o_2, o_4, o_6\}, \{o_3\}\},$$

$$\overline{apr}_{\{a,c\}}(U/D) = \{\{o_1, o_2, o_4, o_5, o_6, o_7, o_8, o_9\}, \{o_3, o_5, o_7, o_8, o_9\}\}.$$

The two nonempty regions are:

$$\text{POS}_{\{a,c\}}(U/D) = \{o_1, o_2, o_3, o_4, o_6\},$$

$$\text{BND}_{\{a,c\}}(U/D) = \{o_5, o_7, o_8, o_9\}.$$

The sizes of approximations and regions can give us some feeling about the degrees of determining decision attributes by the subsets of condition attributes. This topic is further studied in Sect. 4. However, one can also investigate arbitrary pairs of subsets of attributes, which leads to a rough set based framework for considering functional dependencies in information tables [42, 43].

4 Uncertainty Measures

Two classes of uncertainty measures are reviewed. One of them deals with approximations of a single set and the other—with approximations of a partition. The considered measures can be used to evaluate approximations while searching for the best rough set based description of an information table.

4.1 Accuracy and Roughness

Pawlak [1, 2] suggests two numerical measures for characterizing the imprecision of rough set approximations.

Definition 13 Let an approximation space $apr = (U, \text{IND})$ and a subset $X \subseteq U$ be given. The accuracy measure of X in apr is defined as follows:

$$\alpha(X) = \frac{|\underline{apr}(X)|}{|\overline{apr}(X)|}, \tag{18}$$

where $|\cdot|$ denotes the cardinality of $X \neq \emptyset$. For $X = \emptyset$, we put $\alpha(\emptyset) = 1$. The roughness measure is defined as follows:

$$\rho(X) = 1 - \alpha(X). \tag{19}$$

There are inequalities $0 \leq \alpha(X), \rho(X) \leq 1$. Roughness is related to the notion of boundary region as follows:

$$\rho(X) = \frac{|\overline{apr}(X) - \underline{apr}(X)|}{|\overline{apr}(X)|} = \frac{|\text{BND}(X)|}{|\overline{apr}(X)|}. \tag{20}$$

The measures of accuracy and roughness can be compared with various approaches to evaluation of rules in machine learning and data mining [16, 44], where X plays a role of the meaning set of a rule's consequent. Instead of a single antecedent expressed by a formula in the decision logic language $\mathcal{L}$ (see Sect. 2.2), we use a collection of partition classes. Consider an indiscernibility relation induced by a subset of attributes A. Then we can look at $\rho_A(X)$ and $\alpha_A(X)$ as aggregated measures for a collection of rules with antecedents described by conjunctions of descriptors $(a = v)$, where $a \in A$ and $v \in V_a$, corresponding to particular elements of U/A.

Example 9 Continued with Example 6, consider the set X_1. The accuracy and roughness of rough set approximations are given, respectively, by:

$$\alpha_{\{a,c\}}(X_1) = \frac{|\underline{apr}_{\{a,c\}}(X_1)|}{|\overline{apr}_{\{a,c\}}(X_1)|}$$

$$= \frac{|\{o_1, o_2, o_4, o_6\}|}{|\{o_1, o_2, o_4, o_5, o_6, o_7, o_8, o_9\}|} = \frac{1}{2},$$

$$\rho_{\{a,c\}}(X_1) = 1 - \alpha_{\{a,c\}}(X_1) = \frac{1}{2}.$$

Accuracy and roughness can be also defined for some extensions of the standard RST, as the ratios of cardinalities (or other relevant measures) of various versions of lower and upper approximations. It is also worth noting that the standard approximations (as well as many of their extensions) are monotonic with respect to the choice of attributes generating indiscernibility classes, i.e., $\underline{app}_A$ increases (or at least does not decrease) and $\overline{app}_A$ decreases (or at least does not increase) while adding attributes to A. Functions α_A and ρ_A behave monotonically with respect to the subsets of attributes as well. This type of monotonicity is quite intuitive for users and convenient for designing RST based data analysis algorithms.

Example 10 Continued with Example 9, consider the following subsets of attributes: $\emptyset, \{c\}, \{a, b, c\}$. Compare their accuracies with $\alpha_{\{a,c\}}(X_1) = 1/2$:

$$\alpha_\emptyset(X_1) = \frac{|\emptyset|}{|U|} = 0,$$

$$\alpha_{\{c\}}(X_1) = \frac{|\{o_6\}|}{|U|} = \frac{1}{9},$$

$$\alpha_{\{a,b,c\}}(X_1) = \frac{|\{o_1, o_2, o_4, o_5, o_6\}|}{|\{o_1, o_2, o_4, o_5, o_6\}|} = 1.$$

4.2 Attribute Dependencies

A measure of attribute dependency was proposed by Pawlak [2] for describing the accuracy of the approximation of a partition produced by one set of attributes in the approximation space defined by another set of attributes.

Definition 14 Suppose $A, B \subseteq At$ are two not necessarily disjoint subsets of attributes. Consider a task of approximating the partition U/B in the approximation space apr_A. Let $POS_A(U/B)$ denote the positive region of U/B in apr_A. A measure of dependency of B on A is defined as follows:

$$\gamma_A(B) = \frac{|POS_A(U/B)|}{|U|}$$

$$= \frac{1}{|U|} \sum_{X_i \in U/B} |\underline{apr}_A(X_i)|. \tag{21}$$

In case of a decision table with a set of condition attributes C and a set of decision attributes D, $\gamma_C(D)$ gives a degree to which conditions determine decisions. It can be applied, for instance, in the process of attribute selection (or feature selection [45]) aimed at choosing the most meaningful attributes for further analysis. On top of that, RST based data analysis specializes in attribute reduction (which can be compared to feature subset selection [41]), i.e., finding subsets of attributes (called decision reducts [2]) that provide optimal description of decisions. A number of efficient heuristic algorithms were developed to overcome computational cost of searching through the space of all subsets of attributes [46, 47]. This is important because evaluation of single attributes may cause neglecting some important relationships between them.

Let us discuss how γ can be used in attribute reduction. Firstly, note that $\gamma_C(D)$ is monotonic with respect to adding condition attributes into C just like in the case of the accuracy and roughness measures (see Sect. 4.1).

Example 11 Continued with Example 8, consider the subsets of conditions $\emptyset$, $\{c\}$, $\{a, c\}$, $\{a, b, c\}$, and the set of decisions $\{d\}$. We have:

$$\gamma_\emptyset(\{d\}) = \frac{|\emptyset|}{|U|} = 0, \qquad \gamma_{\{a,c\}}(\{d\}) = \frac{|\{o_1, o_2, o_3, o_4, o_6\}|}{|U|} = \frac{5}{9},$$

$$\gamma_{\{c\}}(\{d\}) = \frac{|\{o_6\}|}{|U|} = \frac{1}{9}, \qquad \gamma_{\{a,b,c\}}(\{d\}) = \frac{|U|}{|U|} = 1.$$

Measure $\gamma_C(D)$ is also monotonic (in an opposite way) with respect to D. However, in the attribute reduction task, the most important aspect is to compare the quantities of the form $\gamma_C(D)$ and $\gamma_{C'}(D)$, where $C' \subseteq C$.

Definition 15 For a decision table with condition attributes C and decision attributes D, a subset $C' \subseteq C$ is a decision reduct, if the following holds:

$$\gamma_{C'}(D) = \gamma_C(D), \tag{22}$$

and there are no proper subsets of C', which satisfy the above equality.

Due to monotonicity of γ, we may treat decision reducts as minimum subsets of attributes that do not allow for decrease of determination of decisions. It is also important to note that condition (22) can be equivalently kept under restriction that there are no attributes $c \in C'$ such that $\gamma_{C'-\{c\}}(D) = \gamma_C(D)$.

Let us also consider some extensions of Definition 15. First of all, decision attributes do not need to be fixed. This leads to reconsideration of reducts as pairs of subsets of attributes (A, A') with high degrees of $\gamma_A(A')$ [42, 48]. Secondly, γ can be replaced by different uncertainty measures, which combine RST with other approaches [49, 50]. Thirdly, the equality condition in (22) can be weakened in order to search for smaller subsets of attributes that approximately preserve the attribute dependency degree expressed by γ [26, 41].

5 Conclusion

This chapter reviews the key notions of rough sets, such as representations of concepts in an information table, interpretations of lower and upper approximations of sets and partitions, as well as measures of roughness and attribute dependency. Based on these notions, one can easily study the applications of rough sets, including those discussed in other chapters of this book.

References

1. Pawlak, Z.: Rough sets. Int. J. Comput. Inf. Sci. **11**, 341–356 (1982)
2. Pawlak, Z.: Rough Sets: Theoretical Aspects of Reasoning About Data. Kluwer Academic, Dordrecht (1991)
3. Pawlak, Z., Skowron, A.: Rudiments of rough sets. Inf. Sci. **177**(1), 3–27 (2007)
4. Pawlak, Z., Skowron, A.: Rough sets: some extensions. Inf. Sci. **177**(1), 28–40 (2007)
5. Crespo, F., Peters, G., Weber, R.: Rough clustering approaches for dynamic environments. In: Peters, G., et al. (eds.) Rough Sets: Selected Methods and Applications in Management and Engineering. Springer, Berlin (2012)
6. Lingras, P., Butz, C., Bhalchandra, P.: Financial series forecasting using dual rough support vector regression. In: Peters, G., et al. (eds.) Rough Sets: Selected Methods and Applications in Management and Engineering. Springer, Berlin (2012)
7. Hunter, M.G., Peters, G.: Grounding information technology project critical success factors within the organization: applying rough sets. In: Peters, G., et al. (eds.) Rough Sets: Selected Methods and Applications in Management and Engineering. Springer, Berlin (2012)
8. Peters, G., Tagg, R.: Workflow management supported by rough set concepts. In: Peters, G., et al. (eds.) Rough Sets: Selected Methods and Applications in Management and Engineering. Springer, Berlin (2012)
9. Sikora, M., Sikora, B.: Rough natural hazards monitoring. In: Peters, G., et al. (eds.) Rough Sets: Selected Methods and Applications in Management and Engineering. Springer, Berlin (2012)
10. Ramanna, S., Peters, J.F.: Nearness of associated rough sets. In: Peters, G., et al. (eds.) Rough Sets: Selected Methods and Applications in Management and Engineering. Springer, Berlin (2012)
11. Słowiński, R. (ed.): Intelligent Decision Support, Handbook of Applications and Advances of the Rough Sets Theory. Kluwer Academic, Dordrecht (1992)
12. Lin, T.Y., Lin, T.Y., Cercone, N. (eds.): Rough Sets and Data Mining: Analysis for Imprecise Data. Springer, Berlin (1997)
13. Polkowski, L., Skowron, A. (eds.): Rough Sets in Knowledge Discovery, Parts 1 & 2. Physica-Verlag, Heidelberg (1998)
14. Hassanien, A.E., Suraj, Z., Ślęzak, D., Lingras, P. (eds.): Rough Computing: Theories, Technologies and Applications. IGI Global, Hershey (2007)
15. Bazan, J.: Hierarchical classifiers for complex spatio-temporal concepts. LNCS Trans. Rough Sets IX, LNCS **5390**, 474–750 (2008)
16. Grzymała-Busse, J.W., Ziarko, W.: Rough sets and data mining. In: Wang, J. (ed.) Encyclopedia of Data Warehousing and Mining, 2nd edn., pp. 1696–1701. IGI Global, Hershey (2009)
17. Yao, Y.Y.: Interpreting concept learning in cognitive informatics and granular computing. IEEE Trans. Syst. Man Cybern., Part B, Cybern. **39**, 855–866 (2009)
18. Skowron, A., Stepaniuk, J., Świniarski, R.: Modeling rough granular computing based on approximation spaces. Inf. Sci. **184**, 20–43 (2012)
19. Pawlak, Z.: Information systems, theoretical foundations. Inf. Syst. **6**(3), 205–218 (1981)
20. Kryszkiewicz, M.: Rough set approach to incomplete information systems. Inf. Sci. **112**, 39–49 (1998)
21. Guan, Y.Y., Wang, H.K.: Set-valued information systems. Inf. Sci. **176**, 2507–2525 (2006)
22. Lipski, W. Jr.: On semantic issues connected with incomplete information databases. ACM Trans. Database Syst. **4**, 269–296 (1979)
23. Van Mechelen, I., Hampton, J., Michalski, R.S., Theuns, P. (eds.): Categories and Concepts, Theoretical Views and Inductive Data Analysis. Academic Press, San Diego (1993)
24. Orłowska, E.: Logical aspects of learning concepts. Int. J. Approx. Reason. **2**, 349–364 (1988)
25. Mitchell, T.: Machine Learning. McGraw Hill, New York (1997)
26. Nguyen, H.S.: Approximate Boolean reasoning: foundations and applications in data mining. LNCS Trans. Rough Sets V, LNCS **4100**, 334–506 (2006)

27. Greco, S., Matarazzo, B., Słowiński, R.: Dominance-based rough set approach to decision under uncertainty and time preference. Ann. Oper. Res. **176**(1), 41–75 (2010)
28. Wu, W.Z., Zhang, W.X., Li, H.Z.: Knowledge acquisition in incomplete fuzzy information systems via the rough set approach. Expert Syst. **20**, 280–286 (2003)
29. Skowron, A., Stepaniuk, J.: Tolerance approximation spaces. Fundam. Inform. **27**(2–3), 245–253 (1996)
30. Jensen, R., Shen, Q.: Computational Intelligence and Feature Selection: Rough and Fuzzy Approaches. Wiley, Hoboken (2008)
31. Bazan, J.G., Szczuka, M.S.: The rough set exploration system. LNCS Trans. Rough Sets III, LNCS **3400**, 37–56 (2005)
32. Lingras, P., Peters, G.: Applying rough set concepts to clustering. In: Peters, G., et al. (eds.) Rough Sets: Selected Methods and Applications in Management and Engineering. Springer, Berlin (2012)
33. Ślęzak, D., Wróblewski, J., Eastwood, V., Synak, P.: Brighthouse: an analytic data warehouse for ad-hoc queries. Proc. VLDB Endow. **1**, 1337–1345 (2008)
34. Yao, Y.Y.: A note on definability and approximations. LNCS Trans. Rough Sets VII, LNCS **4400**, 274–282 (2007)
35. Grzymała-Busse, J.W.: LERS—a data mining system. In: Maimon, O., Rokach, L. (eds.) The Data Mining and Knowledge Discovery Handbook, pp. 1347–1351. Springer, Berlin (2005)
36. Yao, Y.Y.: Two views of the theory of rough sets in finite universes. Int. J. Approx. Reason. **15**(4), 291–317 (1996)
37. Yao, Y.Y.: Three-way decisions using rough sets. In: Peters, G., et al. (eds.) Rough Sets: Selected Methods and Applications in Management and Engineering. Springer, Berlin (2012)
38. Ziarko, W.: Variable precision rough set model. J. Comput. Syst. Sci. **46**(1), 39–59 (1993)
39. Yao, Y.Y.: Probabilistic rough set approximations. Int. J. Approx. Reason. **49**, 255–271 (2008)
40. Dubois, D., Prade, H.: Rough fuzzy sets and fuzzy rough sets. Int. J. Gen. Syst. **17**, 191–209 (1990)
41. Widz, S., Ślęzak, D.: Rough set based decision support—models easy to interpret. In: Peters, G., et al. (eds.) Rough Sets: Selected Methods and Applications in Management and Engineering. Springer, Berlin (2012)
42. Mrózek, A.: Rough sets and dependency analysis among attributes in computer implementations of expert's inference models. Int. J. Man-Mach. Stud. **30**(4), 457–473 (1989)
43. Suraj, Z.: Rough set method for synthesis and analysis of concurrent processes. In: Polkowski, L., et al. (eds.) New Developments in Knowledge Discovery in Information Systems, pp. 379–490. Physica-Verlag, Heidelberg (2000)
44. Geng, L., Hamilton, H.J.: Interestingness measures for data mining: a survey. ACM Comput. Surv. **38**(3) (2006)
45. Guyon, I., Aliferis, C., Elisseeff, A.: Causal feature selection. In: Liu, H., Motoda, H. (eds.) Computational Methods of Feature Selection, pp. 63–86. Chapman & Hall/CRC, Boca Raton (2008)
46. Qian, Y., Liang, J., Pedrycz, W., Dang, C.: Positive approximation: an accelerator for attribute reduction in rough set theory. Artif. Intell. **174**(9–10), 597–618 (2010)
47. Banka, H., Mitra, S.: Feature selection, classification and rule generation using rough sets. In: Peters, G., et al. (eds.) Rough Sets: Selected Methods and Applications in Management and Engineering. Springer, Berlin (2012)
48. Ślęzak, D.: Rough sets and functional dependencies in data: foundations of association reducts. LNCS Trans. Comput. Sci. V, LNCS **5540**, 182–205 (2009)
49. Düntsch, I., Gediga, G.: Uncertainty measures of rough set prediction. Artif. Intell. **106**(1), 109–137 (1998)
50. Ślęzak, D.: Various approaches to reasoning with frequency based decision reducts: a survey. In: Polkowski, L., et al. (eds.) New Developments in Knowledge Discovery in Information Systems, pp. 235–288. Physica-Verlag, Heidelberg (2000)

Part II
Methods and Applications in Data Analysis

Applying Rough Set Concepts to Clustering

Pawan Lingras and Georg Peters

Abstract Clustering algorithms are probably the most commonly used methods in data mining. Applications can be found in virtually any domain; prominent areas of application are e.g. bioinformatics, engineering and marketing besides many others. In many applications the classic k-means clustering algorithm is applied. Its fuzzy version, Bezdek's fuzzy c-means has also gained tremendous attention. Another soft computing k-means algorithm based on rough set has been recently introduced by Lingras. This chapter describes how a core concept of rough sets, the lower and upper approximation of a set, can be used in clustering. Rough clusters are shown to be useful for representing groups of highway sections, web users, and supermarket customers.

1 Introduction

The goal of clustering is to group similar objects in one cluster and dissimilar objects in different clusters. Probably the most frequently used clustering algorithm is the classic k-means with applications in virtually any real life domain. The k-means clustering is characterized by non-overlapping, clearly separated ("crisp") clusters with bivalent memberships: an object either belongs to or does not belong to a cluster.

However, many real life applications are characterized by situations where overlapping clusters would be a more suitable representation.

P. Lingras (✉)
Department of Mathematics and Computer Science, Saint Mary's University, Halifax, Canada
e-mail: pawan.lingras@smu.ca

P. Lingras
School of Computational Sciences, Swami Ramanand Teerth Marathwada University, Nanded, India

G. Peters
Department of Computer Science and Mathematics, Munich University of Applied Sciences, 80335 Munich, Germany
e-mail: georg.peters@cs.hm.edu

G. Peters et al. (eds.), *Rough Sets: Selected Methods and Applications in Management and Engineering*, Advanced Information and Knowledge Processing,
DOI 10.1007/978-1-4471-2760-4_2, © Springer-Verlag London Limited 2012

For example, consider seasons. Some days in the season winter might be undoubtedly belong to the "real" winter with snow and freezing temperatures and no indication of spring or even summer.

But at the end of the season winter, in March in the northern hemisphere, spring is "arriving". Or in other words, many days of March are not really winter days any more. They are also not real spring days, these days in March are somehow in-between winter and spring. To address such common real life situations where clusters overlap, fuzzy c-means has been introduced [1].

Another example for the need for overlapping clusters is as follows. For diagnosis of a flu a general practitioner normally requires the temperature, of a patient and whether she has headache and cough (example inspired by Grzymała-Busse [2]). In such a case classic k-means with a bivalent classification (Flu=yes or Flu=no) is fully sufficient.

However, for some special cases these features might not be sufficient to decide if theses patients suffer from flu or not (e.g. further, more detailed diagnoses are required). In such cases rough clustering is an appropriate method since it separates the objects that are definite members of a cluster from the objects that are only possible members of a cluster. In our case most patients are assigned to the clusters Flu=yes or Flu=no. But some, the tricky ones, are labeled as the "we do not know yet" patients.

Note the distinction with fuzzy clustering, where similarities are described by membership degrees while in rough clustering definite and possible members to a cluster are detected.

In contrast to original rough sets [3] which has its foundations in classic set theory, rough clustering is inspired by intervals. It utilizes the fundamental properties of original rough set theory, namely the concept of lower and upper approximations.

For almost a decade rough clustering is attracting increasing attention among researchers [4–6]. In particular, the rough k-means approach for clustering is of interest to several researchers. Lingras and West [7] provided rough k-means algorithm based on an extension of the k-means algorithm [8, 9]. Peters [10] discussed various refinements of Lingras and West's original proposal. The rough k-means [7] and its various extensions [10–12] have been found to be effective in a number of practical applications of clustering.

This chapter first provides the essential concepts of rough k-means. In the following section the foundations of the rough k-means are presented. In Sect. 3 rough clustering is applied to highway, web users, and supermarket data to demonstrate the range of applications. The chapter concludes with a short summary in Sect. 4.

2 Foundations of Rough Clustering

2.1 Adaptation of Rough Set Theory for Clustering

Rough sets were originally proposed using equivalence relations with properties as specified by Pawlak [3, 13]. The core idea is to separate discernible from indis-

Table 1 GP's diagnoses (categories)

Record	Symptoms		Diagnoses
	Temperature	Headache	Flu
1	high	no	yes
2	high	no	no
3	no	no	no

cernible objects and to assign objects to lower and upper approximations of a set $(\underline{A}(X), \overline{A}(X))$.

Yao et al. [14, 15] described various generalizations of rough sets by relaxing the assumptions of an underlying equivalence relation. Such a trend toward generalization is also evident in rough mereology proposed by Polkowski and Skowron [16] and the use of information granules in a distributed environment by Skowron and Stepaniuk [17].

The present study uses such a generalized view of rough sets. If one adopts a more restrictive view of rough set theory, the rough sets developed in this paper may have to be looked upon as interval sets.

In rough clustering we are not considering all the properties of the rough sets [3, 13]. However, the family of upper and lower approximations are required to follow some of the basic rough set properties such as:

1. An object **v** can be part of at most one lower approximation. This implies that any two lower approximations do not overlap.
2. An object **v** that is member of a lower approximation of a set is also part of its upper approximation ($\mathbf{v} \in \underline{A}(\mathbf{x}_i) \rightarrow \mathbf{v} \in \overline{A}(\mathbf{x}_i)$). This implies that a lower approximation of a set is a subset of its corresponding upper approximation ($\underline{A}(X_i) \subseteq \overline{A}(X_i)$).
3. If an object **v** is not part of any lower approximation it belongs to two or more upper approximations. This implies that an object cannot belong to only a single boundary region.

Note that these basic properties are not necessarily independent or complete. However, enumerating them will be helpful in understanding the rough set adaptation of the k-means algorithm.

Let us consider the small decision table (Table 1) depicting three diagnoses of a GP (the example is inspired by Grzymała-Busse [2]).

Although the symptoms of the patients 1 and 2 are indiscernible, patient 1 suffers from flu while patient 2 does not. To indicate this ambiguity, patients with these symptoms are assigned to the upper approximations of the sets Flu=yes and Flu=no. Since the diagnosis of patient 3 is clear this patient is assigned to the lower approximation of the set Flu=no.

Let us continue with our example. In rough k-means, the most widely used rough clustering algorithm, the symptoms are the features and the diagnoses correspond to the labels of the clusters. Hence, we need to map the symptoms on continues feature scales. While this is obvious for the feature temperature (in °C), let us assume that

Table 2 GP's diagnoses
(numeric)

Record	Symptoms		Diagnoses
	Temperature	Headache	Flu
1	40.8	0.3	yes
2	40.3	0.4	no
3	37.1	0.1	no

Fig. 1 Example: rough
clustering results

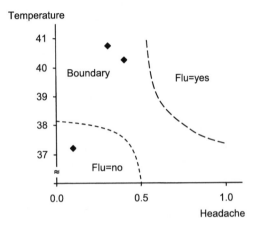

we map the feature headache into an interval from 0 to 1 (0 = no headache, 1 = extremely strong headache). We may get the features as depicted in Table 2.

Figure 1 shows a pictorial representation of the results. Patient 3 is definitely a member of the cluster Flu=no (member of the lower approximation of the set Flu=no). However, the patients 1 and 2 are in "gray zone" (boundary region) between the clusters Flu=no and Flu=yes (members of the upper approximations of the sets Flu=yes and Flu=no).

2.2 Adaptation of k-Means to Rough Set Theory

Classic k-Means   The most popular rough clustering approach has been derived from the classic k-means clustering approach [8, 9].

The name k-means originates from the means of the k clusters that are created from n objects. Let us assume that the objects are represented by m-dimensional vectors.

The objective is to assign these n objects to k clusters. Each of the clusters is also represented by an m-dimensional vector, which is the centroid or mean vector for that cluster. The process begins by randomly choosing k objects as the centroids of the k clusters. The objects are assigned to one of the k clusters based on the minimum value of the distance $d(\mathbf{v}, \mathbf{x})$ between the object vector

$\mathbf{v} = (v_1, \ldots, v_j, \ldots, v_m)$ and the cluster vector $\mathbf{x} = (x_1, \ldots, x_j, \ldots, x_m)$. The distance $d(\mathbf{v}, \mathbf{x})$ is given as follows.

After the assignment of all the objects to various clusters, the new centroid vectors of the clusters are calculated as:

$$x_j = \frac{\sum_{\mathbf{v} \in \mathbf{x}} v_j}{\text{Size of cluster } \mathbf{x}}$$
$$\text{where } 1 \leq j \leq m.$$

The process stops when the centroids of clusters stabilize, i.e. the centroid vectors from the previous iteration are identical to those generated in the current iteration.

Rough k-Means   Incorporating rough sets into k-means clustering requires the addition of the concept of lower and upper approximations.

In particular

(i) the calculation of the centroids needs to be adapted and
(ii) it has to be decided whether an object is assigned to a lower or upper approximation of a cluster.

These items will be addressed in the following paragraphs in more detail.

(i) *Calculation of the Centroids.* Calculation of the centroids of clusters from conventional k-means needs to be modified to include the effects of lower as well as upper approximations.

Basically the objects are weighted based on the different importance of the lower and upper approximations.

Then the modified centroid calculations for rough sets are given by:

IF $\quad \left[\underline{A}(\mathbf{x}) \neq \emptyset \text{ and } \overline{A}(\mathbf{x}) - \underline{A}(\mathbf{x}) = \emptyset \right]$

THEN $\quad \left[x_j = \dfrac{\sum_{\mathbf{v} \in \underline{A}(\mathbf{x})} v_j}{|\underline{A}(\mathbf{x})|} \right]$

ELSE IF $\quad \left[\underline{A}(\mathbf{x}) = \emptyset \text{ and } \overline{A}(\mathbf{x}) - \underline{A}(\mathbf{x}) \neq \emptyset \right]$

THEN $\quad \left[x_j = \dfrac{\sum_{\mathbf{v} \in (\overline{A}(\mathbf{x}) - \underline{A}(\mathbf{x}))} v_j}{|\overline{A}(\mathbf{x}) - \underline{A}(\mathbf{x})|} \right]$

ELSE $\quad \left[x_j = w_{lower} \dfrac{\sum_{\mathbf{v} \in \underline{A}(\mathbf{x})} v_j}{|\underline{A}(\mathbf{x})|} + w_{upper} \dfrac{\sum_{\mathbf{v} \in (\overline{A}(\mathbf{x}) - \underline{A}(\mathbf{x}))} v_j}{|\overline{A}(\mathbf{x}) - \underline{A}(\mathbf{x})|} \right]$

where $1 \leq j \leq m$ and $w_{lower} + w_{upper} = 1$.

The parameters w_{lower} and w_{upper} correspond to the relative importance of lower and upper approximations. If the upper approximation of each cluster were equal to its lower approximation, the clusters would be conventional clusters. Thus, the first condition $[\underline{A}(\mathbf{x}) \neq \emptyset \text{ and } \overline{A}(\mathbf{x}) - \underline{A}(\mathbf{x}) = \emptyset]$ always holds which is identical to conventional centroid calculations.

(ii) *Decide whether an object is assigned to a lower or upper approximation of a cluster.* The next step in the modification of the k-means algorithms for rough sets

Fig. 2 Assigning an object to
an approximation

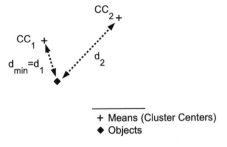

+ Means (Cluster Centers)
◆ Objects

is to design criteria to determine whether an object belongs to the upper or lower approximation of a cluster given as follows.

Basically, an object will be assigned to a lower approximation of a cluster when the distance between the object and the particular cluster center is much smaller than the distances to the remaining other cluster centers (see Fig. 2).

More formally, for each object vector, $\mathbf{v}$, let $d(\mathbf{v}, \mathbf{x}_j)$ be the distance between itself and the centroid of cluster $\mathbf{x}_j$. Then we have two steps to determine the membership of an object:

1. Determine the nearest centroid:

$$d_{min} = d(\mathbf{v}, \mathbf{x}_i) = \min_{1 \le j \le k} d(\mathbf{v}, \mathbf{x}_j).$$

2. Check if further centroids are not significantly farther away than the closest one: Let $T = \{j : d(\mathbf{v}, \mathbf{x}_j)/d(\mathbf{v}, \mathbf{x}_i) \le threshold$ and $i \ne j\}$. Then we get:

   – If $T \ne \emptyset$ then at least one other centroid is similarly close to the object.
   – If $T = \emptyset$ then no other centroids are similarly close to the object.

Hence, we get the following rule for the assignment of the objects to the approximations:

> IF $\left[T \ne \emptyset \right]$
>
> THEN $\left[\mathbf{v} \in \overline{A}(\mathbf{x}_i) \text{ and } \mathbf{v} \in \overline{A}(\mathbf{x}_j), \forall j \in T \right]$
>
> ELSE $\left[\mathbf{v} \in \overline{A}(\mathbf{x}_i) \text{ and } \mathbf{v} \in \underline{A}(\mathbf{x}_i) \right]$

It should be emphasized that the approximation space A is not defined based on any predefined relation on the set of objects. The upper and lower approximations are constructed based on the criteria described above.

While this chapter only describes the rough k-means algorithm, a number of other alternatives based on Kohonen self-organizing maps [18], evolutionary partitive approach [11], and evolutionary k-medoids [19] are also available.

3 Applications of Rough Clustering

The rough k-means has already been applied to real life data in several domains. In this section we particularly address applications in the areas of

- Traffic data (Sect. 3.1),
- Web user data (Sect. 3.2) and
- Supermarket data (Sect. 3.3)

in detail.

3.1 Rough Clustering Highway Sections

Seasonal and permanent traffic counters scattered across a highway network are the major sources of traffic data. These traffic counters measure the traffic volume—the number of vehicles that have passed through a particular section of a lane or highway in a given time period. Traffic volumes can be expressed in terms of hourly or daily traffic. More sophisticated traffic counters record additional information such as the speed, length and weight of the vehicle. Highway agencies generally have records from traffic counters collected over a number of years. In addition to obtaining data from traffic counters, traffic engineers also conduct occasional surveys of road users to get more information.

The permanent traffic counter (PTC) sites are grouped to form various road categories. These categories are used to develop guidelines for the construction, maintenance and upgrading of highway sections. In one commonly used system, roads are categorized on the basis of trip purpose and trip length characteristics [20].

Examples of resulting categories are commuter, business, long distance, and recreational highways. The trip purpose provides information about the road users, an important criterion in a variety of traffic engineering analyzes. Trip purpose information can be obtained directly from the road users, but since all users cannot be surveyed, traffic engineers study various traffic patterns obtained from seasonal and permanent traffic counters and sample surveys of a few road users.

The present study is based on a sample of 264 monthly traffic patterns—variation of monthly average daily traffic volume in a given year—recorded between 1987 and 1991 on Alberta highways. The distribution of PTCs in various regions are determined based on the traffic flow through the provincial highway networks. The patterns obtained from these PTCs represent traffic from all major regions in the province.

The rough set genomes used in the experiment consisted of 264 genes, one gene per pattern. The hypothetical clustering scheme consisted of three categories:

1. Commuter/business,
2. Long distance, and
3. Recreational.

The rough set clustering scheme was expected to specify lower and upper approximations of these categories.

The upper and lower approximations of the commuter/business, long distance, and recreational clusters were also checked against the geography of Alberta highway networks. More details of the experiment can be found in [21].

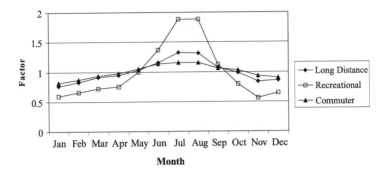

Fig. 3 Monthly patterns for the lower approximations

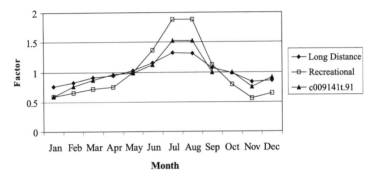

Fig. 4 Monthly pattern that may be long distance or recreational

Figure 3 shows the monthly patterns for the lower approximations of the three groups: commuter/business, long distance, and recreational. The average pattern for the lower approximation of commuter/business cluster has the least variation over the year. The recreational cluster, conversely, has the most variation. The variation for long distance cluster is less than the recreational but more than the commuter/business cluster. Figure 4 shows one of the highway sections near counter number C013201 that may have been Commuter/Business or Long Distance in 1985. It is clear that the monthly pattern for the highway section falls in between the two clusters. The counter C013201 is located on highway 13, 20 km. west of Alberta–Saskatchewan border. It is an alternate route for travel from the city of Saskatoon and surrounding townships to townships surrounding the city of Edmonton. A similar observation can be made in Fig. 5 for highway section C009141 that may have been Long Distance or Recreational in 1991. The counter C009141 is located on highway 9, 141 km. west of Alberta–Saskatchewan border. The traffic on that particular road seems to have higher seasonal variation than a long distance road. Rough set representation of clusters enables us to identify such intermediate patterns.

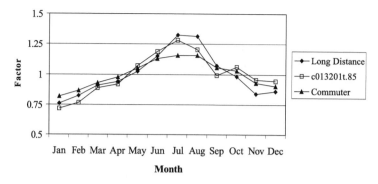

Fig. 5 Monthly pattern that may be commuter/business or long distance

3.2 Rough Clustering Web Users

The study data was obtained from the Web access logs of the first three courses in computing science at Saint Mary's University over a sixteen-week period. Students' attitudes toward the course vary a great deal. It was hoped that the profile of visits would reflect some of the distinctions between the students. For the initial analysis, it was assumed that the visitors could fall into one of the following three categories:

1. Studious: These visitors download the current set of notes. Since they download a limited/current set of notes, they probably study classnotes on a regular basis.
2. Crammers: These visitors download a large set of notes. This indicates that they have stayed away from the classnotes for a long period of time. They are planning for pre-test cramming.
3. Workers: These visitors are mostly working on class or lab assignments or accessing the discussion board.

The rough set clustering scheme was expected to specify lower and upper approximations for these categories.

It was hoped that the variety of user behaviors mentioned above would be identifiable based on the number of Web accesses, types of documents downloaded, and time of day. Certain areas of the Web site were protected and the users could only access them using their IDs and passwords. The activities in the restricted parts of the Web site consisted of submitting a user profile, changing a password, submission of assignments, viewing the submissions, accessing the discussion board, and viewing current class marks. The rest of the Web site was public. The public portion consisted of viewing course information, the lab manual, classnotes, class assignments, and lab assignments.

If the users only accessed the public Web site, their IDs would be unknown. Therefore, the Web users were identified based on their IP address. This also assured that the user privacy was protected. A visit from an IP address started when the first request was made from the IP address. The visit continued as long as the consecutive requests from the IP address had sufficiently small delay.

Table 3 Cardinalities of the clusters for three techniques

Course	Cluster	Lower approximation	Conventional clusters
First	Studious	1412	1814
	Crammers	288	406
	Workers	5350	5399
Second	Studious	1197	1699
	Crammers	443	634
	Workers	1677	3697
Third	Studious	223	318
	Crammers	69	89
	Workers	906	867

The Web logs were preprocessed to create an appropriate representation of each user corresponding to a visit. The abstract representation of a Web user is a critical step that requires a good knowledge of the application domain. Previous personal experience with the students in the course suggested that some of the students print preliminary notes just before a class and an updated copy after the class. Some students view the notes on-line on a regular basis. Some students print all the notes around important days such as midterm and final examinations. In addition, there are many accesses on Tuesdays and Thursdays, when the in-laboratory assignments are due. On and off campus points of access can also provide some indication of a user's objectives for the visit. Based on some of these observations, it was decided to use the following attributes for representing each visitor:

1. On campus/Off campus access.
2. Day time/Night time access: 8 a.m. to 8 p.m. was considered to be the day time.
3. Access during lab/class days or non-lab/class days: All the labs and classes were held on Tuesday and Thursday. The visitors on these days are more likely to be workers.
4. Number of hits.
5. Number of classnotes downloaded.

The first three attributes had binary values of 0 or 1. The last two values were normalized. Since the classnotes were the focus of the clustering, the last variable was assigned higher importance. The resulting rough set clustering schemes were subjectively analyzed. The results were compared with conventional clustering. More details about the experiments can be found in [22].

Table 3 shows the cardinalities of conventional clusters, the modified k-means based on rough set theory. The actual numbers in each cluster vary based on the characteristics of each course. For example, the first term course had significantly more workers than studious visitors, while the second term course had more studious visitors than workers. The increase in the percentage of studious visitors in the second term seems to be a natural progression. Interestingly, the second year

Table 4 The conventional k-means cluster center vectors

Course	Cluster	Campus access	Day night	Lab day	Hits	Doc req
First	Studious	0.67	0.76	0.44	2.97	2.78
	Crammers	0.62	0.72	0.32	4.06	8.57
	Workers	0.67	0.74	0.49	0.98	0.85
Second	Studious	0.00	0.68	0.28	0.67	0.55
	Crammers	0.66	0.72	0.36	2.43	2.92
	Workers	1.00	0.82	0.46	0.66	0.51
Third	Studious	0.69	0.75	0.50	3.87	3.15
	Crammers	0.60	0.71	0.44	5.30	10.20
	Workers	0.62	0.74	0.50	1.41	1.10

course had significantly large number of workers than studious visitors. This seems to be counter-intuitive. However, it can be explained based on the structure of the web sites. Unlike the two first year courses, the second year course did not post the classnotes on the Web. The notes downloaded by these students were usually sample programs that were essential during their laboratory work.

Table 4 shows cluster center vectors from the conventional k-means. It was possible to identify the three clusters as studious, workers, and crammers, from the results obtained using the conventional k-means algorithm. The crammers had the highest number of hits and classnotes in every data set. The average number of notes downloaded by crammers varied from one set to another. The studious visitors downloaded the second highest number of notes. The distinction between workers and studious visitors for the second course was also based on other attributes. For example, in the second data set, the workers were more prone to come on lab days, access Websites from on-campus locations during the daytime.

It is also interesting to note that the crammers had higher ratios of document requests to hits. The workers, on the other hand, had the lowest ratios of document requests to hits. Table 5 shows the modified k-means center vectors. These center vectors are comparable to the conventional centroid vectors. For the second data set, the modified k-means is more sensitive to the differences between studious and crammers in the first three attributes than the conventional k-means.

3.3 Rough Clustering Supermarket Customers

The data used in the study was supplied by a supermarket chain. The data consisted of transactional records from three regions. The first region, S1, consisted of one store in a rural setting. The second rural region (S2) was served by five stores, while the third region was an urban area with six stores. The data was collected over a twenty-six week period: October 22, 2000–April 21, 2001. Lingras and Adams [23] used data on the spending and visits of supermarket customers for clustering

Table 5 The modified k-means cluster center vectors

Course	Cluster	Campus access	Day night	Lab day	Hits	Doc req
First	Studious	0.67	0.75	0.43	3.16	3.17
	Crammers	0.61	0.72	0.33	4.28	9.45
	Workers	0.67	0.75	0.49	1.00	0.86
Second	Studious	0.14	0.69	0.03	0.64	0.55
	Crammers	0.64	0.72	0.34	2.58	3.29
	Workers	0.97	0.88	0.88	0.66	0.49
Third	Studious	0.70	0.74	0.48	4.09	3.91
	Crammers	0.55	0.72	0.43	5.48	10.99
	Workers	0.62	0.75	0.51	1.53	1.13

those customers. The use of average values of these variables may hide some of the important information present in the temporal patterns. Therefore, Lingras and Adams [23] used the weekly time series values. It is possible that customers with similar profiles may spend different amounts in a given week. However, if the values were sorted, the differences between these customers may vanish. For example, three weeks spending of customer A may be CAD 10, CAD 30, and CAD 20. Customer B may spend CAD 20, CAD 10, and CAD 30 in those three weeks. If the two time-series were compared with each other, the two customers may seem to have completely different profiles. However, if the time-series values were sorted, the two customers would have identical patterns. Therefore, the values of these variables for 26 weeks were sorted, resulting in a total of 52 variables. A variety of values for k (number of clusters) were used in the initial experiments. A setting of $k = 5$ seemed to provide a reasonable clustering.

Figure 6 shows the average spending and visit patterns for the lower approximations of the five clusters. The patterns enable us to distinguish between the five types of customers as:

- Loyal big spenders (G1)
- Loyal moderate spenders (G2)
- Semi-loyal potentially big spenders (G3)
- Potentially moderate to big spenders with limited loyalty (G4)
- Infrequent customers (G5)

The patterns of these clusters for the three regions were mostly similar. However, there was an interesting difference in S1 region. Even though for most weeks *loyal moderate spenders* (G2) had higher spending than *semi-loyal potentially big spenders* (G3), the highest spending of G3 was higher than G2. The region has only one store and hence it is likely that *semi-loyal potentially big spenders* do not find it convenient to shop at the supermarket on a regular basis.

While the lower approximations tend to provide distinguishing characteristics of various clusters, the boundary regions of the clusters tend to fall between the lower approximations of two regions. This fact is illustrated in Fig. 7(a).

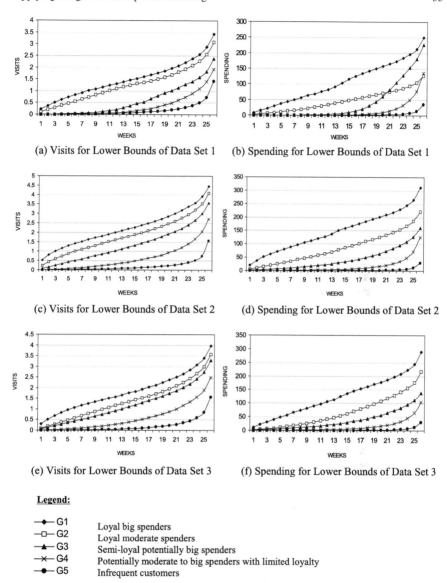

(a) Visits for Lower Bounds of Data Set 1

(b) Spending for Lower Bounds of Data Set 1

(c) Visits for Lower Bounds of Data Set 2

(d) Spending for Lower Bounds of Data Set 2

(e) Visits for Lower Bounds of Data Set 3

(f) Spending for Lower Bounds of Data Set 3

Legend:

◆— G1		
□— G2	Loyal big spenders	
▲— G3	Loyal moderate spenders	
✕— G4	Semi-loyal potentially big spenders	
●— G5	Potentially moderate to big spenders with limited loyalty	
	Infrequent customers	

Fig. 6 Patterns for visits and spending over 26 weeks

There is a large difference between the lower approximations of groups *loyal big spenders* (G1) and *potentially moderate to big spenders with limited loyalty* (G4). However, their boundary regions seem to be less distinct. The boundary regions of G1 and G4 fall between the lower approximations of those groups. The figure also shows the patterns for the overlap of the two groups. Figure 7(b) shows a similar comparison for loyal big spenders (G1) and semi-loyal potentially big spenders (G3).

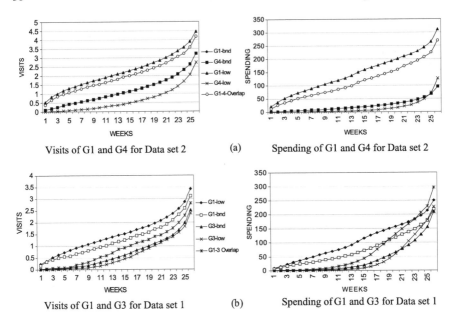

Visits of G1 and G4 for Data set 2   (a)   Spending of G1 and G4 for Data set 2

Visits of G1 and G3 for Data set 1   (b)   Spending of G1 and G3 for Data set 1

Fig. 7 Comparison of two interval clusters

4 Conclusion

In this chapter a brief introduction on rough clustering was given. In particular the rough k-means was described. It was applied to highway section, web user, and supermarket customer data.

Rough sets may provide representation of clusters, where it is possible for an object to belong to more than one cluster. This is of particular interest when buffer zones between clusters are immanent or a "buffer zone" is required to diminish the clustering mistakes. The objects in such a buffer zone need a second look (further information, an expert opinion etc.) before they can eventually be assigned to a cluster.

Hence, the rough k-means has proven to be an important enrichment to clustering approaches, particularly in the direction of soft computing methods.

Acknowledgements The authors would like to thank the Natural Sciences and Engineering Research Council of Canada and the Faculty of Graduate Studies and Research, Saint Mary's University for funding. Data from Alberta Highways, Saint Mary's University, and the supermarket is also appreciated.

References

1. Bezdek, J.: Pattern Recognition with Fuzzy Objective Algorithms. Plenum Press, New York (1981)

2. Grzymala-Busse, J.W.: Rough set theory with applications to data mining. In: Negoita, M.G., Reusch, B. (eds.) Real World Applications of Computational Intelligence, pp. 221–244. Springer, Berlin (2005)
3. Pawlak, Z.: Rough Sets: Theoretical Aspects of Reasoning About Data. Kluwer Academic, Dordrecht (1991)
4. Hirano, S., Tsumoto, S.: Rough clustering and its application to medicine. J. Inf. Sci. **124**, 125–137 (2000)
5. Peters, J.F., Skowron, A., Suraj, Z., Rzasa, W., Borkowski, M.: Clustering: a rough set approach to constructing information granules. In: Proceedings of 6th International Conference on Soft Computing and Distributed Processing (SCDP 2002), pp. 57–61 (2002)
6. Voges, K.E., Pope, N.K., Brown, M.R.: A rough cluster analysis of shopping orientation data. In: Proceedings Australian and New Zealand Marketing Academy Conference, Adelaide, pp. 1625–1631 (2003)
7. Lingras, P., West, C.: Interval set clustering of web users with rough k-means. J. Intell. Inf. Syst. **23**(1), 5–16 (2004)
8. Hartigan, J.A., Wong, M.A.: Algorithm as136: a k-means clustering algorithm. Appl. Stat. **28**, 100–108 (1979)
9. MacQueen, J.: Some methods for classification and analysis of multivariate observations. In: Proceedings of the Fifth Berkeley Symposium on Mathematical Statistics and Probability, vol. 1, pp. 281–297 (1967)
10. Peters, G.: Some refinements of rough k-means. Pattern Recognit. **39**, 1481–1491 (2006)
11. Mitra, S.: An evolutionary rough partitive clustering. Pattern Recognit. Lett. **25**(12), 1439–1449 (2004)
12. Peters, G.: Outliers in rough k-means clustering. In: Pattern Recognition and Machine Intelligence (PReMI 2005). LNCS, vol. 3776, pp. 702–707. Springer, Berlin (2005). [ISI SCI] [SCOPUS]
13. Pawlak, Z.: Rough sets. Int. J. Inf. Comput. Sci. **11**, 145–172 (1982)
14. Yao, Y.Y., Lin, T.Y.: Generalization of rough sets using modal logic. Intell. Autom. Soft Comput. **2**(2), 103–120 (1996)
15. Yao, Y.Y.: Constructive and algebraic methods of the theory of rough sets. Inf. Sci. **109**, 21–47 (1998)
16. Polkowski, L., Skowron, A.: Rough mereology: a new paradigm for approximate reasoning. Int. J. Approx. Reason. **15**(4), 333–365 (1996)
17. Skowron, A., Stepaniuk, J.: Information granules in distributed environment. In: Zhong, N., Skowron, A., Ohsuga, S. (eds.) New Directions in Rough Sets, Data Mining, and Granular-soft Computing. Lecture Notes in Artificial Intelligence, vol. 1711, pp. 357–365. Springer, Tokyo (1999)
18. Lingras, P., Hogo, M., Snorek, M., Leonard, B.: Clustering supermarket customers using rough set based Kohonen networks. In: Proceedings of the Fourteenth International Symposium on Methodologies for Intelligent Systems. Lecture Notes in Artificial Intelligence, vol. 2871, pp. 169–173. Springer, Tokyo (2003)
19. Peters, G., Lampart, M., Weber, R.: Evolutionary rough k-medoids clustering. Trans. Rough Sets **VIII**, 289–306 (2008). LNCS 5084
20. Sharma, S.C., Werner, A.: Improved method of grouping provincewide permanent traffic counters. Transp. Res. Rec. **815**, 13–18 (1981)
21. Lingras, P.: Unsupervised rough set classification using gas. J. Intell. Inf. Syst. **16**(3), 215–228 (2001)
22. Lingras, P., Yan, R., West, C.: Fuzzy c-means clustering of web users for educational sites. In: Proceedings of the Sixteenth Conference of the Canadian Society of Computational Studies of the Intelligence. Advances in Artificial Intelligence, vol. 2671, pp. 557–562. Springer, Tokyo (2003)
23. Lingras, P., Adams, G.: Selection of time-series for clustering supermarket customers. Technical report 2002-006, Department of Mathematics and Computing Science, Saint Mary's University, Halifax, NS, Canada (2002)

Rough Clustering Approaches for Dynamic Environments

Fernando Crespo, Georg Peters, and Richard Weber

Abstract Economies are characterized by constant change. This change has several facets ranging from long term effects like economic cycles and short term financial distortion caused by rumors. It also includes socio-economic technological trends or seasonal alteration and many others. "The only constant is change", the famous saying often credited to the Greek philosopher Heraclitus, summarizes the challenging environment organizations are confronted with. Hence, for any organization, like companies, government agencies or also small family enterprises, one of the main challenges is to discover economic and technological changes as early as possible to smoothly adapt to upcoming new trends or seasonal oscillation. To successfully deal with changing environments dynamic approaches to data mining have gained increasing importance in the last decades. Areas of application range from engineering and management to science and others. In this chapter we introduce to dynamic rough k-means clustering and discuss a real life application in the retail sector.

1 Introduction

Data mining [1] has gained increasing attention in past decades. On the one hand the interest in data mining is driven by progress in information technology making it possible to generate, collect, and store huge amounts of data at collapsing costs. On the other hand increasing competition forces companies to constantly improve their

F. Crespo (✉)
Industrial Engineering School, Universidad de Valparaíso, Brigadier de la Cruz 1050, San Miguel, Santiago, Chile
e-mail: fernando.crespo@uv.cl

G. Peters
Department of Computer Science and Mathematics, Munich University of Applied Sciences, 80335 Munich, Germany
e-mail: georg.peters@cs.hm.edu

R. Weber
Department of Industrial Engineering, Universidad de Chile, República 701, Santiago, Chile
e-mail: rweber@dii.uchile.cl

G. Peters et al. (eds.), *Rough Sets: Selected Methods and Applications in Management and Engineering*, Advanced Information and Knowledge Processing,
DOI 10.1007/978-1-4471-2760-4_3, © Springer-Verlag London Limited 2012

effectiveness and efficiency. Hence, analyzing data to disclose hidden information is a core strategy to gain performance.

Many classic data mining approaches require stable data structures. For example, the classic k-means clustering algorithm is designed to analyze a given set of data. Hence, any significant change in the data structure requires a new analysis.

However, "the only constant is change" is a famous saying which is often credited to the Greek philosopher Heraclitus. Modern economies are characterized by constant change which may appear in the form of cycles or trends.

On a macroeconomic level the Kondratiev waves [2] are an example for long term economic cycles; current major trends are e.g. the aging population or global warming. Many of these macroeconomic changes have direct implications for companies.

Besides these changes companies face countless additional changes, e.g. seasonal cycles. For example, the main buying season for winter garments is in autumn, while summer clothing is mainly sold in spring. In groceries, the sales of sweets increase shortly before Halloween and Christmas while beverages are sought after in a hot summer. Shorter "seasonal" cycles can be observed in, e.g. restaurants. In the morning breakfast is offered which is replaced by a lunch menu around noon and finally at night another set of dishes will be served.

These changes have been intensively addressed especially by time series analysis [3] (moving averages, regression analysis etc.). But also in the field of data mining dynamic systems have gained increasing attention in the past decades [4].

Especially soft computing approaches like fuzzy and rough sets are promising since they address uncertainty which is characteristic for changing environments. Hence, in this chapter we introduce dynamic rough k-means clustering and discuss its performance in real life applications, in particular in the retail sector discovering trends in the grocery business.

The chapter is organized as follows. In the next section we discuss some essentials of dynamic data mining and rough clustering. In Sect. 3 we introduce a dynamic version of the rough k-means clustering algorithm. In the subsequent section we present a case study by applying the dynamic rough k-means clustering algorithm to retail management. The paper concludes with a summary in Sect. 5.

2 Essentials of Dynamic Data Mining and Rough Clustering

2.1 Dynamic Data Mining

Generally speaking, dynamic data mining analyzes changing data structures, ranging from short term alterations to long term trends. Since clustering is a very popular and widely used approach in data mining, its dynamic extensions have also gained great interest. In our chapter we give a brief overview of some selected approaches in this field.

For example, Diday [5] suggested one of the first dynamic cluster methods where groups of objects adapt over time and evolve into meaningful clusters. Karypis et

Fig. 1 Dynamic data mining cycle

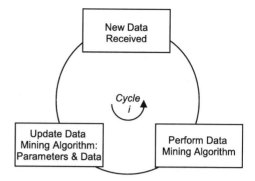

al. [6] developed CHAMELEON, a hierarchical clustering based system, where the merging of clusters on each hierarchy adapts to the changes in the data structure.

A dynamic soft computing approach, utilizing evolutionary algorithms, has been developed by Krishnapuram and Kim [7] who suggested Adaptive Fuzzy Clustering (AFC) to dynamically estimate the respective parameters during classifier design.

In situations where current feature values have insufficient explanatory power to explain the underlying phenomenon an analysis of the respective feature trajectories can be more informative. Examples can be found e.g. in medicine where the development of patients not only depends on their current measurements such as blood pressure and other exams, but also on the development over the relevant past. A method for clustering of such *feature trajectories* has been presented in [8]. Another application is scenario planning where the feature trajectories to be clustered are the relevant economic parameters over time [9].

A prototype-based clustering algorithm called Dynamic Data Assigning Assessment (DDAA) has been proposed by Georgieva and Klawonn [10]. It is based on the noise clustering technique and finds good single clusters one by one and at the same time separates noisy data.

A Dynamic Evolving Neural-Fuzzy Inference System (DENFIS) has been used for dynamic time series prediction [11]. Based on an evolving clustering method (ECM) a first-order Takagi–Sugeno-type fuzzy rule set for prediction is created dynamically.

In contrast to most of the discussed approaches the focus of dynamic rough clustering is on updating cluster parameters over the respective cycles.

Hence, in our paper we follow a dynamic data mining cycle as depicted in Fig. 1. It consists of three major steps:

- In the first step data are collected. If a data set already exists it is refreshed by new data.
- In the next step the parameters of the respective data mining algorithm are set or updated.
- Then, in the third step, the data set at hand is analyzed by the underlying data mining algorithm.

The cycle continues with the first step where new data are received.

Fig. 2 Threshold in rough clustering

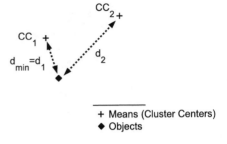

+ Means (Cluster Centers)
◆ Objects

2.2 Rough Clustering

Since Lingras et al. [12–14] introduced rough clustering it has gained increasing attention in academia and practice. In contrast to classic rough set theory rough clustering is not a set based approach but utilizes intervals to approximate the clusters.

Its fundamental idea is to assign objects that are close to a certain cluster center, let's say cluster center CC_1, and far away from all other cluster centers to the lower approximation of the corresponding cluster represented by CC_1. This indicates that the object is quite similar to this cluster and quite dissimilar to all other clusters.

Each object that has quite similar distances to its, at least two, nearest cluster centers is assigned to the upper approximations of these clusters. This indicates that the object is not a typical representative of just one cluster but has characteristics of at least two clusters.

To decide on the assignment of an object to the lower and upper approximations of the clusters we define the threshold ζ.

Let $d_{\min}$ be the distance of the considered object to its closest cluster center CC_j and d_i the distance to all remaining cluster centers CC_i (this implies $j \neq i$).

Then we get the following decision rule:

- If $\min(d_i - d_{\min}) > \zeta$ then assign the considered object to the lower approximation of cluster j,
- Else assign the object to the upper approximations of the clusters j and i with $(d_i - d_{\min}) \leqq \zeta$.

This decision rule is also illustrated in Fig. 2. A possible result of a rough cluster analysis is depicted in Fig. 3. While objects in the lower approximations *surely* belong to the corresponding clusters, objects in the boundary *may* belong to the corresponding clusters.

A possible area of application of rough clustering utilizes the fundamental idea of rough sets. The objects can be classified into three groups.

An object

- surely belongs to a cluster (it is member of its lower approximation),
- undoubtedly does not belong to a cluster (it is not even a member of its upper approximation),
- may belong to a cluster (it is member its upper approximation).

Fig. 3 Two dimensional
rough clustering

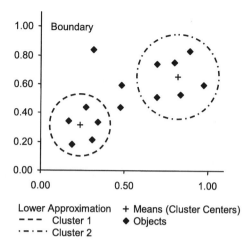

Obviously, the rough cluster algorithm separates objects with clear memberships from objects with unclear status (objects in the boundary). While objects with clear memberships can be processed instantly the objects with unclear status require additional information. Hence, the boundary functions as a "buffer zone" for objects that need a second look.

For further information on rough clustering the reader is referred to the corresponding chapter in this book.

3 Dynamic Rough k-Means Clustering

3.1 Foundations of Dynamic Soft Computing Clustering Methods

Fuzzy sets as well as rough sets are established methods in the field of soft computing. Therefore, a well established approach for dynamic fuzzy clustering [15] based on Bezdek's fuzzy c-Means [16] has been the basis for dynamic rough clustering.

The main idea of this branch of dynamic clustering methods in the soft computing domain [17] is to dynamically adapt an already obtained classifier with respect to the changes in the structure of newly arriving data.

The adaption of the classifier can be considered as a good compromise between the following two extreme solutions:

1. Neglect the changes in the analyzed phenomenon and apply the classifier without any modifications,
2. Perform the cluster analysis again from scratch whenever new data has arrived.

The first option would lead to "antiquated" classifiers that no longer represent the current data structure and therefore produce inaccurate results. Running the cluster analysis from scratch each time when the data have possibly changed as proposed in

Fig. 4 Emerging clusters (small data set)

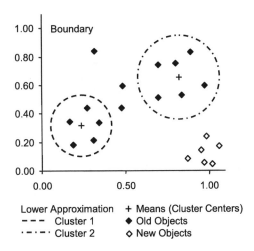

the second option could be intricate and even more importantly would not disclose any information about the characteristics of the underlying change.

Along the lines with dynamic fuzzy clustering in dynamic rough clustering three selected changes are addressed:

1. A new cluster emerges (Sect. 3.2),
2. An established cluster cannot allure enough new members and is therefore considered as obsolete (Sect. 3.3),
3. Changing uncertainties within the clusters' structures. This requires an adaption of the classifier parameters (Sect. 3.4).

To illustrate these changes we discuss a simple two dimensional data set as depicted in Fig. 3.

3.2 Emerging Clusters

Consider the following example. In a new cycle six fresh objects are collected (see Fig. 4). Unfortunately, they do not fit well into the given classifier that was obtained by clustering the original data set. In fact, they seem to establish a new cluster.

An additional, illustrative three-dimensional example [18] with a large number of data is given in the Figs. 5 and 6. Figure 5 shows the initial data set consisting of four clusters $C_1, \ldots, C_4$.

Then fresh data are received establishing the new cluster C_5 (Fig. 6). The dynamic rough clustering algorithm detects this new cluster so that the presented solution is obtained.

Based on our examples we can derive the following rule to detect emerging clusters:

– *If a reasonable number of new objects are far away from existing cluster centers we assume that a new cluster has emerged.*

Fig. 5 Emerging clusters
(large data set): initial setting
[18]

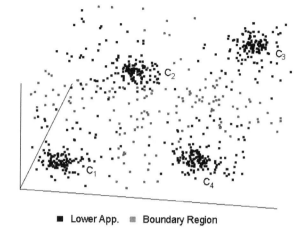

■ Lower App. ▧ Boundary Region

Fig. 6 Emerging clusters
(large data set): initial
setting + new data [18]

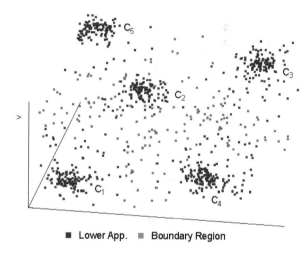

■ Lower App. ▧ Boundary Region

For a detailed definition of a *reasonable number of new objects are far away from existing cluster centers* the reader is referred to [17].

3.3 Obsolete Clusters

Consider Fig. 7 which shows the data after new objects have appeared. Obviously, the structure of these new objects differs from the old data set. Only one cluster is refreshed by new objects while the other cluster has not gained any new members. In such a case we consider the latter cluster as obsolete.

Based on our example we derive the following rule to detect obsolete clusters:

– *If an existing cluster is not refreshed by a reasonable number of new objects in each cycle we assume that the cluster is obsolete.*

Fig. 7 Obsolete clusters

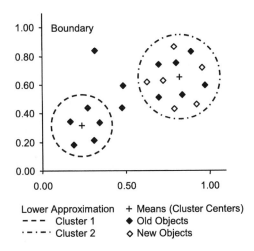

Lower Approximation   + Means (Cluster Centers)
– – –   Cluster 1   ◆ Old Objects
· – · – · Cluster 2   ◇ New Objects

The main challenge is to define the criterion *reasonable number of new members* to keep the cluster alive (see [17] for a suggestion).

In dynamic rough clustering the obsolete cluster will be removed by deleting the members of its lower approximation. In the next cycle the number of clusters is reduced by one.

Note also, that—in certain circumstances—it might be useful to keep a cluster alive although it is not refreshed sufficiently according to a given criterion. Therefore, the concept of obsolete clusters has to be applied thoughtfully and always needs a domain expert to make a final decision on whether a cluster should be kept alive or should be deleted.

3.4 Changing Uncertainties

Now consider new data as depicted in Fig. 8. Obviously, the data do not call for a new cluster. They also do not lead to obsolete clusters since both clusters get sure new members. But the cluster on the rights seems to be blurrier than in its initial state.

However, it can be a reasonable objective to keep the relationship between sure and possible members of a cluster constant, for example, when an expert applies the well-known 80/20 principle. Eighty percent of the objects should be assigned to lower approximations of the clusters. Therefore their assignment is clear. Only the remaining twenty percent need further special treatment.

We define the quotient of the number of sure objects (objects in lower approximations) over the number of objects in the boundary as degree of uncertainty. Then our objective is to keep the uncertainty constant by adapting the initial parameters of the rough cluster algorithm.

Based on our example we derive the following rule to detect changes of uncertainty:

Fig. 8 Changing uncertainty

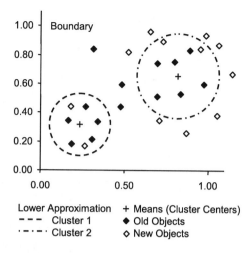

Lower Approximation   + Means (Cluster Centers)
- - -   Cluster 1   ◆ Old Objects
·—·—· Cluster 2   ◇ New Objects

- *If the quotient of the number of sure objects over the number of objects in the boundary changes significantly we assume that the uncertainty of the cluster has changed.*

Along the lines with the previous cases, the main challenge is to define the criterion *changes significantly* to assume a change in the uncertainty (see [17] for a suggestion).

Note, beside the discussed case, where a cluster becomes blurrier, the opposite is also possible, i.e. a cluster becomes less blurry.

4 Case Study—Dynamic Retail Management

The dynamic soft computing clustering algorithms have already been successfully applied to several data sets. While the dynamic fuzzy c-means has been used e.g. to improve traffic management [15], dynamic rough clustering was employed in the retail sector analyzing purchase data to detect changes in the buying behavior of customers at grocery stores [17]. Due to confidentiality issues, we only report principle results but cannot present the results in their very detail.

4.1 Data and Initial Settings

During a period of two months the sales data of a medium-sized Chilean supermarket were stored for the nine Mondays of that period. For each transaction (purchase) we had basically the information provided on its sales ticket, i.e. day and time of purchase and the chosen products together with their respective price. On average about 6,000 transactions were recorded within the 16 opening hours each day. As a

Table 1 Initial solution

Class	Cat1	Cat2	Cat3	Cat4	Cat5	Cat6	Cat7	Cat8	Cat9	Nlower	Nupper
1	21327	1607	494	3617	4841	9964	817	7602	216	153	342
2	2729	368	74	488	539	325	240	703	100	5018	5311
3	16001	914	373	3411	2600	988	5086	3416	340	115	277
4	13897	1255	3684	1827	2018	715	456	3057	271	200	446
5	130826	7904	1812	14918	17177	6839	3437	170192	1062	12	32
6	52551	16182	1297	5443	5725	1749	1305	9217	401	55	167
7	37194	4430	12228	4577	7487	2517	1334	10040	458	49	100
8	68111	5605	2346	24603	15731	29316	3291	24652	677	23	61
									Total	5625	6736

preprocessing step the more than 10,000 different stock-keeping-units at the super-market have been grouped into 9 categories, such as e.g. vegetables, perfumery, bakery, and dairy products. Finally each transaction is described by a nine-dimensional feature vector where each feature value corresponds to the total amount of money spent within the respective category.

4.2 Experiments and Results

The analysis of buying patterns was performed weekly, i.e. each Monday constitutes a new iteration. The basic (static) rough k-means revealed 8 classes for the 5,995 transactions from the first Monday as is shown Table 1 where the nine categories are indicated as Cat1, . . . , Cat9 for confidentiality reasons. The value for each category is measured in local currency (Chilean pesos; 1 USD ≈ 500 Chilean pesos). Nlower and Nupper are the numbers of objects in each class' lower and upper approximations, respectively.

Applying the proposed dynamic rough k-means to the second Monday's transactions yields the result shown in the Table 2.

As can be seen, class 5 from the initial segmentation has been eliminated. This result together with the updated class structure of the remaining classes provides useful insights for category management at the grocery store.

An in-depth analysis of the results would go beyond the scope of this chapter. Therefore, we restrain from presenting the remaining experiments in detail but only summarize in Fig. 9 how the number of classes evolves over the further iterations.

The analysis of customers' buying behavior using dynamic rough k-means revealed several interesting insights. Creation and elimination of classes as well as changing preferences among categories and knowledge about the segments' sizes provide the basis for better decision making in the retail industry. These results can be used to further optimize the daily and seasonal offers in the groceries and more efficiently manage the supply chain of the company.

Table 2 First iteration of the dynamic rough k-means

Class	Cat1	Cat2	Cat3	Cat4	Cat5	Cat6	Cat7	Cat8	Cat9	Nlower	Nupper
1	23165	1539	519	3842	5619	11031	889	7682	273	255	583
2	2651	342	77	471	562	343	238	679	114	9873	10396
3	16176	796	433	3012	3524	1218	5556	3304	398	195	474
4	14779	1275	4042	1892	2565	986	491	3133	331	348	786
5	58271	17815	1666	6004	8641	3118	1358	11717	604	81	239
6	38358	4105	15289	4466	8444	3461	1430	7593	597	87	181
7	86334	5811	3213	29445	20917	33034	3856	23620	1195	28	90
									Total	10867	12749

Fig. 9 Evolution of number of classes

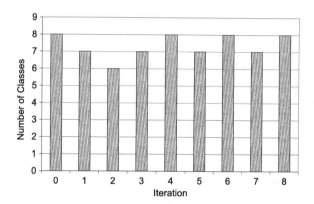

5 Conclusions

In many real-world applications data change over time. These effects might be seasonal like the altering buying patterns of retail customers over one year or they might be trends like the aging populations in many mature economies. To address such situations dynamic data mining provides a rich range of methods. In particular, dynamic cluster algorithms have been successfully applied in several projects.

Classic cluster algorithms that are used as part of their dynamic extension are crisp and only allow full membership or non-membership. However, changes in the data structure are often of continuous rather than of disruptive nature. To address this continuous characteristics soft computing methods, like fuzzy or rough approaches, are very promising. While dynamic fuzzy clustering addresses neighborhood relations the here presented dynamic rough clustering algorithm categorizes the objects into three groups: members, non-members, and possible members.

The main advantage of such a categorization is that objects that can be treated immediately are separated from objects with unclear status to clusters. These objects need to have a second look before they can be assigned to a cluster. Obviously, this characteristic makes the dynamic rough clustering algorithm very suitable for changing data structures with continuous, transitional states.

The case study on analyzing seasonal buying patterns in groceries confirms this. So, dynamic rough clustering helps to discover changing structures timely and supports the management to react to changing environments pro-actively.

Acknowledgements Support from the Chilean Instituto Sistemas Complejos de Ingeniera (ICM: P-05-004-F, CONICYT: FBO16) is greatly acknowledged (www.isci.cl).

References

1. Han, J., Kamber, M.: Data Mining: Concepts and Technique. Morgan Kaufmann, San Francisco (2000)
2. Korotayev, A.V., Tsirel, S.V.: A spectral analysis of world GDP dynamics: Kondratieff waves, Kuznets swings, Juglar and Kitchin cycles in global economic development, and the 2008–2009 economic crisis. Struct. Dyn. **4**, 3–57 (2010)
3. Hamilton-Paterson, J.: Time Series Analysis. Princeton University Press, Princeton (1994)
4. Guajardo, J., Weber, R., Miranda, J.: A model updating strategy for predicting time series with seasonal patterns. Appl. Soft Comput. **10**, 276–283 (2010)
5. Diday, E.: The dynamic cluster method in non-hierarchical clustering. Int. J. Parallel Program. **2**, 61–88 (1973)
6. Karypis, G., Han, E., Kumar, V.: Chameleon: a hierarchical clustering algorithm using dynamic modeling. Computer **32**(8), 68–75 (1999)
7. Krishnapuram, R., Kim, J.: A note on the Gustafson–Kessel and adaptive fuzzy clustering algorithms. IEEE Trans. Fuzzy Syst. **7**, 453–461 (1999)
8. Joentgen, A., Mikenina, L., Weber, R., Zimmermann, H.J.: Dynamic fuzzy data analysis based on similarity between functions. Fuzzy Sets Syst. **105**, 81–90 (1999)
9. Weber, R.: Fuzzy clustering in dynamic data mining—techniques and applications. In: Advances in Fuzzy Clustering and Its Applications, pp. 315–332. Wiley, Hoboken (2007)
10. Georgieva, O., Klawonn, F.: Dynamic data assigning assessment clustering of streaming data. Appl. Soft Comput. **8**, 1305–1313 (2008)
11. Kasabov, N., Song, Q.: DENFIS: dynamic, evolving neural-fuzzy inference systems and its application for time-series prediction. IEEE Trans. Fuzzy Syst. **10**, 144–154 (2002)
12. Lingras, P., West, C.: Interval set clustering of web users with rough k-means. Technical report 2002-002, Department of Mathematics and Computer Science, St. Mary's University, Halifax, Canada (2002)
13. Lingras, P., Yan, R., West, C.: Comparison of conventional and rough k-means clustering. In: International Conference on Rough Sets, Fuzzy Sets, Data Mining and Granular Computing. LNAI, vol. 2639, pp. 130–137. Springer, Berlin (2003)
14. Lingras, P., West, C.: Interval set clustering of web users with rough k-means. J. Intell. Inf. Syst. **23**, 5–16 (2004)
15. Crespo, F., Weber, R.: A methodology for dynamic data mining based on fuzzy clustering. Fuzzy Sets Syst. **150**, 267–284 (2005)
16. Bezdek, J.: Pattern Recognition with Fuzzy Objective Algorithms. Plenum Press, New York (1981)
17. Peters, G., Weber, R., Crespo, F.: Uncertainty modeling in dynamic clustering—a soft computing perspective. In: Proceedings WCCI 2010 IEEE World Congress on Computational Intelligence, pp. 3206–3211 (2010)
18. Nowatzke, R.: Analysis of dynamic rough clustering. Bachelor thesis, Munich University of Applied Sciences (2009)

Feature Selection, Classification and Rule Generation Using Rough Sets

Haider Banka and Sushmita Mitra

Abstract In this chapter we present two applications using rough sets. The first application deals with an evolutionary-rough feature selection algorithm for classifying microarray gene expression patterns. Since the data typically consists of a large number of redundant features, an initial redundancy reduction of the attributes is done to enable faster convergence. Rough set theory is employed to generate reducts, which represent the minimal sets of non-redundant features capable of discerning between all objects, in a multi-objective framework. The effectiveness of the algorithm is demonstrated on three cancer datasets. The second application is concerned with the dependencies among the attributes, their significance, and evaluation performed using intelligent data analysis tool. The predictive model, based on rough set approach generates fewer number of decision rules. It is found that without considering lag attribute for stock price movement decision table, the number of decision rules generated reduces significantly considering to the lag attribute taking into consideration. Ignoring the lag attribute does not affect the degree of dependency while the rest of the conditional attributes are same. The results are also compared with the neural network based algorithm. Rough confusion matrix is used to evaluate the predicted classification performances.

1 Introduction

Computational Molecular Biology is an interdisciplinary subject involving fields as diverse as biology, computer science, information technology, mathematics, physics, statistics, and chemistry. Aspects of this subject that relate to information science, are the focus of Bioinformatics [1, 2]. One needs to analyze and interpret

H. Banka (✉)
Department of Computer Science and Engineering, Indian School of Mines, Dhanbad 826004, Jharkhand, India
e-mail: banka.h.cse@ismdhanbad.ac.in

S. Mitra
Machine Intelligence Unit, Indian Statistical Institute, Kolkata 700108, India
e-mail: sushmita@isical.ac.in

G. Peters et al. (eds.), *Rough Sets: Selected Methods and Applications in Management and Engineering*, Advanced Information and Knowledge Processing,
DOI 10.1007/978-1-4471-2760-4_4, © Springer-Verlag London Limited 2012

the vast amount of data that are available, involving the decoding of around 24,000–30,000 human genes. Specifically, high-dimensional feature selection is important for characterizing gene expression data involving many attributes—indicating that data mining methods hold promise in this direction.

Unlike a genome, which provides only static sequence information, microarray experiments produce gene expression patterns that provide dynamic information about cell function. This information is useful while investigating complex interactions within the cell. For example, data mining methods can ascertain and summarize the set of genes responding to a certain level of stress in an organism [1]. Microarray technologies have been utilized to evaluate the level of expression of thousands of genes in colon, breast and blood cancer classification [3–6], as well as clustering [7, 8].

In addition to the combinatorial approach for solutions, there also exists scope for soft computing; especially, for generating low-cost, low-precision, good solutions. *Soft computing* is a consortium of methodologies that works synergistically and provides flexible information processing capability for handling real life ambiguous situations [9]. Its aim is to exploit the tolerance for imprecision, uncertainty, approximate reasoning, and partial truth in order to achieve tractability, robustness, and low-cost solutions. Recently various soft computing methodologies (like fuzzy logic, neural networks, genetic algorithms and rough sets) have been applied to handle the different challenges posed by data mining [10], involving large heterogeneous datasets.

One of the important problems in extracting and analyzing information from large databases is the associated high complexity. Feature selection is helpful as a preprocessing step for reducing dimensionality, removing irrelevant data, improving learning accuracy and enhancing output comprehensibility. There are two basic categories of feature selection algorithms, viz., filter and wrapper models. The filter model selects feature subsets independently of any learning algorithm, and relies on various measures of the general characteristics of the training data. The wrapper model uses the predictive accuracy of a predetermined learning algorithm to determine the goodness of the selected subsets, and is computationally expensive. Use of fast filter models for efficient selection of features, based on correlation for relevance and redundancy analysis, has been reported in literature [11, 12] for high-dimensional data.

Microarray data is a typical example presenting an overwhelmingly large number of features (genes), the majority of which are not relevant to the description of the problem and could potentially degrade the classification performance by masking the contribution of the relevant features. The key informative features represent a base of reduced cardinality, for subsequent analysis aimed at determining their possible role in the analyzed phenotype. This highlights the importance of feature selection, with particular emphasis on microarray data. Recent approaches in this direction include probabilistic neural networks [13], support vector machines [14], neuro-fuzzy computing [15], and neuro-genetic hybridization [16].

Rough set theory [17] provides an important and mathematically established tool, for this sort of dimensionality reduction in large data. A basic issue addressed, in relation to many practical applications of knowledge databases, is the following. An information system consisting of a domain U of objects/observations and a set A of attributes/features induces a partitioning (classification) of U by A. A block of the partition would contain those objects of U that share identical feature values, i.e. are *indiscernible* with respect to the given set A of features. But the whole set A may not always be necessary to define the classification/partition of U. Many of the attributes may be superfluous, and we may find *minimal* subsets of attributes which give the same classification as the whole set A. These subsets are called *reducts* in rough set theory. In terms of feature selection, therefore, reducts correspond to the *minimal feature sets* that are *necessary* and *sufficient* to represent a *correct* decision about classification of the domain. One is thus provided with another angle of addressing the problem of dimensionality, based on the premise that the initial set of features may render objects of the domain indiscernible, due to lack of complete information.

The task of finding reducts is reported to be NP-hard [18]. The high complexity of this problem has motivated investigators to apply various approximation techniques to find near-optimal solutions. There are some studies reported in literature, e.g. [19, 20], where genetic algorithms (GAs) [21] have been applied to find reducts.

Genetic algorithms provide an efficient search technique in a large solution space, based on the theory of evolution. It involves a set of evolutionary operators, like selection, crossover and mutation. A population of chromosomes is made to evolve over generations by optimizing a fitness function, which provides a quantitative measure of the fitness of individuals in the pool. When there are two or more conflicting characteristics to be optimized, often the single-objective GA requires an appropriate formulation of the single fitness function in terms of an additive combination of the different criteria involved. In such cases *multi-objective* GAs MOGAs [22] provide an alternative, more efficient, approach to searching for optimal solutions.

Each of the studies in [19, 20] employs a single objective function to obtain reducts. The essential properties of a reduct are (i) to classify among all elements of the universe with the same accuracy as the starting attribute set, and at the same time (ii) to be of small cardinality. A close observation reveals that these two characteristics are of a conflicting nature. Hence the determination of reducts is better represented as a two-objective optimization problem. This idea was first mooted in [23], and a preliminary study was conducted.

In this present work, we consider microarray data consisting of three sets of two-class cancer samples. Since such data typically contains a large number of features, most of which are not relevant, an initial redundancy reduction is done on the (attribute) expression values. The idea is to retain only *those* genes that play a major role in arriving at a decision about the output classes. This preprocessing aids faster convergence, mainly because the initial population is now located nearer the optimal solution in the huge search space. Reducts or minimal features are then generated from these reduced sets, using MOGA. Among the different multi-objective algorithms, it is observed that Non-dominated Sorting Genetic Algorithm (NSGA-II) [24] has the features required for a good MOGA. NSGA-II is adapted here to handle large datasets more effectively.

Stock market plays a vital role in the economic performance. Typically, it is used to infer the economic situation of a particular nation [25]. However, information regarding a stock market is normally incomplete, uncertain and vague, making it a challenge to predict the future economic performance. More specifically, the stock market's movements are analyzed and predicted in order to retrieve knowledge that could guide investors on when to buy, to sell and to hold a stock. With the emergence of various data mining and computational intelligence techniques, there are more and more applications appearing in the areas of financial and economic prediction especially in stock market movement such as genetic algorithm based [26–28], neural networks based [29], and rough based [30] to name a few.

Forecasting is essentially taking historical data, analyzing patterns and relationships between it, and production a system or acquiring results that facilitate the prediction of future events [31, 32]. Stock market dataset are basically time-series data. Various tools are used for stock market time-series but there is no consensus for the best models. Neural network techniques are predominantly popular for financial and forecasting [33–35]. Other soft computing techniques like fuzzy sets [36, 37], genetic algorithm [28] and Bayesian networks [38] also offers some methods for time-series data analysis. Recently, soft computing techniques are becoming popular for financial and economic prediction. Rough set theory offers a powerful mathematical framework to acquire information about data that cannot be categorized with traditional set theory [39, 40]. Rough sets has been applied to various financial and economic predictions [41–46] and is used for the discovery of data dependencies, evaluates the importance of attributes, discovers the patterns of data, reduces all redundant objects and attributes, and seeks the minimum subset of attributes.

The objective of this chapter is to modify the already existing stock market predictive model based on rough set approach and to construct a rough set data model that would significantly reduce the total number of generated decision rules as compared to [47], keeping the degree of dependency intact. The creation of information table usually consists of several market indicators like opening price, closing price, highest price, lowest price, trading, volume, moving average of price, upward price change, downward price change. These indicator acts as the conditional attributes of decision table which have been clearly shown in stock price movement decision table [47] and [48]. It has been found that the total no of rules generated reduces nearly $1/3$ without considering lag attribute for data analysis. A batch back-propagation learning algorithm is used to train a 3-layer feed forward neural network. The batch-mode of back-propagation learning is especially used to perform classification with a 3-layer feed-forward neural network approach. Rule extraction techniques have been applied to automatically discover temporal rule with high predictive accuracy, from trained neural network. Rules are extracted first by grouping similarly weighted links, eliminating insignificant groups, and then forming rules from the remaining groups through an exhaustive search [49].

The chapter is organized as follows. Section 2 describes the relevant preliminaries on rough set theory, multi-objective genetic algorithms, and microarray gene expression data, and an overview of stock market. We presume that the readers are

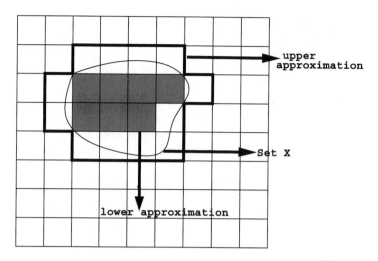

Fig. 1 Lower and upper approximations of a rough set

sufficiently familiar with the basics of classical GA [21], and hence do not go into its details here. The first application on feature selection is described in detail in Sect. 3 along with the basic components of the algorithm in its subsections. The second part on rule generation is described in Sect. 4 along with experimental study. Finally, Sect. 5 concludes the chapter.

2 Preliminaries

In this section we briefly discuss the basic concepts of rough set theory, Multi-Objective Genetic Algorithms (MOGA), and microarray gene expression data.

2.1 Rough Set Theory

Rough sets [17] constitute a major mathematical tool for managing uncertainty that arises from granularity in the domain of discourse—due to incomplete information about the objects of the domain. The granularity is represented formally in terms of an *indiscernibility* relation that partitions the domain. If there is a given set of *attributes* ascribed to the objects of the domain, objects having the same attribute values would be indiscernible, and would belong to the same block of the partition. The intention is to approximate a *rough* (imprecise) concept in the domain, by a pair of *exact* concepts. These exact concepts are called the lower and upper approximations, and are determined by the indiscernibility relation. The lower approximation is the set of objects definitely belonging to the rough concept, whereas the upper approximation is the set of objects possibly belonging to the same. Figure 1 provides an illustration of a rough set with its approximations. The formal definitions of the above notions and others required for the present work are given below.

Definition 1 An *Information System* $\mathcal{A} = (U, A)$ consists of a non-empty, finite set U of objects (cases, observations, etc.) and a non-empty, finite set A of attributes a (features, variables), such that $a : U \rightarrow V_a$, where V_a is a value set. We shall deal with information systems called *decision tables*, in which the attribute set has two parts ($A = C \cup D$) consisting of the *condition* and *decision* attributes (in the subsets C, D of A respectively). In particular, the decision tables we take will have a single decision attribute d, and will be *consistent*, i.e., whenever objects x, y are such that for each condition attribute a, $a(x) = a(y)$, then $d(x) = d(y)$.

Definition 2 Let $B \subset A$. Then a *B-indiscernibility relation* $\text{IND}(B)$ is defined as

$$\text{IND}(B) = \{(x, y) \in U : a(x) = a(y), \forall a \in B\}. \tag{1}$$

It is clear that $\text{IND}(B)$ partitions the universe U into equivalence classes

$$[x_i]_B = \{x_j \in U : (x_i, x_j) \in \text{IND}(B)\}, \quad x_i \in U. \tag{2}$$

Definition 3 The *B-lower* and *B-upper approximations* of a given set X ($\subseteq U$) are defined, respectively, as follows:

$$\underline{B}X = \{x \in U : [x]_B \subseteq X\},$$
$$\overline{B}X = \{x \in U : [x]_B \cap X \neq \phi\}.$$

The *B-boundary* region is given by $BN_B(X) = \overline{B}X \setminus \underline{B}X$.

Reducts   In a decision table $\mathcal{A} = (U, C \cup D)$, one is interested in eliminating redundant *condition* attributes, and actually *relative* (D)-reducts are computed.

Let $B \subseteq C$, and consider the *B-positive region* of D, viz., $\text{POS}_B(D) = \bigcup_{[x]_D} \underline{B}[x]_D$. An attribute $b \in B$ ($\subseteq C$) is *D-dispensable* in B if $\text{POS}_B(D) = \text{POS}_{B \setminus \{b\}}(D)$, otherwise b is *D-indispensable* in B. Here B is said to be *D-independent* in $\mathcal{A}$, if every attribute from B is *D*-indispensable in B.

Definition 4 B ($\subseteq C$) is called a *D-reduct* in $\mathcal{A}$, if B is *D*-independent in $\mathcal{A}$ and $\text{POS}_C(D) = \text{POS}_B(D)$.

Notice that, as decision tables with a single decision attribute d are taken to be consistent, $U = \text{POS}_C(d) = \text{POS}_B(D)$, for any d-reduct B.

Discernibility Matrix   D-reducts can be computed with the help of *D-discernibility matrices* [18]. Let $U = \{x_1, \ldots, x_m\}$. A *D-discernibility matrix* $M_D(\mathcal{A})$ is defined as an $m \times m$ matrix of the information system $\mathcal{A}$ with the (i, j)th entry c_{ij} given by

$$c_{ij} = \{a \in C : a(x_i) \neq a(x_j), \text{ and } (x_i, x_j) \notin \text{IND}(D)\}, \quad i, j \in \{1, \ldots, m\}. \tag{3}$$

A variant of the discernibility matrix, viz., *distinction table* [19] is used in our work to enable faster computation.

Definition 5 A *distinction table* is a *binary* matrix with dimensions $\frac{(m^2-m)}{2} \times N$, where N is the number of attributes in A. An entry $b((k,j),i)$ of the matrix corresponds to the attribute a_i and pair of objects (x_k, x_j), and is given by

$$b((k,j),i) = \begin{cases} 1 & \text{if } a_i(x_k) \neq a_i(x_j), \\ 0 & \text{if } a_i(x_k) = a_i(x_j). \end{cases} \tag{4}$$

The presence of a '1' signifies the ability of the attribute a_i to discern (or distinguish) between the pair of objects (x_k, x_j).

2.2 Multi-objective Genetic Algorithms (MOGA)

Most real-world search and optimization problems typically involve multiple objectives. A solution that is better with respect to one objective requires a compromise in other objectives. Let us consider the decision-making problem regarding the purchase of a car. It is expected that an inexpensive car is likely to be less comfortable. If a buyer is willing to sacrifice cost to some extent, (s)he can find another car with a better comfort level than the cheapest one. Thus in problems with more than one conflicting objective there exists no single optimum solution. Rather, there exists a set of solutions which are all optimal involving trade-offs between conflicting objectives. For example, the various factors to be optimized in the problem of buying a car include the total finance available, distance to be driven each day, number of passengers riding in the car, fuel consumption and cost, depreciation value, road conditions where the car will be mostly driven, physical health of the passengers, social status, etc.

Unlike single-objective optimization problems, the multiple-objective GA tries to optimize two or more conflicting characteristics represented by fitness functions. Modeling this situation with single-objective GA would amount to heuristic determination of a number of parameters involved in expressing such a scalar-combination-type fitness function. MOGA, on the other hand, generates a set of *Pareto-optimal* solutions [22] which simultaneously optimize the conflicting requirements of the multiple fitness functions.

Among the different multi-objective algorithms, it is observed that Non-dominated Sorting Genetic Algorithm (NSGA-II) [24] possesses all the features required for a good MOGA. It has been shown that this can converge to the global Pareto front, while simultaneously maintaining the diversity of population. We describe here the characteristics of NSGA-II, like non-domination, crowding distance and crowding selection operator. This is followed by the actual algorithm.

Non-domination   The concept of optimality, behind the multi-objective optimization, deals with a set of solutions. The conditions for a solution to be *dominated* with respect to the other solutions are given below.

Definition 6 If there are M objective functions, a solution $x^{(1)}$ is said to *dominate* another solution $x^{(2)}$, if both conditions (a) and (b) are true:

(a) The solution $x^{(1)}$ is *no worse* than $x^{(2)}$ in *all* the M objective functions.
(b) The solution $x^{(1)}$ is *strictly better* than $x^{(2)}$ in *at least one* of the M objective functions.

Otherwise the two solutions are *non-dominating* to each other. When a solution i dominates solution j, then *rank* $r_i < r_j$.

The major steps for finding the non-dominated set in a population P of size $|P|$ are outlined below.

1. Set solution counter $i = 1$ and create an empty non-dominated set P'.
2. **For** a solution $j \in P$ ($j \neq i$), check if solution j dominates solution i.
   If yes **then go to** Step 4.
3. **If** more solutions are left in P, increment j by one and **go to** Step 2
   Else set $P' = P' \cup \{i\}$.
4. Increment i by one.
   If $i \leq |P|$ **then go to** Step 2 **else** declare P' as the non-dominated set.

After all the solutions of P are checked, the members of P' constitute the non-dominated set at the first level (front with rank = 1). In order to generate solutions for the next higher level (dominated by the first level), the above procedure is repeated on the reduced population $P = P - P'$. This is iteratively continued until $P = \emptyset$.

Crowding Distance   In order to maintain diversity in the population, a measure called *crowding distance* is used. This assigns the highest value to the boundary solutions and the average distance of two solutions $[(i + 1)$th and $(i - 1)$th] on either side of solution i along each of the objectives. The following algorithm computes the crowding distance d_i of each point in the front $\mathcal{F}$.

1. Let the number of solutions in $\mathcal{F}$ be $l = |\mathcal{F}|$ and assign $d_i = 0$ for $i = 1, 2, \ldots, l$.
2. **For** each objective function f_k, $k = 1, 2, \ldots, M$, sort the set in its worse order.
3. Set $d_1 = d_l = \infty$.
4. **For** $j = 2$ to $(l - 1)$ increment d_j by $f_{k_{j+1}} - f_{k_{j-1}}$.

Crowding Selection Operator   *Crowded tournament selection* operator is defined as follows. A solution i wins tournament with another solution j if any one of the following is true:

– Solution i has better rank, i.e., $r_i < r_j$.
– Both the solutions are in the same front, i.e., $r_i = r_j$, but solution i is less densely located in the search space, i.e., $d_i > d_j$.

NSGA-II The multi-objective algorithm NSGA-II is characterized by the use of the above-mentioned three characteristics while generating the optimal solution. Let us now outline the main steps of NSGA-II [24].

1. Initialize the population randomly.
2. Calculate the multi-objective fitness function.
3. Rank the population using the dominance criteria of Sect. 2.2.
4. Calculate the crowding distance based on Sect. 2.2.
5. Do selection using crowding selection operator of Sect. 2.2.
6. Do crossover and mutation (as in conventional GA) to generate children population.
7. Combine parent and children population.
8. Replace the parent population by the best members of the combined population. Initially, members of lower fronts replace the parent population. When it is not possible to accommodate all the members of a particular front, then that front is sorted according to the crowding distance. Selection of individuals is done on the basis of higher crowding distance. The number selected is that required to make the new parent population size the same as the size of the old one.

2.3 Microarray and Gene Expression Data

Microarrays are used in the medical domain to produce molecular profiles of diseased and normal tissues of patients. Such profiles are useful for understanding various diseases, and aid in more accurate diagnosis, prognosis, treatment planning, as well as drug discovery.

DNA microarrays (gene arrays or gene chips) [1] usually consist of thin glass or nylon substrates containing specific DNA gene samples spotted in an array by a robotic printing device. Researchers spread fluorescently labeled m-RNA from an experimental condition onto the DNA gene samples in the array. This m-RNA binds (hybridizes) strongly with some DNA gene samples and weakly with others, depending on the inherent double helical characteristics. A laser scans the array and sensors to detect the fluorescence levels (using red and green dyes), indicating the strength with which the sample expresses each gene.

The logarithmic ratio between the two intensities of each dye is used as the gene expression data. The relative abundance of the spotted DNA sequences in a pair of DNA or RNA samples is assessed by evaluating the differential hybridization of the two samples to the sequences on the array. Gene expression levels can be determined for samples taken (i) at multiple time instants of a biological process (different phases of cell division) or (ii) under various conditions (tumor samples with different histopathological diagnosis). Each sample corresponds to a high-dimensional row vector of its gene expression profile.

2.4 Stock Market

Most stocks are traded on exchanges, which are places where buyers and sellers meet and decide on a price. The purpose of a stock market is to facilitate the exchange of securities between the buyers and sellers, reducing the risk of investing. A stock market is nothing more than a super-sophisticated farmer's market linking buyers and sellers. The primary market is where the securities are created by means of an IPO, while in secondary markets, investor's trade previously-issued securities without the involvement of the issuing companies. The secondary market is what people are referring to when they talk about the stock market. The trading of a company's stock does not directly involve that particular company. Stock price changes every day as a result of market forces—demand and supply. If more people want to buy a stock (demand) than sell it (supply), then the price moves up. Conversely, if more people want to sell a stock than buy it, there would be greater supply than demand, and the price would fall. So, it is very hard to predict the stock price movement. The only think we can say is that stocks are volatile and can change its price extremely rapidly. For more details about stock market, one can refer to [50]. This paper deals with stock price predictive model based on rough set approach.

An extensive review of the use of rough set analysis for financial and economic prediction can be found in [47]. Rough sets were also used for marketing decision support systems in Swedish retail business [51], tourism shopping [52], business failure prediction [53], predicting insolvency insurance companies [54] and business failure prediction in Greece [55]. The results obtained in [55] were found to be satisfactory as compared to classical discriminant analysis and logic analysis. Susmaga et al. used rough sets in an attempt to identify and pick top stock performers [31] while Shen and Loh predicted stock market movements by retrieving knowledge that would guide investors to decide when to buy and sell [48]. JingTao Yao et al. [56] applied rough set for the discovery of decision rules from time-series data collected from New Zealand stock exchange and presented a unique ranking system for the decision rules based on both strength of the rule and stability of the rule. The ranking system gave the user confidence regarding market decisions. Ziarko et al. [57], Golan and Edwards [58, 59] applied the rough sets model to discover strong trading rules, which reflect highly repetitive patterns in data, from historical database of the Toronto stock exchange.

3 Evolutionary Reduct Generation

Over the past few years, there has been a good amount of study in effectively applying GAs to find reducts. We describe here the reduct generation procedure, incorporating initial redundancy reduction, in a multi-objective framework. NSGA-II is adapted to handle large datasets more effectively. We focus our analysis to two-class problems.

3.1 Redundancy Reduction for Microarray Data

Gene expression data typically consists of a small number of samples with very large number of features, of which many are redundant. We consider here two-class problems, particularly, diseased and normal samples, or two varieties of diseased samples. In other words, there is a single decision attribute d having only two members in its value set V_d. We first do a redundancy reduction on the (attribute) expression values, to retain only *those* genes that play a highly decisive role in choosing in favor of either output class. Note that this preprocessing phase is a simple, fast, heuristic thresholding, with the objective of generating an initial crude redundancy reduction among features. Subsequent reduct generation with MOGA (as explained in Sects. 3.2–3.4) determines the actual, refined minimal feature sets that are necessary and sufficient to represent a correct classification decision.

Normalization leads to scaling of intensities, thereby enabling comparison of expression values between different microarrays within an experiment. *Preprocessing* aims at eliminating the ambiguously expressed genes (neither too high nor too low), as well as the constantly expressed genes across the tissue classes. During reduct generation we select an *appropriate minimal* set of differentially expressed genes, across the classes, for subsequent efficient classification.

1. Attribute-wise normalization by

$$a'_j(x_i) = \frac{a_j(x_i) - \min_j}{\max_j - \min_j}, \quad \forall i, \qquad (5)$$

where $\max_j$ and $\min_j$ correspond to the maximum and minimum gene expression values for attribute a_j over all samples. This constitutes the normalized gene dataset, i.e., (continuous) attribute value table.

2. Choose thresholds Th_i and Th_f, based on the idea of quantiles [10]. Let the N patterns be sorted in the ascending order of their values along the jth axis. In order to determine the partitions, we divide the measurements into a number of small class intervals of equal width δ and count the corresponding class frequencies fr_c. The position of the kth partition value ($k = 1, 2, 3$ for four partitions) is calculated as

$$Th_k = l_c + \frac{R_k - cfr_{c-1}}{fr_c} * \delta, \qquad (6)$$

where l_c is the lower limit of the cth class interval, $R_k = \frac{N*k}{4}$ is the rank of the kth partition value, and cfr_{c-1} is the cumulative frequency of the immediately preceding class interval, such that $cfr_{c-1} \le R_k \le cfr_c$. Here we use $Th_i = Th_1$ and $Th_f = Th_3$.

3. Convert the attribute value table to binary (0/1) form as follows:
   If $a'(x) \le Th_i$ **Then** put '0',
   Else If $a'(x) \ge Th_f$ **Then** put '1',
   Else put '*' (don't care).

4. Find the average occurrences of '*' over the entire attribute value table. Choose this as threshold Th_a.

5. Remove from the table those attributes for which the number of '*'s are $\geq Th_a$. This is the *modified* (reduced) *attribute value table* $\mathcal{A}_r$.

3.2 d-Distinction Table

For a decision table $\mathcal{A}$ with N condition attributes and a single decision attribute d, the problem of finding a d-reduct is equivalent to finding a minimal subset of columns R ($\subseteq \{1, 2, \ldots, N\}$) in the distinction table [cf. Sect. 2, Definition 5, Eq. (4)], satisfying

$$\forall (k, j) \; \exists i \in R : b((k, j), i) = 1, \quad \text{whenever } d(x_k) \neq d(x_j).$$

So, in effect, we may consider the distinction table to consist of N columns, and rows corresponding to only those object pairs (x_k, x_j) such that $d(x_k) \neq d(x_j)$. Let us call this shortened distinction table, a *d-distinction table*. Note that, as $\mathcal{A}$ is taken to be consistent, there is no row with all 0 entries in a d-distinction table.

Accordingly, to find d-reducts in the present case, the reduced attribute value table $\mathcal{A}_r$ (as obtained in Sect. 3.1) is used for generating the d-distinction table. d, as mentioned earlier, has the two output classes as the only members in its value set V_d.

- As object pairs corresponding to the same class do not constitute a row of the d-distinction table, there is a considerable reduction in its size thereby leading to a decrease in computational cost.
- Additionally,
  If either of the objects in a pair, has '*' as an entry under an attribute in table $\mathcal{A}_r$
  Then in the distinction table, put '0' at the entry for that attribute and pair.
- The entries '1' in the matrix correspond to the attributes of interest for arriving at a classification decision.

Let the number of objects initially in the two classes be m_1 and m_2 respectively. Then the number of rows in the d-distinction table becomes $(m_1 * m_2) < \frac{m*(m-1)}{2}$, where $m_1 + m_2 = m$. This reduces the complexity of fitness computation to $O(N * m_1 * m_2)$.

3.3 Using MOGA

Algorithms reported in literature, e.g. in [19, 20], vary more or less in defining the fitness function, and typically use combined single objective functions. Upon closely observing the nature of the reduct, we find that one needs to concentrate on generating a minimal set of attributes that are necessary and sufficient in order to arrive at an acceptable (classification) decision. These two characteristics of reducts, being conflicting to each other, are well-suited for multi-objective modelling. This idea was explored and a preliminary study using simple datasets done in [23]. In order to optimize the pair of conflicting requirements, the fitness function of [19] was split in a two-objective GA setting. We use these two objective functions in the present work in a modified form.

The reduct candidates are represented by binary strings of length N, where N is the number of condition attributes. In the bit representation, a '1' implies that the corresponding attribute is present while '0' means that it is not. So, if there are three attributes a_1, a_2, a_3 (i.e. $N = 3$), $\vec{v} = (1, 0, 1)$ in the search space of the GA would actually indicate the reduct candidate $\{a_1, a_3\}$. As we are looking for *minimal* non-redundant attribute sets, an objective then is to obtain a minimal number of 1's in a solution. We note that a reduct is a minimal set of attributes that *discerns between all objects* [cf. Eq. (4)]. Now $\vec{v}$ would discern between an object pair (k, j) (say), provided at least one of the attributes present in $\vec{v}$ assigns a 1 to the pair, i.e. in the d-distinction table, $b((k, j), i) = 1$, for some a_i in $\vec{v}$. Thus the second objective is to maximize the number of such object pairs for a solution.

Accordingly, two *fitness functions* f_1 and f_2 are considered for each individual. We have

$$f_1(\vec{v}) = \frac{N - L_{\vec{v}}}{N} \tag{7}$$

and

$$f_2(\vec{v}) = \frac{C_{\vec{v}}}{(m^2 - m)/2}, \tag{8}$$

where $\vec{v}$ is the reduct candidate, $L_{\vec{v}}$ represents the number of 1's in $\vec{v}$, m is the number of objects, and $C_{\vec{v}}$ indicates the number of object combinations $\vec{v}$ can discern between. The fitness function f_1 gives the candidate credit for containing less attributes (fewer 1's), while the function f_2 determines the extent to which the candidate can discern among objects.

Thus, by generating a reduct we are focusing on that minimal set of attributes which can essentially distinguish between all patterns in the given set. In this manner, a reduct is mathematically more meaningful as the most appropriate set of non-redundant features selected from a high-dimensional data.

Crowding binary tournament selection of Sect. 2.2 is used. One-point crossover is employed with probability $p_c = 0.7$. Probability p_m of mutation on a single position of individual was taken as 0.05. Mutation of one position means replacement of '1' by '0', or '0' by '1'. The probability values were chosen after several experiments.

3.4 The Algorithm

In this chapter NSGA-II is modified to effectively handle large datasets. Since we are interested in inter-class distinction, the fitness function of Eq. (8) is modified as

$$f_2(\vec{v}) = \frac{C_{\vec{v}}}{m_1 * m_2}, \tag{9}$$

where m_1 and m_2 are the number of objects in the two classes. The basic steps of the proposed algorithm are summarized as follows.

1. Redundancy reduction is made for the high-dimensional microarray data, as described in Sect. 3.1, to get the reduced attribute value table $\mathcal{A}_r$.
2. d-distinction table is generated from $\mathcal{A}_r$ for the two classes being discerned.
3. A random population of size n is generated.
4. The two fitness values f_1, f_2, for each individual, are calculated using Eqs. (7), (9).
5. Non-Domination Sorting is done as discussed in Sect. 2.2, to identify different fronts.
6. Crowding sort based on crowding distance is performed to get a wide spread of the solution.
7. Offspring solution of size n is created using *fitness* tournament selection, crossover and mutation operators. This is a modification of crowded tournament selection of Sect. 2.2, with f_1 being accorded a higher priority over f_2 during solution selection from the same front. This implies precedence to the classification efficiency of a solution over its cardinality. Specifically, for $r_i = r_j$ we favor solution i if $f_{1_i} > f_{1_j}$ (instead of $d_i > d_j$).
8. Select the best populations of size $\frac{n}{2}$ each from both the parent and offspring solutions, based on non-dominated sorting, to generate a combined population of size n. This modification enables effective handling of larger population sizes in case of large datasets, along with computational gain.
9. *Steps 3 to 7* are *repeated* for a pre-specified number of generations.

3.5 Experimental Results

We have implemented the proposed minimal feature selection algorithm on microarray data consisting of three different cancer samples. Availability of literature about performance of other related algorithms on these datasets, summarized in Table 1, prompted us to select them for our study. All results are averaged over several (3–5) runs involving different random seeds. No significant change was observed in the performance, using different seeds.

The *Colon Cancer* data (http://microarray.princeton.edu/oncology) is a collection of 62 gene expression measurements from colon biopsy samples. There are 22 normal (class C2) and 40 colon cancer (class C1) samples, having 2000 genes (features). 50% of the samples $(20 + 11 = 31)$ was considered as the training set, while the remaining 50% $(20 + 11 = 31)$ constituted the test set.

The *Lymphoma* (http://llmpp.nih.gov/lymphoma/data/figure1/figure1.cdt) dataset provides expression measurements from 96 normal and malignant lymphocyte samples, containing 42 cases of diffused large B-cell lymphoma (DLBCL) (class C2) and 54 cases of other types (class C1). There are 4026 genes present. Here also, 50% of the samples $(27 + 21 = 48)$ was considered as the training set, while the remaining 50% $(27 + 21 = 48)$ constituted the test set.

Table 1 Usage details of the two-class microarray data

Data used	# Attributes	Classes	# Samples
Colon	2000	Colon cancer	40
		Normal	22
Lymphoma	4026	Other type	54
		B-cell lymphoma	42
Leukemia	7129	ALL	47
		AML	25

The *Leukemia* dataset (http://www.genome.wi.mit.edu/MPR) is a collection of gene expression measurements from 38 leukemia samples. There are 27 cases of acute lymphoblastic leukemia (ALL) and 11 cases of acute myeloblastic leukemia (AML). An independent test set, composed of 20 ALL and 14 AML samples, was used for evaluating the performance of the classifier. The gene expression measurements were taken from high density oligonucleotide microarrays containing 7129 genes (attributes).

After the initial redundancy reduction, by the procedure outlined in Sect. 3.1, the feature sets were reduced to

- Colon dataset: 1102 attributes for the normal and cancer classes,
- Lymphoma dataset: 1867 attributes for normal and malignant lymphocyte cells, and
- Leukemia dataset: 3783 attributes for classes ALL and AML.

3.6 Reduct Generation and Classification

The MOGA of Sect. 3.4 is run on the d-distinction table by using the fitness functions of Eqs. (7)–(8), with different population sizes, to generate reducts upon convergence. Results are provided in Table 2 for the *minimal* reduct, on the three sets of two-class microarray gene expression data, after 15,000 generations. Note that a reduct implies 100% discrimination over the training set, consisting of object pairs from the d-distinction table. The corresponding recognition scores (%) (on test set) by the powerful k-nearest neighbors (k-NN) classifier [60], for different values of k, are also presented in the table. We do not use other classifiers like ID-tree which typically deal with symbolic (non-numeric) data. Neural nets were not explored since our objective was to focus on the classification ability of the reducts generated, and not to further improve upon the recognition at the expense of increased computational complexity.

It is observed that the number of features get reduced considerably with the evolutionary progression of reduct generation. A larger initial population size leads to a smaller size of reducts faster, and hence a correspondingly higher fitness value.

Table 2 Reduct generation and classification of gene expression data using multi-objective GA

Dataset	Population size	Min. reduct size	k-nearest neighbors classification (%) on test set					
			$k = 1$			$k = 3$		
			C1	C2	Net	C1	C2	Net
Colon:	50	10	80.0	90.9	83.9	75.0	90.9	80.6
# Genes 2000	100	9	90.0	90.9	90.3	90.0	90.9	90.3
Reduce to 1102	200	8	85.0	90.9	87.1	90.0	81.8	87.1
	300	8	75.0	72.7	74.2	80.0	72.7	77.4
Lymphoma:	50	2	92.6	90.5	91.7	96.3	95.2	95.8
# Genes 4026	100	3	92.6	90.5	91.7	96.3	95.2	95.8
Reduce to 1867	200	3	96.3	90.5	93.8	96.3	95.2	95.8
	300	2	92.6	90.5	91.7	96.3	95.2	95.8
Leukemia:	50	3	100.0	85.7	94.1	100.0	78.6	91.2
# Genes 7129	100	3	100.0	78.6	91.2	95.0	85.7	91.2
Reduce to 3783	150	2	90.0	71.4	82.4	90.0	100.0	94.1
	180	2	95.0	71.4	85.3	100.0	71.4	88.2
			$k = 5$			$k = 7$		
			C1	C2	Net	C1	C2	Net
Colon:	50	10	75.0	81.8	77.4	75.0	72.7	74.2
continued...	100	9	90.0	81.8	87.1	90.0	63.6	80.6
	200	8	90.0	90.9	90.3	95.0	81.8	90.3
	300	8	80.0	63.6	74.2	80.0	63.6	74.2
Lymphoma:	50	2	96.3	95.2	95.8	96.3	95.2	95.8
continued...	100	3	96.3	95.2	95.8	96.3	95.2	95.8
	200	3	96.3	95.2	95.8	96.3	95.2	95.8
	300	2	96.3	95.2	95.8	96.3	95.2	95.8
Leukemia:	50	3	100.0	78.6	91.2	100.0	71.4	88.2
continued...	100	3	100.0	78.6	91.2	100.0	78.6	91.2
	150	2	90.0	85.7	88.2	90.0	85.7	88.2
	180	2	100.0	71.4	88.2	100.0	71.4	88.2

However the associated computational complexity also increases, with a larger size of population, thereby resulting in a limitation in terms of available space and time.

Here we plot the reduct size versus the number of misclassifications over the training set (as obtained from the object pairs in the d-distinction table) at the end of 15,000 generations.

We found that with increase in number of generations, the $f_1(\vec{v})$ component of Eq. (7) gains precedence over the $f_2(\vec{v})$ component of Eq. (8) in the fitness function. Thereby the number of minimal reducts (having 100% discrimination between

Table 3 Comparative performance as number of misclassification

Dataset	Leukemia		Colon		
# Genes:	2	3	8	9	10
# Misclassification for:					
Evolutionary-rough	2	2	3	3	5
# Genes:	2	4	2	4	8
# Misclassification for:					
RSA	4	2	8.5 ± 0.58	6.5 ± 1.73	5.0 ± 1.41

training samples) decreases, as compared to those having less number of attributes but incapable of perfect discrimination.

3.7 Comparison

Feature selection has been reported in literature [13–15]. Huang [13] used a probabilistic neural network for feature selection, based on correlation with class distinction. In case of *Leukemia* data, there is 100% correct classification with a ten-genes set. For *Colon* data, a ten-genes set produces a classification score of 79.0%. From Table 2 we obtain a correct classification of 90.3% with a nine-genes set, whereas the reduced attribute size comes down to two or three for *Leukemia* data.

Chu et al. [15] employ a t-test based feature selection with a fuzzy neural network. A five-genes set provides 100% correct classification for *Lymphoma* data. We determine from Table 2, a misclassification on just two samples from the test data using a two-genes set for *Lymphoma*.

Cao et al. [14] apply saliency analysis to support vector machines for gene selection in tissue classification. The importance of genes is ranked by evaluating the sensitivity of the output to the inputs, in terms of the partial derivative. The Recursive Saliency Analysis (RSA) algorithm is developed to remove irrelevant genes in case of the *Leukemia* and *Colon* data. Table 3 lists a comparative study of RSA with the proposed evolutionary-rough method, in terms of the number of misclassification on the test data.

We also made a comparative study with some other logically similar fitness functions [19, 20], involving combinations of

$$f_1(\vec{v}) = \frac{1}{L_{\vec{v}}}, \tag{10}$$

$$f_2(\vec{v}) = \begin{cases} \frac{C_{\vec{v}}}{(m^2-m)/2} & \text{if } C_{\vec{v}} < (m^2 - m)/2, \\ \left(\frac{C_{\vec{v}}}{(m^2-m)/2} + \frac{1}{2}\right) * \frac{1}{2} & \text{if } C_{\vec{v}} = (m^2 - m)/2, \end{cases} \tag{11}$$

as adapted to the multi-objective framework. There was no observable improvement in performance here while using the multi-objective algorithm, as compared to that employing the functions of Eqs. (7) and (8).

Table 4 Comparative performance on gene expression data using single-objective GA

Dataset	Min. Reduct Size	k-nearest neighbors classification (%) on test set										
		$k=1$			$k=3$			$k=5$			$k=7$		
		C1	C2	Net	C1	C2	Net	C1	C2	Net	C1	C2	Net
Colon	15	75.0	63.6	71.0	70.0	36.4	58.1	75.0	0.0	48.4	90.0	9.1	61.3
Lymphoma	18	85.2	71.4	79.2	81.5	90.5	85.4	92.6	81.0	87.5	92.6	85.7	89.6
Leukemia	19	90.0	50.0	73.5	90.0	57.1	76.5	95.0	14.3	61.7	100.0	14.3	64.7

Reduct generation with single-objective (classical) GA [19] was also investigated for different population sizes. The fitness function

$$F_t = \alpha_1 f_1(\vec{v}) + \alpha_2 f_2(\vec{v}) \qquad (12)$$

was used, in terms of Eqs. (7) and (8), with the parameters $\alpha_1 = \alpha_2 = 1$. Additionally, we investigated with $0 < \alpha_1, \alpha_2 < 1$ for $\alpha_1 = 1 - \alpha_2$. Sample results are provided in Table 4 for population size of 100, with optimal values being generated for $\alpha_1 = 0.9$. It is observed that, for different choices of α_1 and α_2, the size of the minimal reduct was 15, 18, 19 for *Colon*, *Lymphoma*, *Leukemia* data respectively. This is more than the reduct size generated by the proposed multi-objective approach illustrated in Table 2. Moreover, the classification performance in Table 4 is also observed to be poorer. Comparison is provided for the same set of parameter initializations, with runs over same number of generations, using similar objective functions. It is observed that the plots stabilize at a larger reduct size in case of single-objectives, as compared to the case of multi-objective optimization. Moreover there is a convergence to noticeably homogeneous solutions in the population, in case of the single-objective GA, resulting in stagnation of performance.

Principal component analysis (PCA) [60] based data reduction technique has been very popular in data mining [10]. Eigenvectors of the covariance matrix of a dataset identify a linear projection, that produces uncorrelated features. PCA allows extraction of the most relevant eigenvalues and eigenvectors, which provide a good approximation for the discrimination. We employed PCA to generate an optimal set of n_o transformed features (eigenvalues), subject to a threshold of 99% approximation for the decision function. These features were subsequently evaluated using a k-NN classifier (for $k = 1, 3, 5, 7$) on the test set. The best performance (% recognition scores) for the three cancer datasets were as follows.

- *Colon*: $k = 1$ with $n_o = 7$ eigenvalues, C1 = 90.0, C2 = 66.7, *Net* = 80.7
- *Lymphoma*: $k = 3$ with $n_o = 8$ eigenvalues, C1 = 95.5, C2 = 96.3, *Net* = 95.8
- *Leukemia*: $k = 1$ with $n_o = 8$ eigenvalues, C1 = 100.0, C2 = 64.3, *Net* = 85.3

Our evolutionary-rough strategy is found to work better in all cases.

4 Rule Generation Using Rough Set Data Model

Rough set analysis of data is used to obtain preliminary information. Methods like approximation reduct and core generation, classification, and rule generation can be performed on data to gain knowledge. Redundant attributes are any attributes that could be eliminated without affecting the degree of dependency between remaining attributes and the decision. The degree of dependency is a measure used to convey the ability to discern objects from each other. The minimum subset of attributes preserving the dependency degree is termed as reducts. The computation of the core and reduct generation from a decision table is a way of selecting relevant attribute [61, 62]. A straighter manner for selecting relevant attribute is to assign a measure of relevance to each attribute and choose the attribute with higher values. The generated reducts are used to generate decision rules. The decision rule, at its left side, is a combination of attributes values such that the set of all objects matching this combination have the decision value given at the rules's right side [47]. The rule derived from reducts can be used to classify the data. The set of rules is referred to as a classifier and can be used to classify new and unseen data in the validation phase.

The rough set predictive model basically consists of three distinct phases:

1. *Pre-processing phase* includes tasks such as extra variable addition and computation, decision class assignments, data cleaning attribute creation attribute selection and discretization.
2. *Analysis and rule generation phase* includes the generation of preliminary knowledge, such as computation of object reducts from data, derivation of rules from reducts and rule evaluation
3. *Classification and prediction phase* utilizes the rule generated from the previous phase to predict the stock price movement.

Several market indicators have been considered in Table 5 such as Last, High, Low, Trade, Volume, Average, Momentum, Disparity in five days, Price Oscillator, RSI and ROC which has been clearly defined in [47]. The proposed rough set data model is found to generate fewer number of decision rules which will guide the investors when to buy, to sell and to hold a stock.

4.1 Experimental Results

In order to analyze data with rough set, data sets consisting of daily movements of a stock traded by the Gulf Bank of Kuwait (GBK)[1] are collected from the website of the Kuwait Stock Exchange [63]. The data set consists of three years time-series historical data starting from 2004–2006.

---

[1] http://www.kuwaitse.com/portal/Stock/Stock.aspx?Stk=102.

Table 5 Calculated daily stock movement decision table (ticker: GBK, year 2007)

Date m/dd	Last	High	Low	Tr	Value	Average	Mo	Disparity	OSCP	RSI	ROC	D
1/01	1720	1720	1700	10	178700	1756	60	97.95	50.60	99.94	3.382	0
1/02	1720	1720	1700	10	178700	1784	60	96.41	50.58	99.94	4.261	0
1/03	1720	1720	1700	10	178700	1808	20	95.13	50.54	99.94	4.438	0
1/14	1800	1800	1780	9	209200	1776	20	101.35	50.49	99.92	4.44	1
1/15	1780	1780	1760	25	168050	1768	0	100.68	50.48	99.92	0	1
1/16	1780	1800	1760	20	128750	1760	0	101.14	50.49	99.92	−3.37	1
1/30	1700	1700	1700	5	170000	1692	0	100.47	50.46	99.89	−3.53	−1
1/31	1700	1720	1680	13	101900	1688	−20	100.71	50.45	99.89	−2.35	−1
2/03	1700	1700	1660	20	271650	1680	−20	101.19	50.53	99.88	−2.35	−1
2/04	1700	1700	1680	45	1441050	1672	−20	101.67	50.52	99.88	−3.53	−1

Tr = Trade, Mo = Momentum, D = Decatt

The attribute used in the creation of rough set decision table is same as those of [47], except without taking the lag attribute into consideration as discussed earlier. The decision attribute indicates the future direction of the data set is represented by the following formulae:

$$\text{Decatt} = \frac{\sum_{i=1}^{i=n}((n+1)-i) \cdot \text{sign}[\text{close}(i) - \text{close}(0)]}{\sum_{i=1}^{n} i}$$

The sign function considered in the decision formulae is actually signum function which returns three values +1, 0 and −1. In the decision formulae, close(0) is today's closing price and close(i) is the ith closing price in the future. The value of Decatt ranges between −1 to +1. A value of +1 indicates that every day up to n days in the future, the market closed higher than today. Similarly, −1 indicates that every day up to n days in the future, the market closed lower than today. Table 5 shows the corresponding calculated daily stock movement using the attribute described there.

Discretization of continuous-valued attributes, reduct generation, rule generation are performed using the same algorithm described in [47]. We reach the minimum number of reducts that contains a combination of attributes which has the same discrimination factor. The final generated reducts sets which are used to generate the list of rules for the classification are: Last, high, trade, momentum, disparity in five days, OSCP.

A natural use of a set of rules is to measure how well the ensemble of rules is able to classify new and unseen objects. The measure the performance of the rules is to assess how well the rules do in classifying new cases. So, we apply the rules produced from the training data set to test case data set.

The samples of rule generated are presented in more readable format in Table 6. A comparison is performed with the total number of rule generated using neural networks, rough set taking lag attribute into account and without considering lag attribute which is shown in Table 7.

Table 6 A sample set of generated rules

Rule	Rule form	
R1	Last = (1680 or 1700)	and
	High = (1680 or 1700)	and
	Trade = (5 or 10)	and
	Momentum = (−20 or 0)	and
	Disparity in 5 days = (95.132 or 96.412)	and
	OSCP = (50.464 or 50.521) d = 0	
R2	Last = (1700 or 1720)	and
	High = (1700 or 1720)	and
	Trade = (5 or 10)	and
	Momentum = (−20 or 0)	and
	Disparity in 5 days = (96.412 or 100.472)	and
	OSCP = (50.464 or 50.521) d = 0	
R3	Last = (1720 or 1800)	and
	High = (1720 or 1800)	and
	Trade = (10 or 20)	and
	Momentum = (0 or 60)	and
	Disparity in 5 days = (100.472 or 101.674)	and
	OSCP = (50.521 or 50.598) d = 1.0	
R4	Last = (1680 or 1700)	and
	High = (1680 or 1700)	and
	Trade = (5 or 10)	and
	Momentum = (0 or 60)	and
	Disparity in 5 days = (96.412 or 100.472)	and
	OSCP = (50.464 or 50.521) d = 1.0	
R5	Last = (1680 or 1700)	and
	High = (1680 or 1700)	and
	Trade = (20 or 45)	and
	Momentum = (−20 or 0)	and
	Disparity in 5 days = (95.132 or 96.412)	and
	OSCP = (50.521 or 50.598) d = −1.0	

It can be observed that the number of rule generated without using lag attribute has been reduced significantly. Measuring the performance of the rules generated from the training dataset in terms of their ability to classify new and unseen objects is also important. Rough confusion matrix is used to measure the performance between the predicted classes and actual classes which is shown in Table 8.

Table 7 Number of
generated rules

Methods	Generated rule numbers
Neural networks	630
Rough set (with lag attribute)	371
Rough set (without lag attribute)	112

5 Conclusion

We have described an evolutionary-rough feature selection algorithm, using redundancy reduction for effective handling of high-dimensional microarray gene expression data. This serves as an interesting study in Bioinformatics. The NSGA-II has been modified to more effectively handle large data.

Since microarray data typically consists of a large number of redundant attributes, we have done an initial preprocessing for redundancy reduction. The objective was to retain only those genes that play a major role in discerning between objects. This preprocessing aids faster convergence along the search space. Moreover, a reduction in the rows (object pairs) of the distinction table was made by restricting comparisons only between objects belonging to different classes—giving the d-distinction table. This is intuitively meaningful, since our objective here is to determine the reducts that can discern between objects belonging to different classes. A further reduction in computational complexity is thereby achieved.

Selection of the most frequently occurring attributes amongst the reducts may prove significant for biologists. This is because the attributes in the *core* [17] (the intersection of the reducts) could be the relevant genes responsible for a certain medical condition. For example, let us consider the results presented in Table 2, to illustrate selection of important attributes (or genes) in the reducts. It is found that generally gene IDs *Hsa*.8147, *Hsa*.1039 occurred most frequently amongst the reducts in case of *Colon* data. Similar analysis on *Lymphoma* data lead to a focus on genes $1559X$, $1637X$. In case of *Leukemia* data, the genes $U46499$, $M28130$, $Y00787$ are found to be in the core. In the next phase, we plan to collaborate with biological experts toward validating these findings.

Microarray Bioinformatics has aided in a massive parallelization of experimental biology [1], and the associated explosion of research has led to astonishing progress in our understanding of molecular biology. Future hybrid approaches, combining powerful algorithms and interactive visualization tools with the strengths of fast processors, hold further promise for enhanced performance.

Table 8 Rough confusion matrix

Actual	Predict class 1	Predict class 2	Predict class 3	Accuracy
Class 1 (-1)	17	13	0	0.556
Class 2 (0)	0	3	0	1.0
Class 3 ($+1$)	0	3	15	0.857

This chapter presents a comparative study of an already existing generic stock market predictive model based on rough set approach using a data set consisting of daily movement of a stock traded by the Gulf Bank of Kuwait with respect to rough set data model proposed in this chapter. This data model would guide the investors whether to buy, to sell and to hold a stock. The generic stock market predictive model considered lag attribute in the decision table for rough set data analysis. This chapter analyze rough set predictive model without taking lag attribute into consideration in the decision table. Ignoring lag attribute does not affect the degree of dependency also. The creation of information table usually consists of several market indicators. These indicator acts as the conditional attributes of decision table. The result shows significant reduction in rule generation as compared to generic stock market prediction model. Moreover, the results obtained are compared to that of neural networks algorithm. Rough confusion matrix is used to evaluate the performance of the predicted classes. Thus, rough set theory offers a powerful mathematical framework for decision rule generation of various financial and economic predictions. The majority of this research applies rules derived from reducts to various decision tasks. Performing reducts on the data can significantly reduce the amount of information required in order to discern between the decision rules. A future research can be implemented with hybridization approach of other soft computing techniques using rough set as reducts generator.

References

1. Special Issue on Bioinformatics. Computer **35**(7) (2002)
2. Special Issue on Bioinformatics, Part I: Advances and Challenges. Proc. IEEE **90**(11) (2002)
3. Cho, S.B., Won, H.H.: Data mining for gene expression profiles from DNA microarray. Int. J. Softw. Eng. Knowl. Eng. **13**, 593–608 (2003)
4. Won, H.H., Cho, S.B.: Ensemble classifier with negatively correlated features for cancer classification. J. KISS Softw. Appl. **30**, 1124–1134 (2003)
5. Ando, S., Iba, H.: Artificial immune system for classification of cancer: applications of evolutionary computing. In: Lecture Notes in Computer Science, vol. 2611, pp. 1–10 (2003)
6. Futschik, M.E., Reeve, A., Kasabov, N.: Evolving connectionist systems for knowledge discovery from gene expression data of cancer tissue. Artif. Intell. Med. **28**, 165–189 (2003)
7. Roth, V., Lange, T.: Bayesian class discovery in microarray datasets. IEEE Trans. Biomed. Eng. **51**, 707–718 (2004)
8. Turkeli, Y., Ercil, A., Sezerman, O.U.: Effect of feature extraction and feature selection on expression data from epithelial ovarian cancer. In: Proceedings of the 25th Annual International Conference of the IEEE Engineering in Medicine and Biology Society, vol. 4, pp. 3559–3562 (2003)
9. Zadeh, L.A.: Fuzzy logic, neural networks, and soft computing. Commun. ACM **37**, 77–84 (1994)
10. Mitra, S., Acharya, T.: Data Mining: Multimedia, Soft Computing, and Bioinformatics. Wiley, New York (2003)
11. Yu, L., Liu, H.: Feature selection for high-dimensional data: a fast correlation-based filter solution. In: Proceedings of the Twentieth International Conference on Machine Learning (ICML-2003), Washington, DC, 2003

12. Yu, L., Liu, H.: Efficient feature selection via analysis of relevance and redundancy. J. Mach. Learn. Res. **5**, 1205–1224 (2004)
13. Huang, C.J.: Class prediction of cancer using probabilistic neural networks and relative correlation metric. Appl. Artif. Intell. **18**, 117–128 (2004)
14. Cao, L., Lee, H.P., Seng, C.K., Gu, Q.: Saliency analysis of support vector machines for gene selection in tissue classification. Neural Comput. Appl. **11**, 244–249 (2003)
15. Chu, F., Xie, W., Wang, L.: Gene selection and cancer classification using a fuzzy neural network. In: Proceedings of 2004 Annual Meeting of the North American Fuzzy Information Processing Society (NAFIPS 2004), vol. 2, pp. 555–559 (2004)
16. Karzynski, M., Mateos, A., Herrero, J., Dopazo, J.: Using a genetic algorithm and a perceptron for feature selection and supervised class learning in DNA microarray data. Artif. Intell. Rev. **20**, 39–51 (2003)
17. Pawlak, Z.: Rough Sets, Theoretical Aspects of Reasoning About Data. Kluwer Academic, Dordrecht (1991)
18. Skowron, A., Rauszer, C.: The discernibility matrices and functions in information systems. In: Slowiński, R. (ed.) Intelligent Decision Support, Handbook of Applications and Advances of the Rough Sets Theory, pp. 331–362. Kluwer Academic, Dordrecht (1992)
19. Wroblewski, J.: Finding minimal reducts using genetic algorithms. Technical Report 16/95, Warsaw Institute of Technology—Institute of Computer Science, Poland (1995)
20. Bjorvand, A.T.: 'Rough Enough'—a system supporting the rough sets approach. In: Proceedings of the Sixth Scandinavian Conference on Artificial Intelligence, Helsinki, Finland, pp. 290–291 (1997)
21. Goldberg, D.E.: Genetic Algorithms in Search, Optimization and Machine Learning. Addison-Wesley, Reading (1989)
22. Deb, K.: Multi-objective Optimization Using Evolutionary Algorithms. Wiley, London (2001)
23. Anand, A.: Representation and learning of inexact information using rough set theory. Master's thesis, Department of Mathematics, Indian Institute of Technology, Kanpur, India (2002)
24. Deb, K., Agarwal, S., Pratap, A., Meyarivan, T.: A fast and elitist multi-objective genetic algorithm: NSGA-II. IEEE Trans. Evol. Comput. **6**, 182–197 (2002)
25. Shamsuddin, S.M., Jaaman, S.H., Darus, M.: Neuro-rough trading rules for mining Kuala Lumpur composite index. Eur. J. Sci. Res. **28**(2), 278–286 (2009)
26. Bauer, R.J.: Genetic Algorithms and Investment Strategies. Wiley, New York (1994)
27. Kuo, R.J., Chen, C.H., Hwang, Y.C.: An intelligent stock trading decision support system through integration of genetic algorithm based fuzzy neural network and artificial neural network. Fuzzy Sets Syst. **118**(1), 21–45 (2001)
28. Leigh, W., Purvis, R., Ragusa, J.M.: Forecasting the nyse composite index with technical analysis, pattern recognition, neural network and genetic algorithm: a case study in romantic decision support. Decis. Support Syst. **32**(4), 361–377 (2002)
29. Mani, G., Quah, K.K., Mahfoud, S., Barr, D.: An analysis of neural-network forecasts from a large-scale, real-world stock selection system. In: Proceedings of the IEEE/IAFE 1995 Conference on Computational Intelligence for Financial Engineering (CIFER95), IEEE, New Jersey, pp. 72–78 (1995)
30. Skalko, C.: Rough sets help time the oex. J. Comput. Intell. Finance **4**(6), 20–27 (1996)
31. Susmaga, R., Michalowski, W., Slowinski, R.: Identifying regularities in stock portfolio tilting—a technical report. International Institute for Applied System Analysis (1997)
32. Taylor, S.: Modelling Financial Time-series. Wiley, New York (1986)
33. Refenes, A.N., Zapranis, A., Francis, G.: Stock performance modeling using neural networks—a comparative-study with regression-models. Neural Netw. **7**(2), 375–388 (1994)
34. Yao, J.T., Teng, N., Poh, H.L., Tan, C.L.: Forecasting and analysis of marketing data using neural networks. J. Inf. Sci. Eng. **14**(4), 523–545 (1998)
35. Yao, J.T., Tan, C.L., Li, Y.: Option prices forecasting using neural networks. Omega **28**(4), 455–466 (2000)
36. Tarrazo, M., Gutierrez, L.: Economic expectations, fuzzy sets and financial planning. Eur. J. Oper. Res. **126**(1), 89–105 (2000)

37. Zhang, J., Hsu, W., Lee, M.L.: Image mining: issues, frameworks and techniques. In: Proceedings of the 2nd International Workshop on Multimedia Data Mining and the ACM SIGKDD Conference (MDM/KDD'01), San Francisco, USA, pp. 13–20 (2001)
38. Gemela, J.: Financial analysis using Bayesian networks. Appl. Stoch. Models Bus. Ind. **17**(1), 57–67 (2001)
39. Pawlak, Z.: Rough sets. Int. J. Comput. Inf. Sci. **11**, 341–356 (1982)
40. Pawlak, Z., Grzymala-Busse, J., Slowinski, R., Ziarko, W.: Rough sets. Commun. ACM **38**(11), 89–95 (1995)
41. Herbert, J., Yao, J.T.: Time-series data analysis with rough sets. In: Proceedings of the 4th International Conference on Computational Intelligence in Economics and Finance, pp. 908–911 (2005)
42. Kim, K.J., Han, I.: The extraction of trading rules from stock market data using rough sets. Expert Syst. **18**(4), 194–202 (2001)
43. Tremba, J., Lin, T.Y.: Attribute transformations for data mining ii: applications to economic and stock market data. Int. J. Intell. Syst. **17**(2), 223–233 (2002)
44. Tay, F.E., Shen, L.: Economic and financial prediction using rough sets model. Eur. J. Oper. Res. **141**, 641–659 (2002)
45. Ang, K.K., Quek, C.: Stock trading using rspop: a novel rough set-based neuro-fuzzy approach. IEEE Trans. Neural Netw. **17**, 1301–1315 (2006). doi:10.1109/TNN.2006.875996
46. Ahn, B.S., Cho, S.S., Kim, C.Y.: The integrated methodology of rough set theory and artificial neural network for business failure prediction. Expert Syst. Appl. **18**, 65–74 (2000)
47. Hameed, A., Hassanien, A.E., Abraham, A.: A generic scheme for generating prediction rules using rough set. Neural Netw. World **18**(3), 181–198 (2008)
48. Shen, L., Loh, H.T.: Applying rough sets to market timing decisions. Decis. Support Syst. **37**(4), 583–597 (2004)
49. Nehamiah, H.K., Kannan, A., Vijaya, K., Jane, Y.N., Merin, J.B.: Employing clinical data sets for intelligent temporal rule mining and decision making, a comparative study. ICGST-BIME **7**(1), 37–45 (2007)
50. http://www.investopedia.com/university/stocks/
51. Kumar, A., Agrawal, D.P.: Advertising data analysis using rough sets model. Int. J. Inf. Technol. Decis. Mak. **4**(2), 263–276 (2005)
52. Law, R., Au, N.: Relationship modeling in tourism shopping: a decision rules induction approach. Tour. Manag. **21**(3), 241–249 (2000)
53. Beynon, M.J., Peel, M.J.: Variable precision rough set theory and data discretisation: an application to corporate failure prediction. Omega **29**(6), 561–576 (2001)
54. Segovia, V.M.J., Gil, F.J.A., Heras, M.A.: Using rough set to predict insolvency of nonlife insurance companies. Insur. Math. Econ. **32**(1), 162–163 (2003)
55. Dimitras, A.I., Slowinski, R., Susmaga, R., Zopounid, C.: Business failure prediction using rough sets. Eur. J. Oper. Res. **114**(2), 263–280 (1999)
56. Yao, J., Herbert, J.P.: Financial time-series analysis with rough sets. Appl. Soft Comput. **9**(3), 1000–1007 (2009)
57. Ziarko, W., Golan, R., Edwards, D.: An application of datalogic/r knowledge discovery tool to identify strong predictive rules in stock market data. In: Proceedings of AAAI Workshop on Knowledge Discovery in Databases, Washington, DC, pp. 89–101 (1993)
58. Golan, R.H., Ziarko, W.: A methodology for stock market analysis utilizing rough set theory. In: Proceedings of the IEEE/IAFE Computational Intelligence for Financial Engineering, pp. 32–40 (1995)
59. Golan, R.: Stock market analysis utilizing rough set theory. Ph.D. thesis, Department of Computer Science, University of Regina, Canada
60. Tou, J.T., Gonzalez, R.C.: Pattern Recognition Principles. Addison-Wesley, London (1974)
61. Skowron, A., Rauszer, C.: The discernibility matrices and functions in information systems. In: Slowinski, R. (ed.) Intelligent Decision Support, Handbook of Applications and Advances of the Rough Sets Theory, pp. 331–362. Kluwer Academic, Dordrecht (1992)

62. Bazan, J., Nguyen, H.S., Nguyen, S.H., Synak, P., Wroblewski, J.: Rough set algorithms in classification problem. In: Polkowski, L., Tsumoto, S., Lin, T.Y. (eds.) Rough Set Methods and Applications: New Developments in Knowledge Discovery in Information Systems, pp. 49–88. Physica-Verlag, Heidelberg (2000)
63. http://www.kuwaitse.com/portal/Stock/Stock.aspx?Stk=102

Part III
Methods and Applications in Decision Support

Three-Way Decisions Using Rough Sets

Yiyu Yao

Abstract A fundamental notion of rough sets is the approximation of a set by a triplet of positive, boundary, and negative regions, which leads to three-way decisions or ternary classifications. Rules from the positive region are used for making a decision of acceptance, rules from the negative region for making a decision of rejection, and rules from the boundary region for making a decision of non-commitment or deferment. This new view captures an important aspect of rough set theory and may find many practical applications.

1 Introduction

In rough set theory, there exist at least two formulations of approximations of a set that represents a concept. A set is approximated either by a pair of lower and upper approximations or by a triplet of positive, boundary and negative regions [1]. Although the two formulations are mathematically equivalent and differ only in forms, they offer very different hints for decision-making or classification using rough sets.

In the qualitative classical rough set model, rules derived, respectively, from the lower and upper approximations are called *certain rules* and *possible rules* by Grzymała-Busse [2], and are called *certain decision rules* and *uncertain decision rules* by Pawlak [3]. Wong and Ziarko [4] give another characterization, they call rules derived from both positive and negative regions *deterministic decision rules* and rules from the boundary region *undeterministic decision rules*. Theses characterizations of rules, in terms of *certain* versus *possible* [2], *deterministic* versus *nondeterministic* [4], and *certain* versus *uncertain* [3], correctly reflect qualitative natures of rules. Unfortunately, they are no longer applicable to quantitative probabilistic rough set models. Rules from both probabilistic positive and negative regions are not certain nor deterministic, but with certain tolerable degrees of errors [5].

Although the three regions in qualitative and quantitative models have different statistical characteristics, they share the same semantics interpretation. The positive

Y. Yao (✉)

Department of Computer Science, University of Regina, Regina, Saskatchewan, Canada S4S 0A2
e-mail: yyao@cs.uregina.ca

G. Peters et al. (eds.), *Rough Sets: Selected Methods and Applications in Management and Engineering*, Advanced Information and Knowledge Processing,
DOI 10.1007/978-1-4471-2760-4_5, © Springer-Verlag London Limited 2012

region is intended to be a set of instances of a concept; it has no error in the case of a qualitative model and has errors that are below a given level in the case of a quantitative model. The negative region is intended to be a set of non-instances of the concept; again, it has no error in the case of a qualitative model and has errors that are below another given level in the case of a quantitative model. The boundary region is intended to be a set of objects that we have difficulty in deciding, beyond reasonable levels of doubt, whether they are instances or non-instances of the concept. In other words, rules derived from the corresponding regions of qualitative and quantitative models have the same intended uses and make the same decisions; they only differ in their accuracy or confidence in making such decisions.

From a viewpoint of semantics of the three regions, the region based formulation offers a new interpretation of rough set theory in terms of three-way decisions and a ternary classification [6, 7]. Rules from the positive region are used for making a decision of acceptance, rules from the negative region for making a decision of rejection, and rules from the boundary region for making a decision of non-commitment or deferment. In the qualitative classical rough set model, decisions of acceptance and rejection must be made without any error; in quantitative probabilistic models, acceptance and rejection are associated with some tolerance levels of errors.

The notion of three-way decisions is applicable to both qualitative and quantitative models. It more precisely reflects the philosophy of rough sets in approximating a concept. In addition, it establishes a link between rough set theory and hypothesis testing in statistics [8, 9]. The main objective of this chapter is to investigate the notion of three-way decisions and its potential applications.

2 Qualitative Three-Way Decisions

Suppose that a finite universe of objects U is described by a finite set of attributes At. That is, each object is described by a conjunction of atomic conditions of the form ($attribute\_name = attribute\_value$). For a subset of attributes $A \subseteq At$, it defines an equivalence relation on U. Given an object $x \in U$, the set of objects with the same description as x, based on A, is the equivalence class containing x, written $[x]_A$.

A subset $C \subseteq U$ of objects represents a concept, namely, C consists of all objects to which the concept applies. Based on the description of an object, we can make one of the following three decisions or classifications with respect to $C \subseteq U$:

- Positive decision: classify an object x into the positive region POS(C), if *all* objects with the same description as x are in C, i.e., $[x]_A \subseteq C$;
- Boundary decision: classify an object x into the boundary region BND(C), if *at least one* object with the same description as x is in C and, at the same time, not *all* objects with the same description as x are in C, i.e., $[x]_A \cap C \neq \emptyset \wedge \neg([x]_A \subseteq C)$;
- Negative decision: classify an object x into the negative region NEG(C), if *none* of objects with the same description as x is in C, i.e., $[x]_A \cap C = \emptyset$.

Formally, the three regions are given by:

$$POS(C) = \{x \in U \mid [x]_A \subseteq C\},$$
$$BND(C) = \{x \in U \mid [x]_A \cap C \neq \emptyset \wedge \neg([x]_A \subseteq C)\}, \tag{1}$$
$$NEG(C) = \{x \in U \mid [x]_A \cap C = \emptyset\}.$$

They are pair-wise disjoint and form a partition of the universe U.

Let $\text{Des}(x)$ denote the description of x with respect to a subset of attributes $A \subseteq At$, namely, $\text{Des}(x) = \bigwedge_{a \in A}(a = I_a(x))$, where $I_a(x)$ is the value of x on attribute a. For simplicity, we also use C to denote the concept, or the name of the concept, whose instances are the subset of objects $C \subseteq U$. The region based formulation offers a new interpretation of rules in terms of three-way decisions and a ternary classification [6, 7]:

- rule of acceptance:

$$[x]_A \subseteq POS(C),$$
$$\text{Des}(x) \to \text{accept } x \in C;$$

- rule of deferment:

$$[x]_A \subseteq BND(C),$$
$$\text{Des}(x) \to \text{neither accept nor reject } x \in C;$$

- rule of rejection:

$$[x]_A \subseteq NEG(C),$$
$$\text{Des}(x) \to \text{reject } x \in C.$$

They clearly show that rules from different regions are meant for making different classification decisions. Based on the description of an object, one uses a rule of acceptance to accept an object to be an instance of C, uses a rule of rejection to reject an object to be an instance of C, and uses a rule of deferment to neither accept nor reject but to defer such a definite decision.

By the definition of three regions of the qualitative rough set model, decisions of acceptance and rejection are made without any error; whenever in doubt, a deferment decision is made. Based on this observation, three-way decisions of Pawlak rough set model are of qualitative nature and are therefore called qualitative three-way decisions.

3 Quantitative Probabilistic Three-Way Decisions

Decision-theoretic rough set models are quantitative probabilistic extensions of the qualitative classical rough set model [10–13]. A pair of thresholds on conditional probability is used to obtain probabilistic positive, boundary and negative regions.

Suppose that $Pr(C|[x]_A)$ denotes the conditional probability of an object in C given that the object is in $[x]_A$. It may be roughly estimated based on the cardinality of set as follows:

$$Pr(C|[x]_A) = \frac{|C \cap [x]_A|}{|[x]_A|}, \tag{2}$$

where $|\cdot|$ denotes the cardinality of a set. With conditional probability, Pawlak three regions can be equivalently expressed as:

$$
\begin{aligned}
POS(C) &= \{x \in U \mid Pr(C|[x]_A) \geq 1\}, \\
BND(C) &= \{x \in U \mid 0 < Pr(C|[x]_A) < 1\}, \\
NEG(C) &= \{x \in U \mid Pr(C|[x]_A) \leq 0\}.
\end{aligned} \tag{3}
$$

They use the two extreme probability values of 0 and 1. A main result of the decision-theoretic rough set model is the introduction of a pair of thresholds on conditional probability, to replace 0 and 1 in this definition of Pawlak three regions, for defining three probabilistic positive, boundary and negative regions: for $0 \leq \beta < \alpha \leq 1$,

$$
\begin{aligned}
POS_{(\alpha,\beta)}(C) &= \{x \in U \mid Pr(C|[x]_A) \geq \alpha\}, \\
BND_{(\alpha,\beta)}(C) &= \{x \in U \mid \beta < Pr(C|[x]_A) < \alpha\}, \\
NEG_{(\alpha,\beta)}(C) &= \{x \in U \mid Pr(C|[x]_A) \leq \beta\}.
\end{aligned} \tag{4}
$$

Pawlak model may be viewed as a special of probabilistic models in which $\beta = 0$ and $\alpha = 1$.

From three probabilistic regions, we can obtain three types of quantitative probabilistic rules:

- rule of acceptance:

$$[x]_A \subseteq POS_{(\alpha,\beta)}(C),$$
$$Des(x) \rightarrow \text{accept } x \in C;$$

- rule of deferment:

$$[x]_A \subseteq BND_{(\alpha,\beta)}(C),$$
$$Des(x) \rightarrow \text{neither accept nor reject } x \in C;$$

- rule of rejection:

$$[x]_A \subseteq NEG_{(\alpha,\beta)}(C),$$
$$Des(x) \rightarrow \text{reject } x \in C.$$

Probabilistic three-way decisions are of a quantitative nature, which produces a quantitative rough set model. By definition of probabilistic regions, decisions of acceptance and rejection are associated with some errors. In other words, in a probabilistic model one accepts or rejects the hypothesis that $x \in C$, rather than $x \in C$ is true or false as in the Pawlak model. Thus, the naming of three types of rule becomes more meaningful.

4 Interpretation and Computation of Thresholds

For practical applications of probabilistic rough sets, it is necessary to interpret the meaning of the pair of thresholds, (α, β), and to provide a method for estimating or computing them. The formulation of decision-theoretic rough set models in fact solves these problems based on the Bayesian decision theory [14]; a particular decision of choosing the positive region, boundary region or negative region is made with minimum risk.

With respect to a concept $C \subseteq U$, we have a set of two states $\Omega = \{C, C^c\}$ indicating that an object is in C and not in C, respectively. Corresponding to three-way decisions, we have a set of three actions $\mathcal{A} = \{a_P, a_B, a_N\}$, where a_P, a_B and a_N represent the three actions in classifying an object x, namely, deciding $x \in \text{POS}(C)$, deciding $x \in \text{BND}(C)$ and deciding $x \in \text{NEG}(C)$, respectively. The loss function regarding the risk or cost of actions in different states is given by a 3×2 matrix:

	C (P)	C^c (N)
a_P (P)	λ_{PP}	λ_{PN}
a_B (B)	λ_{BP}	λ_{BN}
a_N (N)	λ_{NP}	λ_{NN}

In the matrix, P, B and N inside the parentheses are used as subscripts to label various loss. In particular, λ_{PP}, λ_{BP} and λ_{NP} denote the losses incurred for taking actions a_P, a_B and a_N, respectively, when an object belongs to C, and λ_{PN}, λ_{BN} and λ_{NN} denote the losses incurred for taking the same actions when the object does not belong to C.

A loss function for different actions is typically given by experts in a particular domain. For example, in medical decision making, losses may be interpreted based on the harms of treating patients who do not have the disease and the benefits of treating patients with the disease. One may intuitively interpret losses as costs measured in terms of the amount of money, although putting a monetary value is not always easy in practice. The estimation of losses is much domain dependent and needs careful investigation based on domain knowledge when applying the decision-theoretic rough set model.

Given the loss matrix, the expected losses associated with taking different actions for objects in $[x]$ can be expressed as:

$$
\begin{aligned}
R(a_P|[x]_A) &= \lambda_{PP} \Pr(C|[x]_A) + \lambda_{PN} \Pr(C^c|[x]_A), \\
R(a_B|[x]_A) &= \lambda_{BP} \Pr(C|[x]_A) + \lambda_{BN} \Pr(C^c|[x]_A), \\
R(a_N|[x]_A) &= \lambda_{NP} \Pr(C|[x]_A) + \lambda_{NN} \Pr(C^c|[x]_A).
\end{aligned} \tag{5}
$$

The Bayesian decision procedure suggests the following minimum-risk decision rules:

(P) If $R(a_P|[x]_A) \leq R(a_N|[x]_A) \wedge R(a_P|[x]_A) \leq R(a_B|[x]_A)$, decide $x \in \text{POS}(C)$;

(B) If $R(a_B|[x]_A) \leq R(a_P|[x]_A) \wedge R(a_B|[x]_A) \leq R(a_N|[x]_A)$, decide $x \in \text{BND}(C)$;

(N) If $R(a_N|[x]_A) \leq R(a_P|[x]_A) \wedge R(a_N|[x]_A) \leq R(a_B|[x]_A)$, decide $x \in$ NEG(C).

Tie-breaking criteria are added so that each object is put into only one region. Since $\Pr(C|[x]) + \Pr(C^c|[x]) = 1$, we can simplify the rules based only on the probabilities $\Pr(C|[x])$ and the loss function λ.

Consider a special kind of loss functions with:

$$\text{(c0)} \quad \lambda_{PP} \leq \lambda_{BP} < \lambda_{NP}, \qquad \lambda_{NN} \leq \lambda_{BN} < \lambda_{PN}. \tag{6}$$

That is, the loss of classifying an object x belonging to C into the positive region POS(C) is less than or equal to the loss of classifying x into the boundary region BND(C), and both of these losses are strictly less than the loss of classifying x into the negative region NEG(C). The reverse order of losses is used for classifying an object not in C. Under condition (c0), the decision rules can be re-expressed as:

(P) If $\Pr(C|[x]_A) \geq \alpha$ and $\Pr(C|[x]_A) \geq \gamma$, decide $x \in$ POS(C);
(B) If $\Pr(C|[x]_A) \leq \alpha$ and $\Pr(C|[x]_A) \geq \beta$, decide $x \in$ BND(C);
(N) If $\Pr(C|[x]_A) \leq \beta$ and $\Pr(C|[x]_A) \leq \gamma$, decide $x \in$ NEG(C);

where the parameters α, β and γ are computed from the loss function as:

$$\begin{aligned}
\alpha &= \frac{(\lambda_{PN} - \lambda_{BN})}{(\lambda_{PN} - \lambda_{BN}) + (\lambda_{BP} - \lambda_{PP})}, \\
\beta &= \frac{(\lambda_{BN} - \lambda_{NN})}{(\lambda_{BN} - \lambda_{NN}) + (\lambda_{NP} - \lambda_{BP})}, \\
\gamma &= \frac{(\lambda_{PN} - \lambda_{NN})}{(\lambda_{PN} - \lambda_{NN}) + (\lambda_{NP} - \lambda_{PP})}.
\end{aligned} \tag{7}$$

In other words, from a loss function one can practically interpret and systematically determine the required threshold parameters.

Consider now an additional condition on a loss function:

$$\text{(c1)} \quad (\lambda_{PN} - \lambda_{BN})(\lambda_{NP} - \lambda_{BP}) > (\lambda_{BN} - \lambda_{NN})(\lambda_{BP} - \lambda_{PP}). \tag{8}$$

It follows form (c0) and (c1) that $0 \leq \beta < \gamma < \alpha \leq 1$. After tie-breaking, the following simplified rules are obtained:

(P) If $\Pr(C|[x]) \geq \alpha$, decide $x \in$ POS(C);
(B) If $\beta < \Pr(C|[x]) < \alpha$, decide $x \in$ BND(C);
(N) If $\Pr(C|[x]) \leq \beta$, decide $x \in$ NEG(C).

The parameter γ is no longer needed. Thus, (α, β)-probabilistic positive, negative and boundary regions are given, respectively, by:

$$\begin{aligned}
\text{POS}_{(\alpha,\beta)}(C) &= \{x \in U \mid \Pr(C|[x]_A) \geq \alpha\}, \\
\text{BND}_{(\alpha,\beta)}(C) &= \{x \in U \mid \beta < \Pr(C|[x]_A) < \alpha\}, \\
\text{NEG}_{(\alpha,\beta)}(C) &= \{x \in U \mid \Pr(C|[x]_A) \leq \beta\}.
\end{aligned} \tag{9}$$

The derivation shows that decision-theoretic rough set models have a solid theoretical basis on one hand and a systematic practical way of computing the required thresholds on the other.

5 Further Analysis of Three-Way Decisions

In probabilistic rough set models, acceptance decisions are made with certain level of incorrect acceptance errors and rejection decisions are made with another level of incorrect rejection errors. They are similar to the two types of errors of two-way decisions or binary classifications. Although a deferment decision does not cause an incorrect acceptance nor an incorrect rejection, it introduces two new types of errors, namely, deferment of positive and deferment of negative. A further analysis of three-way decisions in terms of different types of error would bring new insights.

The expression of a loss function by a 3×2 matrix suggests that the results of three-way decisions can be classified into six groups, with rows representing decisions and columns representing the true membership of an object, as follows:

	C (positive)	C^c (negative)
accept	correct acceptance	incorrect acceptance
defer	deferred positive	deferred negative
reject	incorrect rejection	correct rejection

Rules of acceptance, deferment and rejection can be characterized by the six groups of classification results.

For a rule of acceptance, $[x]_A \subseteq POS_{(\alpha,\beta)}(C)$,

$$Des(x) \to accept\ x \in C,$$

its rate of correct acceptance (or accepted positive) and rate of incorrect acceptance (or accepted negative) are given, respectively, by:

$$accuracy(Des(x) \to accept\ x \in C) = \frac{|[x]_A \cap C|}{|[x]_A|} \geq \alpha,$$

$$e_{ia}(Des(x) \to accept\ x \in C) = \frac{|[x]_A \cap C^c|}{|[x]_A|} \leq 1 - \alpha. \tag{10}$$

They are also referred to as the accuracy (or confidence) and the incorrect acceptance error of a rule of acceptance, and are linked together by $accuracy(\cdot) + e_{ia}(\cdot) = 1$. A decision of acceptance is made beyond an α-level confidence or equivalently below an $(1 - \alpha)$-level incorrect acceptance error rate.

For a rule of rejection, $[x]_A \subseteq NEG_{(\alpha,\beta)}(C)$,

$$Des(x) \to reject\ x \in C,$$

its rate of correct rejection (or rejected negative) and rate of incorrect rejection (or rejected positive) are given, respectively, by:

$$accuracy(Des(x) \to reject\ x \in C) = \frac{|[x]_A \cap C^c|}{|[x]_A|} \geq 1 - \beta,$$

$$e_{ir}(Des(x) \to reject\ x \in C) = \frac{|[x]_A \cap C|}{|[x]_A|} \leq \beta. \tag{11}$$

They are also referred to as the accuracy (or confidence) and the incorrect rejection error rate of a rule of rejection, and are linked together by $accuracy(\cdot) + e_{ir}(\cdot) = 1$.

A decision of rejection is made beyond an $(1 - \beta)$-level confidence or equivalently below an β-level incorrect rejection error rate.

For a deferment rule, $[x]_A \subseteq \text{BND}_{(\alpha,\beta)}(C)$,

$$\text{Des}(x) \rightarrow \text{neither accept nor reject } x \in C,$$

its error rate of deferred positive and error rate of deferred negative are given, respectively, by:

$$e_{dp}(\text{Des}(x) \rightarrow \text{neither accept nor reject } x \in C) = \frac{|[x]_A \cap C|}{|[x]_A|},$$

$$e_{dn}(\text{Des}(x) \rightarrow \text{neither accept nor reject } x \in C) = \frac{|[x]_A \cap C^c|}{|[x]_A|}. \tag{12}$$

They are linked by $e_{dp}(\cdot) + e_{dn}(\cdot) = 1$. By definition of boundary region, $\beta \leq e_{dp}(\cdot) \leq \alpha$ and $1 - \alpha \leq e_{dn}(\cdot) \leq 1 - \beta$. A deferment decision is made when one fails to achieve an above α-level confidence for acceptance (or equivalently a below $(1 - \alpha)$-level incorrect acceptance error rate) and, at the same time, an above $(1 - \beta)$-level confidence for rejection (or equivalently a below β-level incorrect rejection error rate). In other words, a deferment decision is made when one is neither confident for an acceptance nor confident for a rejection.

6 Applications of Three-Way Decisions

Three-way decisions have been introduced and investigated from different perspectives and various considerations in many fields. Typically, decisions of acceptance and rejection are made when available information or evidence is sufficient to warrant such a decision beyond certain levels of doubt, above certain levels of confidence, or below certain levels of error. A deferred decision is made when available information or evidence is insufficient. In order to change from a deferred decision into a decision of acceptance or rejection, one must collect new information, search for new evidence, or conduct new testings and experiments.

6.1 Three-Way Decisions in Various Fields

Weller [15] discusses three-way decisions in the editorial peer review process of many journals. An editor typically makes a three-way decision about a manuscript, namely, acceptance, rejection, or further revision, based on comments from reviewers; the final decision of the third category is subject to comments from reviewers in additional round(s) of review.

Wald [9] introduces and examines a framework of a sequential test of a statistical hypothesis based on three-way decisions. At any stage of the experiment, a three-way decision is made, namely, to accept the hypothesis being tested, to reject the hypothesis, and to continue the experiment by making an additional observation. The process is terminated when one of the first two decisions is made; another trial is performed if the third decision is made; the process is continued until eventually either the first or the second decision is made.

Three-way decisions have been investigated from other perspectives in applications of statical inference and decision-making. Woodward and Naylor [16] discuss Bayesian methods in statistical process control. A pair of threshold values on the posterior odds ratio is used to make a three-stage decision about a process: *accept without further inspection*, *adjust (reject) and continue inspecting*, or *continue inspecting*. Forster [17] considers the importance of model selection criteria with a three-way decision: *accept*, *reject* or *suspend judgment*. Goudey [18] examines three-way statistical inference that supports three possible actions for an environmental manager: *act as if there is no problem*, *act as if there is a problem*, or *act as if there is not yet sufficient information to allow a decision*.

The sequential three-way decision-making strategy is commonly used in medical decision making [19, 20]. Pauker and Kassirer [20] discuss a threshold approach to clinical decision-making. A pair of a "testing" threshold and a "test-treatment" threshold is used, with testing threshold being less than the test-treatment threshold. If the probability of disease is smaller than the testing threshold, there should be no treatment and no further testing; if the probability of disease is greater than the test-treatment threshold, treatment should be given without further testing. If the probability is between the two thresholds, a test should be performed so that a decision may be made depending on its results.

Three-way decisions offered by rough sets and probabilistic rough sets have been used by many authors. Herbert and Yao [21–23] study three-way decision-making in an integrated framework of decision-theoretic rough sets and game-theoretic rough sets. Li, Zhang and Swan [24, 25] use three-way decisions in the design of information retrieval systems and intelligent agents systems, where a document is classified into one of three probabilistic regions, namely, relevant, nonrelevant, or possible relevant. Zhao and Zhu [26] and Zhou, Yao and Luo [27] apply results of decision-theoretic rough set models for email spam filtering. In contract to a binary classification, email is put into one of three folders by making a decision of accepting it as legitimate email, rejecting it as legitimate email (or equivalently accepting it as spam), and deferring decision (or treating it as suspected spam). Liu, Yao and Li [28] apply decision-theoretic rough sets for modeling three-way investment decision-making, consisting of "investment, non-investment or further investigation". Ślęzak et al. [29] consider a three-way decision when choosing data packs for query optimization; they classify data packs into the relevant, irrelevant, and suspect data packs. Lingras, Chen and Miao [30] and Yu et al. [31, 32] examine rough clustering in which the quality of a cluster is quantified and interpreted by using various losses of decision-theoretic rough set models. Yang et al. [33, 34] study three-way decision-making with decision-theoretic rough sets in the context of incomplete information systems and multi-agent systems.

Equivalence class	a	b	c	d	$\Pr(C|X_i)$	$\Pr(C^c|X_i)$
X_1	1	1	0	1	0.90	0.10
X_2	0	1	1	0	0.60	0.40
X_3	0	0	1	1	0.40	0.60
X_4	1	1	1	0	0.80	0.20
X_5	0	1	0	1	0.20	0.80

Table 1 An information table

6.2 Generalizations of Decision-Theoretic Rough Set Models

Practical applications of three-way decision-making require further generalizations of the basic decision-theoretic rough set model. Abd El-Monsef and Kilany [35] consider five disjoint regions by generalizing three-region based decision-theoretic rough set model, which leads to five-way decision-making. In general, one may consider m-way decision-making with $m \geq 2$. Liu et al. [36] and Zhou [37] examine multiple-category decision-theoretic rough set models. Liu, Li and Ruan [38] discuss probabilistic model criteria for two-stage decision-making with decision-theoretic rough sets. Yao and Zhou [39] propose a naive Bayesian rough set model, and Liu, Li and Liang [40] use logistic regression, for estimating the required probabilities in decision-theoretic rough set models.

Attribute reduction within decision-theoretic rough set models is another important issue that has been investigated by many authors. For example, Yao and Zhao [41] present a study of several types of reducts; Jia et al. [42] propose cost-based optimal reducts; Li et al. [43] investigate positive-region based reducts. These new classes of reducts are generalizations of reducts of the classical model of rough sets and the basic model of decision-theoretic rough sets. They can be easily related to, and interpreted by, more practical notions such as costs, loss and benefits.

6.3 An Illustrative Example

A simple example is used to demonstrate the main ideas of three-way decision-making using rough sets.

Consider an information table given by Table 1. For clarity, we use a processed information table in which equivalence classes X_i's and conditional probabilities of a concept C, $\Pr(C|X_i)$ and $\Pr(C^c|X_i)$, are given. In the table, each object is described by four attributes a, b, c and d. Based on descriptions of objects, it can be seen that Pawlak positive and negative regions are both the empty set and Pawlak boundary region is the entire universe. Thus, qualitative three-way decisions are of limited value and one needs to use quantitative probabilistic three-way decisions.

The loss function depends crucially on a particular application. It may be influenced by the semantics of the application problem, the expert perception of various risks, and/or expert tolerance levels of risk. In the following, we derive two sets of classification rules for two experts.

Suppose that one expert gives the following loss function:

	C (P)	C^c (N)
a_P (P)	$\lambda_{PP} = 0$	$\lambda_{PN} = 10$
a_B (B)	$\lambda_{BP} = 5$	$\lambda_{BN} = 3$
a_N (N)	$\lambda_{NP} = 14$	$\lambda_{NN} = 0$

It can be observed that the expert is more concerned about both incorrect acceptance and incorrect acceptance. This loss function satisfies conditions (c0) and (c1). By the calculation of α and β, we have:

$$\alpha = \frac{(\lambda_{PN} - \lambda_{BN})}{(\lambda_{PN} - \lambda_{BN}) + (\lambda_{BP} - \lambda_{PP})} = \frac{(10 - 3)}{(10 - 3) + (5 - 0)} = 0.58,$$

$$\beta = \frac{(\lambda_{BN} - \lambda_{NN})}{(\lambda_{BN} - \lambda_{NN}) + (\lambda_{NP} - \lambda_{BP})} = \frac{(3 - 0)}{(3 - 0) + (14 - 5)} = 0.25.$$

By using the pair of thresholds, three probabilistic regions are given by:

$$\text{POS}_{(0.58, 0.25)}(C) = X_1 \cup X_2 \cup X_4,$$
$$\text{BND}_{(0.58, 0.25)}(C) = X_3,$$
$$\text{NEG}_{(0.58, 0.25)}(C) = X_5.$$

Finally, the following set of three-way classification rules are obtained:

- Rule of acceptance:

$$(a = 1) \wedge (b = 1) \wedge (c = 0) \wedge (d = 1) \rightarrow \text{accept } x \in C,$$
$$(a = 0) \wedge (b = 1) \wedge (c = 1) \wedge (d = 0) \rightarrow \text{accept } x \in C,$$
$$(a = 1) \wedge (b = 1) \wedge (c = 1) \wedge (d = 0) \rightarrow \text{accept } x \in C,$$

- Rule of deferment:

$$(a = 0) \wedge (b = 0) \wedge (c = 1) \wedge (d = 1) \rightarrow \text{neither accept nor reject } x \in C,$$

- Rule of rejection:

$$(a = 0) \wedge (b = 1) \wedge (c = 0) \wedge (d = 1) \rightarrow \text{reject } x \in C,$$

where the left hand side of a rule is the description of an object x in the right hand side of the rule.

Suppose that another expert gives a different loss function:

	C (P)	C^c (N)
a_P (P)	$\lambda_{PP} = 0$	$\lambda_{PN} = 8$
a_B (B)	$\lambda_{BP} = 2$	$\lambda_{BN} = 2$
a_N (N)	$\lambda_{NP} = 8$	$\lambda_{NN} = 0$

In this case, the expert is indifferent to incorrect acceptance and incorrect acceptance and is less concerned about a deferred decision. Again, the loss function satisfies conditions (c0) and (c1). Thresholds α and β can be computed as follows:

$$\alpha = \frac{(\lambda_{PN} - \lambda_{BN})}{(\lambda_{PN} - \lambda_{BN}) + (\lambda_{BP} - \lambda_{PP})} = \frac{(8 - 2)}{(8 - 2) + (2 - 0)} = 0.75,$$

$$\beta = \frac{(\lambda_{BN} - \lambda_{NN})}{(\lambda_{BN} - \lambda_{NN}) + (\lambda_{NP} - \lambda_{BP})} = \frac{(2 - 0)}{(2 - 0) + (8 - 2)} = 0.25.$$

Accordingly, the three probabilistic regions are given by:

$$POS_{(0.75, 0.25)}(C) = X_1 \cup X_4,$$
$$BND_{(0.75, 0.25)}(C) = X_2 \cup X_3,$$
$$NEG_{(0.75, 0.25)}(C) = X_5.$$

They lead to the following set of three-way classification rules:

- Rule of acceptance:

$$(a = 1) \wedge (b = 1) \wedge (c = 0) \wedge (d = 1) \rightarrow \text{accept } x \in C,$$
$$(a = 1) \wedge (b = 1) \wedge (c = 1) \wedge (d = 0) \rightarrow \text{accept } x \in C,$$

- Rule of deferment:

$$(a = 0) \wedge (b = 1) \wedge (c = 1) \wedge (d = 0) \rightarrow \text{neither accept nor reject } x \in C,$$
$$(a = 0) \wedge (b = 0) \wedge (c = 1) \wedge (d = 1) \rightarrow \text{neither accept nor reject } x \in C,$$

- Rule of rejection:

$$(a = 0) \wedge (b = 1) \wedge (c = 0) \wedge (d = 1) \rightarrow \text{reject } x \in C.$$

In comparison with the case of the first expert, one rule of acceptance is changed into a rule of deferment. This reflects the second expert's perception of losses or costs of different classification actions.

In general, different loss functions may produce different thresholds, and hence different sets of three-way classification rules. It may also happen that different loss functions produce the same thresholds. In the two examples, two different loss functions produce two different values for threshold α but the same value for threshold β. Consequently, they produce different sets of rules of acceptance and deferment, but the same set of rules of rejection.

7 Conclusion

The notion of three-way decisions has been investigated and used in many different fields. It provides a more practical framework of decision-making with insufficient information or evidence. Three-way decision-making may be interpreted and formulated in many different ways and from various perspectives. Probabilistic rough set models provide one such formulation and interpretation.

Three-way decisions are based on three regions of rough set models. They perhaps better capture the classification philosophy of rough set theory. They are particularly useful and semantically meaningful for interpreting probabilistic rough set models in which probabilistic positive and negative regions are associated with uncertainty. Through the notion of three-way decisions, in terms of acceptance, rejection and deferment, it is possible to establish a useful link between rough set classification and hypothesis testing in statistics. One may expect to see more applications of three-way decisions using rough sets.

References

1. Pawlak, Z.: Rough Sets: Theoretical Aspects of Reasoning About Data. Kluwer Academic, Boston (1991)
2. Grzymała-Busse, J.W.: Knowledge acquisition under uncertainty—a rough set approach. J. Intell. Robot. Syst. **1**, 3–16 (1988)
3. Pawlak, Z.: Rough sets, decision algorithms and Bayes' theorem. Eur. J. Oper. Res. **136**, 181–189 (2002)
4. Wong, S.K.M., Ziarko, W.: Algorithm for inductive learning. Bull. Acad. Pol. Sci., Sér. Sci. Tech. **34**, 271–276 (1986)
5. Yao, Y.Y.: Three-way decision: an interpretation of rules in rough set theory. In: Proceedings of the 4th International Conference on Rough Sets and Knowledge Technology. LNCS (LNAI), vol. 5589, pp. 642–649 (2009)
6. Yao, Y.Y.: Three-way decisions with probabilistic rough sets. Inf. Sci. **180**, 341–353 (2010)
7. Yao, Y.Y.: The superiority of three-way decisions in probabilistic rough set models. Inf. Sci. **181**, 1080–1096 (2011)
8. Ślęzak, D.: Rough sets and Bayes factor. In: Transactions on Rough Sets III. LNCS (LNAI), vol. 3400, pp. 202–229 (2005)
9. Wald, A.: Sequential tests of statistical hypotheses. Ann. Math. Stat. **16**, 117–186 (1945)
10. Yao, Y.Y.: Probabilistic approaches to rough sets. Expert Syst. **20**, 287–297 (2003)
11. Yao, Y.Y.: Probabilistic rough set approximations. Int. J. Approx. Reason. **49**, 255–271 (2008)
12. Yao, Y.Y., Wong, S.K.M.: A decision theoretic framework for approximating concepts. Int. J. Man-Mach. Stud. **37**, 793–809 (1992)
13. Yao, Y.Y., Wong, S.K.M., Lingras, P.A.: Decision-theoretic rough set model. In: Ras, Z.W., Zemankova, M., Emrich, M.L. (eds.) Methodologies for Intelligent Systems, vol. 5, pp. 17–24. North-Holland, New York (1990)
14. Duda, R.O., Hart, P.E.: Pattern Classification and Scene Analysis. Wiley, New York (1973)
15. Weller, A.C.: Editorial Peer Review: Its Strengths and Weaknesses. Information Today Inc., Medford (2001)
16. Woodward, P.W., Naylor, J.C.: An application of Bayesian methods in SPC. The Statistician **42**, 461–469 (1993)
17. Forster, M.R.: Key concepts in model selection: performance and generalizability. J. Math. Psychol. **44**, 205–231 (2000)
18. Goudey, R.: Do statistical inferences allowing three alternative decision give better feedback for environmentally precautionary decision-making. J. Environ. Manag. **85**, 338–344 (2007)
19. Lurie, J.D., Sox, H.C.: Principles of medical decision making. Spine **24**, 493–498 (1999)
20. Pauker, S.G., Kassirer, J.P.: The threshold approach to clinical decision making. N. Engl. J. Med. **302**, 1109–1117 (1980)

21. Herbert, J.P., Yao, J.T.: Criteria for choosing a rough set model. Comput. Math. Appl. **57**, 908–918 (2009)
22. Herbert, J.P., Yao, J.T.: Game-theoretic rough sets. Fundam. Inform. **108**, 267–286 (2011)
23. Herbert, J.P., Yao, J.T.: Analysis of data-driven parameters in game-theoretic rough sets. In: Proceedings of the 6th International Conference on Rough Sets and Knowledge Technology. LNCS (LNAI), vol. 6954, pp. 447–456 (2011)
24. Li, Y., Zhang, C., Swan, J.R.: Rough set based model in information retrieval and filtering. In: Proceeding of the 5th International Conference on Information Systems Analysis and Synthesis, pp. 398–403 (1999)
25. Li, Y., Zhang, C., Swan, J.R.: An information filtering model on the Web and its application in JobAgent. Knowl.-Based Syst. **13**, 285–296 (2000)
26. Zhao, W.Q., Zhu, Y.L.: An email classification scheme based on decision-theoretic rough set theory and analysis of email security. In: Proceedings of 2005 IEEE Region 10 TENCON (2005). doi:10.1109/TENCON.2005.301121
27. Zhou, B., Yao, Y.Y., Luo, J.G.: A three-way decision approach to email spam filtering. In: Proceedings of the 23rd Canadian Conference on Artificial Intelligence. LNCS (LNAI), vol. 6085, pp. 28–39 (2010)
28. Liu, D., Yao, Y.Y., Li, T.R.: Three-way investment decisions with decision-theoretic rough sets. Int. J. Comput. Intell. Syst. **4**, 66–74 (2011)
29. Ślęzak, D., Wróblewski, J., Eastwood, V., Synak, P.: Brighthouse: an analytic data warehouse for ad-hoc queries. Proc. VLDB Endow. **1**, 1337–1345 (2008)
30. Lingras, P., Chen, M., Miao, D.Q.: Rough cluster quality index based on decision theory. IEEE Trans. Knowl. Data Eng. **21**, 1014–1026 (2009)
31. Yu, H., Chu, S.S., Yang, D.C.: Autonomous knowledge-oriented clustering using decision-theoretic rough set theory. In: Proceedings of the 5th International Conference on Rough Sets and Knowledge Technology. LNCS (LNAI), vol. 6401, pp. 687–694 (2010)
32. Yu, H., Liu, Z.G., Wang, G.Y.: Automatically determining the number of clusters using decision-theoretic rough set. In: Proceedings of the 6th International Conference on Rough Sets and Knowledge Technology. LNCS (LNAI), vol. 6954, pp. 447–456 (2011)
33. Yang, X.P., Song, H.G., Li, T.J.: Decision making in incomplete information system based on decision-theoretic rough sets. In: Proceedings of the 6th International Conference on Rough Sets and Knowledge Technology. LNCS (LNAI), vol. 6954, pp. 495–503 (2011)
34. Yang, X.P., Yao, J.T.: A multi-agent decision-theoretic rough set model. In: Proceedings of the 5th International Conference on Rough Sets and Knowledge Technology. LNCS (LNAI), vol. 6401, pp. 711–718 (2010)
35. Abd El-Monsef, M.M.E., Kilany, N.M.: Decision analysis via granulation based on general binary relation. Int. J. Math. Math. Sci. **2007**, 12714 (2007). doi:10.1155/2007/12714
36. Liu, D., Li, T.R., Hu, P., Li, H.X.: Multiple-category classification with decision-theoretic rough sets. In: Proceedings of the 5th International Conference on Rough Sets and Knowledge Technology. LNCS (LNAI), vol. 6401, pp. 703–710 (2010)
37. Zhou, B.: A new formulation of multi-category decision-theoretic rough sets. In: Proceedings of the 6th International Conference on Rough Sets and Knowledge Technology. LNCS (LNAI), vol. 6954, pp. 514–522 (2011)
38. Liu, D., Li, T.R., Ruan, D.: Probabilistic model criteria with decision-theoretic rough sets. Inf. Sci. **181**, 3709–3722 (2011)
39. Yao, Y.Y., Zhou, B.: Naive Bayesian rough sets. In: Proceedings of the 5th International Conference on Rough Sets and Knowledge Technology. LNCS (LNAI), vol. 6401, pp. 719–726 (2010)
40. Liu, D., Li, T.R., Liang, D.C.: A new discriminant analysis approach under decision-theoretic rough sets. In: Proceedings of the 6th International Conference on Rough Sets and Knowledge Technology. LNCS (LNAI), vol. 6954, pp. 476–485 (2011)
41. Yao, Y.Y., Zhao, Y.: Attribute reduction in decision-theoretic rough set models. Inf. Sci. **178**, 3356–3373 (2008)

42. Jia, X.Y., Li, W.W., Shang, L., Chen, J.J.: An optimization viewpoint of decision-theoretic rough set model. In: Proceedings of the 6th International Conference on Rough Sets and Knowledge Technology. LNCS (LNAI), vol. 6954, pp. 457–465 (2011)
43. Li, H.X., Zhou, X.Z., Zhao, J.B., Liu, D.: Attribute reduction in decision-theoretic rough set model: a further investigation. In: Proceedings of the 6th International Conference on Rough Sets and Knowledge Technology. LNCS (LNAI), vol. 6954, pp. 466–475 (2011)

Rough Set Based Decision Support—Models Easy to Interpret

Sebastian Widz and Dominik Ślęzak

Abstract Rapid evolution of technology allows people to record more data than ever. Gathered information is intensively used by data analysts and domain experts. Collections of patterns extracted from data compose models (compact representations of discovered knowledge), which are at the heart of each decision support system. Models based on mathematically sophisticated methods may achieve high accuracy but they are hardly understandable by decision-makers. Models relying on symbolic, e.g. rule based methods can be less accurate but more intuitive. In both cases, feature subset selection leads to an increase of interpretability and practical usefulness of decision support systems. In this chapter, we discuss how rough sets can contribute in this respect.

1 Introduction

Technology brings us every day almost unlimited amount of information. As a result, one can now suffer not from a lack of information but from its overload. Choosing the right data and the right way of decision making is crucial to both commercial and research projects. The concept of a decision support system (further abbreviated as DSS) was introduced to assist decision-makers with such choices.

Since their very beginning, DSSs have been constantly evolving with respect to both the underlying methodologies and the major areas of applications. Nowadays,

S. Widz
Systems Research Institute, Polish Academy of Sciences, Newelska 6, 01-447 Warsaw, Poland

S. Widz (✉)
XPLUS SA, Gżegżółki 4, 02-804 Warsaw, Poland
e-mail: sebastian.widz@xplus.pl

D. Ślęzak
Institute of Mathematics, University of Warsaw, Banacha 2, 02-097 Warsaw, Poland

D. Ślęzak
Infobright Inc., Poland, Krzywickiego 34 pok. 219, 02-078 Warsaw, Poland
e-mail: slezak@infobright.com

G. Peters et al. (eds.), *Rough Sets: Selected Methods and Applications in Management and Engineering*, Advanced Information and Knowledge Processing,
DOI 10.1007/978-1-4471-2760-4_6, © Springer-Verlag London Limited 2012

DSSs are used in a number of fields, such as investment [1], cost accounting [2], marketing [3], production [4], supply chain management [5] and many others [6].

Each DSS is based on a model by which we understand a compact representation of knowledge. Models vary with respect to required level of human interaction, from static, predefined black boxes that work on the input-output basis to models that interact with domain experts in process of discovering patterns. The discovered patterns are usually stored as sets of rules and constitute so called expert systems.

The above process is often referred to as the knowledge discovery in databases (further abbreviated as KDD) [7]. It consists of steps such as selection of the most representative features (also referred to as, e.g. attributes, variables, or dimensions), analysis of dependencies between them, as well as extraction, evaluation and interpretation of the most meaningful patterns. All these steps are typical for the DSS model design. They should be performed with extensive use of data mining tools and, whenever possible, interaction with domain experts. The ability to interact during the DSS model design is highly important because, after all, decision making should take into account human knowledge, experience and intuition.

Data mining tools should be treated as complementary to the interaction framework. They can be divided into *symbolic* and *non-symbolic* methods [8]. Symbolic methods focus on finding relationships within data, typically reported in form of rules in a feature-value language. Rules are built using basic logical operators. Examples include rule induction methods such as learning if-then rules [9] or decision trees [10]. Non-symbolic methods (also referred to as sub-symbolic or numeric) are based on more mathematically advanced paradigms. They are focused on classification properties of data rather than data patterns or if-then dependencies. Examples of non-symbolic methods include neural networks [11] and support vector machines [12].

Non-symbolic methods may achieve high accuracy but they are hard to understand by decision-makers. Symbolic methods may be easier to modify by involving domain knowledge. In both cases, feature selection—one of the above-mentioned steps of KDD—leads to an increase of interpretability and usefulness of DSSs. Even the most complicated methods yield clearer outcomes when applied to data with significantly less features. Sometimes it is even worth working with a number of less accurate sub-models learned from far smaller feature subsets, in order to expose different aspects of the problem and the underlying data to decision-makers. It is worth doing even given an additional requirement of fusion of such sub-models into the final decision model, which might require additional explanation to decision-makers interested in technical details.

Rough sets [13, 14] have proven to be a successful tool in feature selection (see e.g. [15, 16]). The rough set approach is based on *decision reducts*—irreducible subsets of features, which determine specified decision classes in (almost) the same degree as the original set of features. Determining decisions can be interpreted analogously to, e.g. functional or multivalued dependencies in relational databases. Subsets of features providing exactly the same degree of determination as the original set are often referred to as *crisp* decision reducts, in opposite to so called *approximate* decision reducts [17, 18] where some controlled decrease of determination is allowed. By specifying a threshold for allowed decrease of determination, one can address the balance between decision model's simplicity and accuracy. Indeed, it is easier to search for smaller subsets of features yielding simpler sub-models under loosened constraints for decision determination, although too weak constraints may also cause poorer accuracy. However, as stated above, even relatively less accurate sub-models may lead toward a very accurate final model, if the processes of sub-models' design are synchronized.

We refer the reader to, e.g. [19, 20] for other extensions of decision reducts. In all cases a reduct is assumed to exclude redundant features, on top of those necessary to meet predefined criteria. Accordingly, rough sets provide an example of feature subset selection (further abbreviated as FSS) methodology [21, 22].

The identified feature subsets can be employed as an input to the other data mining algorithms or can be directly used as a classifier, by utilizing them to generate decision rules (see e.g. [23]). It is worth noting that during the DSS design phase one can choose which of the data mining techniques will be later applied in the model, both generally (e.g. symbolic or non-symbolic methods) and in more detail (e.g. neural networks or support vector machines). Therefore, one may attempt to adjust the above-mentioned feature subset criteria and optimization goals to specific data mining algorithms to be used later. For example, default optimization function refers to the subsets' cardinality, but more specific goal in case of symbolic methods may be to minimize the number of induced decision rules (see e.g. [24]). Furthermore, the criteria of feature elimination may refer to the measures of determining decision or preserving information about decision by feature subsets, which may mean something different for classification models learned from each of the algorithms.

The feature subset search methods, including those based on rough sets, can produce one or more results. Then, each of the subsets can be used to produce a classifier. In case of a single classifier approach, one is supposed to choose the best-found feature subset as a base for the decision model. On the other hand, a larger number of best-found feature subsets can produce multiple classifiers, which is in line with the classifier ensembles—a popular and powerful idea in machine learning [25, 26].

Classifier ensembles perform usually better than their components used independently. Combining several classifiers is efficient especially if they are substantially different from each other. One of the approaches is to construct many different classifiers based on the least overlapping subsets, which goes along perfectly with the above observations on the rough set based FSS methods [27]. This way, one can better represent data to people, as they can observe multiple subsets of features providing roughly the same or complementary information. In fact, the feature subsets applied in ensembles can be relatively smaller than in case of a single feature subset approach, if we can guarantee that combination of less accurate classifier components (further referred to as base classifiers) will lead back to a satisfactory level of determining the decision or preserving information about the decision. This is important because the outcomes of even most complicated non-symbolic data mining methods become better understandable if computed over smaller subsets of features.

Chapter organization: Section 2 introduces the basics of DSSs. Section 3 describes various types of FSS, including methods based on rough sets. Section 4 shows how to use ensembles of feature subsets in DSS model design. Section 5 discusses an example of a rough set inspired technique of extracting such ensembles from data. Section 6 summarizes our observations.

2 Decision Support Systems

DSSs are often identified with terms such as business intelligence [28], data warehousing [29], online analytical processing [30], online analytical mining [31], enterprise resource planning [32] and statistical analysis [33]. Indeed, the DSS platforms incorporate all those technologies as corresponding to their particular layers. However, a DSS as a whole should be understood as the system that supports people in their decision processes, with its architecture based on three main components: dialog, data and modeling, as presented in Fig. 1. The distinction of such three components is often referred to as the DDM paradigm [34]. The dialog component of DSSs should allow non-technical decision-makers to easily interact with the system. The data component should allow access to a variety of data sources. The modeling component should provide tools for the analysis and problem modeling. It is important to note that the last of the above components includes the design phase of the decision process. It is the most important element which should allow interactive creation of a model which becomes, as already mentioned, a compact representation of the knowledge discovered in data.

Depending on the nature of a decision problem, the model can take various forms imposed by the applied methods. Prediction (classification, regression), segmentation (clustering) and relationship discovering (association) are the typical data mining tasks reflecting the needs of the DSS models. However, according to the principles of the KDD process employed at this stage of the DSS creation, the prior step should always be related to FSS. This step has a tremendous impact on the final DSS quality and performance. It provides decision-makers with a better insight into data dependencies. It becomes a powerful tool especially when combined with domain knowledge. On one hand, the system can initialize the design process with the set of selected features of the highest importance. On the other hand, domain experts can modify the feature subsets according to their knowledge and preferences through interfaces.

With respect to the model components and the way people interact with them, DSSs can be divided into *knowledge-*, *model-* and *data-driven* [35].[1] In a knowledge-driven DSS, decision support comes from the knowledge or patterns discovered in data. The discovery process is based on data mining and statistical techniques. Interaction with such systems usually involves high knowledge about the applied techniques, as well as domain knowledge in the field of analysis. On

---

[1] The meaning of terms *knowledge-driven*, *model-driven* and *data-driven* may be confusing for the readers with some background in data mining. For example, the knowledge-driven DSSs do not necessarily assume the usage of any type of domain ontology. As another example, the data-driven DSSs do have much in common with the data mining algorithms.

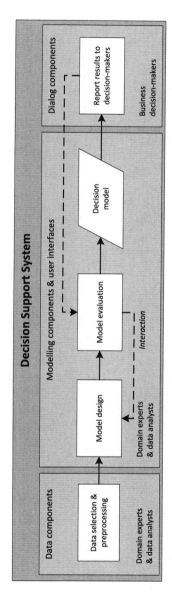

Fig. 1 DSS architecture

the other hand, an appropriate support at the level of feature subsets chosen for the model creation may ease this kind of interaction to a large extent. In case of the model-driven category, decision support comes from the build-in decision model (e.g. financial models) that is based on some previous research in a particular domain. The manipulation of the embedded model is done by changing its parameter values however the principal model characteristic remains static. The business intelligence term what-if analysis is the most elementary example here. Interaction with such systems involves knowledge about the model and the meaning of its variables. Finally, in a data-driven DSS, decision support comes from the information system designed to present the data via different kinds of reports used as input for making strategic decisions and controlling daily operations. Data warehouses, management information systems and various business intelligence tools are examples of such systems. Usually, the decision-maker has no influence on the model. Any changes in the model would require utilization of the IT resources. In present DSS applications these categories are usually mixed.

DSSs can deal with three categories of problems: *structured, semi-structured* and *unstructured* [36].[2] The first category relates to problems with already well-established procedures of reaching the optimal solution, both with respect to the planning of particular stages of data preparation, analysis and interpretation, as well as specific techniques applied at each of those stages. Semi- and unstructured problems are characterized respectively as the ones with an unknown optimal solution or no solution at all. While structured problems can be solved in an automatic fashion, semi- and unstructured problems require individual judgment. In such cases, domain knowledge is frequently used in decision-making process [37].

In case of semi-structured problems it is especially important to do what we have already mentioned in Section 1—that is to combine the existing data mining algorithms and expert system components with simple interfaces allowing domain experts to modify the core model(s) based on their experience. On one hand, the use of data mining can help in the data preparation process, e.g. choosing important features from the data set (the already-discussed FSS processes), choosing representative instances or concepts from data (instance selection) or generating additional information in order to improve the analytical process (feature extraction). On the other hand, data mining methods provide tools for data analysis, e.g. create a set of symbolic rules that could explain dependencies in data. Possibilities of improvement that can be introduced to the model based on domain expert remarks exist in both cases. Similar routines should be followed in case of unstructured problems, provided that the system can support the whole process of the decision model design.

Analytical solutions of unstructured problems start with data preparation. As it is unknown how to perform it optimally, the process of data gathering might result in collection of any data that could possibly help in problem solving. Such attitude

---

[2]Coincidentally, the terms *structured, semi-structured* and *unstructured* are also used for categorizing data formats in data mining and databases. However, although there are some high level analogies, these two categorizations should not be confused with each other.

can cause an excessive growth of data size, in terms of the number of instances and features. For a human, it is often impossible to discover all dependencies and patterns hidden in such data. Hence, it is important to combine all mentioned decision system components. The use of data mining tools together with simple interfaces should allow both initial automatic "pre-model" construction and further model improvements. In the case of FSS, this may mean changing the discovered subsets by interactive and iterative removals and additions of some features according to domain knowledge.

3 Feature Subset Selection and Rough Sets

FSS is an important step in many knowledge discovery and decision support applications. It establishes the basis for better problem understanding, as well as more efficient classification, prediction and approximation models [38]. In real world, the challenge that all decision-makers must face is where to focus their attention. When too many details are provided, one has to decide which aspects of a considered problem are relevant. Such choices are usually made based on domain knowledge. FSS may establish a very helpful framework with this respect.

Feature subsets can be searched using various approaches, following *filter*, *wrapper*, or *embedded* paradigms [21]. In the filter approach, the feature subset(s) are selected as a preprocessing step [39]. Selected features or feature subsets are then used by a learning algorithm to construct a decision support model. Feature subset evaluation is part of the selection process and it does not depend on the learning algorithm. Filter methods do not incorporate learning. In other words, the phase of learning a decision model based on the previously found feature subset(s) may have nothing in common with the criteria and algorithms employed in the phase of FSS.

In the wrapper approach, FSS is performed in combination with the learning algorithm [40]. First, the subset candidate is selected and used by the algorithm in order to evaluate its performance. If the obtained accuracy satisfies the assumed level, the search process stops and the selected feature subset (or subsets) is used for model construction, otherwise the inner loop sends feedback to the so called feature selector and the process is repeated. The mechanism of generating candidate feature subsets is external to the learning algorithm, but its performance strictly depends on the above mentioned feedback, thus only the best found subsets (i.e.: the subsets being the bases for the most accurate classifiers) are used by the model.

In the embedded approach, FSS is a part of the training process and feature relevance is obtained from the objective of the learning algorithm [41]. In contrast to filter and wrapper, embedded methods can be used in two ways: in order to explicitly construct a classifier, or to provide some feature subset(s) for further stages. In the first case, the learning algorithm leads to the decision model while reducing the feature dimensionality. In the second case, the obtained features the input to other methods of model construction. However, the criteria used for FSS should be then carefully synchronized with the specifics of the learning methods applied later. The basic schema of all three FSS methods is presented in Fig. 2.

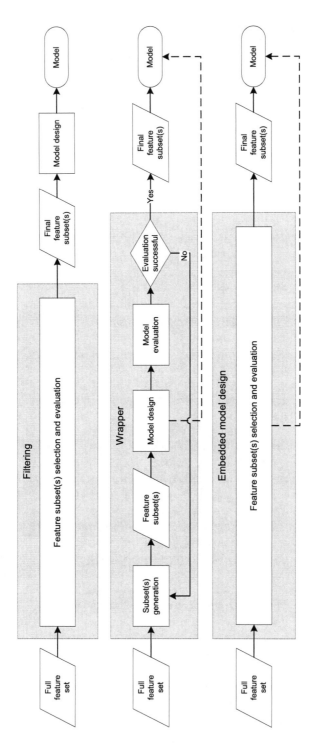

Fig. 2 Filter, wrapper and embedded FSS

Traditional wrapper approaches are often criticized because of massive amounts of calculations required to find a feature subset satisfying the accuracy threshold specified for the learning method. Coarse search techniques may cause overfitting, which means that the classifier may recognize only the data used during learning process [22]. The main drawback of filter approaches relates to ignoring the effects of selected features on the accuracy of further applied learning algorithms. Some methods attempt to solve this issue by defining feature selection criteria that resemble specific classifier learning mechanisms as much as possible. The usage of feature selectors as an input to the learning processes is common aspect of filters and wrappers. It exposes an additional phase, which can be used by domain experts to investigate the proposed feature subsets and modify them according to their preferences. A lack of such phase may be considered a drawback of embedded approaches, unless the interaction can be conducted both with respect to feature subsets and algorithms using them to derive decision models.

The rough set based FSS methods are usually regarded as an example of the filter approach (see e.g. [42]). There are numerous rough set based algorithms aimed at searching for decision reducts, which are irreducible subsets of features that satisfy predefined criteria of (approximate) determination of decision features [14]. Those criteria are verified on the training data and can encode more or less directly the risk of misclassification by if-then rules with their left sides referring to the values of investigated feature subsets and their right sides referring to decisions [43]. Discovered decision reducts can be followed by arbitrary learning algorithms. The general focus on the space of feature subsets rather than on single features has resulted in a number of intelligent search techniques documented in rough set literature (see e.g. [19, 23]).

The rough set based FSS methods can also be interpreted as an example of the embedded approach. This is because decision reducts may be used explicitly for generating the sets of if-then rules constituting a classifier. We refer the reader to [27, 44] for more details on how rules generated within the rough set framework can be interpreted for the purposes of classification and decision support. Regardless of specific interpretations, it is worth noting that decision reducts with a smaller number of features usually generate a smaller amount of rules. It is also quite easy to explicitly redefine the optimization goal to minimize the number of generated rules while searching for the most valuable decision reducts (see e.g. [24]). In such cases, we obtain shorter and better supported rules that tend to be more robust and practically meaningful, with their accuracy level guaranteed by the (approximate) decision determination constraints.

4 Ensembles of Classifiers and Feature Subsets

Rough sets allow expressing the discovered knowledge in the domain terms, either at the level of identified feature subsets or their corresponding decision rules. Such knowledge representation may help domain experts to interact with DSSs by means of changing rules or adding/removing features according to their preferences. However, it is often hard to decide how to modify a given feature subset. Moreover, such modification may cause changes that can be too unpredictable in the model's performance. Therefore, it is worth considering models based on multiple feature subsets or, in other words, the ensembles of feature subsets, as they may provide more insight into data dependencies and enable to represent knowledge from different perspectives.

In machine learning, the term *ensemble* refers to multiple instances of algorithms that work together to improve the decision model's performance [45, 46]. Outputs of each of the algorithms in the ensemble are combined using various techniques into one common result. The rationale for such approach is that it is more difficult to optimize the design of a general model than in case of combination of relatively simpler classifiers focusing on particular aspects of data and the corresponding DSS requirements. Using the classifier ensembles as decision models offers a simple yet efficient technique for obtaining increased levels of final accuracy. Figure 3 illustrates a high-level architecture of the ensemble decision model.

Ensemble accuracy depends both on the quality of the problem decomposition and individual accuracies of base classifiers. Decomposition refers to the way base classifiers are trained. Individual accuracies are very important but, as shown in [47, 48], in order to improve final accuracy some form of diversity among base classifiers must exist. Indeed, if all base classifiers behave in nearly the same way, little is achieved by combining their mechanisms.

In machine learning, diversity is usually considered by means of classifiers' *output*. Classifiers are regarded as different from the output perspective, if they address different, mutually complementary classification aspects or subspaces of instances. A popular method based on diversity of classification aspects is decomposing a multi-class classification problem into a set of two-class sub-problems, each of them handled by a different base classifier [49]. Another example relates to usage of domain knowledge to decompose the nature of decisions into a hierarchy of layers that can be addressed more easily [50]. On the other hand, among a number of rough set inspired methods based on the output diversity understood by means of subspaces of instances, there are ensembles of decision bireducts—families of irreducible feature subsets determining decisions subject to minimally overlapping sets of outliers [51].

Diversity can also be expressed in terms of the algorithms' *design* and classifiers' *input* [26]. Both these aspects can strengthen the above-discussed output complementarity, although they may have different implications for interactions with people. The design aspect of diversity relates to the types of algorithms used to train base classifiers. Although it may highly improve the overall model's accuracy, the model's clarity may decrease, making interactions harder. When it comes to the input aspect of diversity the situation is quite the opposite. From this perspective, classifiers are considered different when they produce their predictions based on different feature subsets or different instance subspaces. Our further considerations are focused on ensembles optimized by means of input diversity because this particular type of diversity is especially important for DSS performance in practice. However,

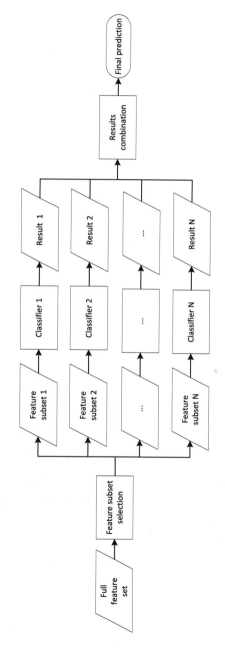

Fig. 3 Prediction model based on the ensemble of feature subsets

increase of input diversity is expected to imply the same for output diversity as a desired side effect.

Out of a number of methodologies of classifier ensemble construction, let us focus on boosting [52] and bagging [25]. Both algorithms are based on manipulating the training set samples. Boosting method works by repeatedly running a learning algorithm on variously distributed training data. In each iteration, the number of instances misclassified by a previously produced classifier is used to prepare the training set for the next iteration, by prioritizing misclassified cases. The classifier constructed in the next iteration is focused on instances with higher priority value. In the case of bagging (bootstrap aggregating), the data sets created from the original training set may be mutually disjointed or minimally overlapped. The base classifiers are trained over the sample of instances. Classifiers are built independently, while in boosting each classifier is influenced by the performance of those that were built prior to its construction.

At the beginning of this section we informally introduced another methodology, which may be referred to as the ensemble feature selection (further abbreviated as EFS). In the traditional FSS, the goal is to find the best feature subset for the learning method. EFS has the goal of finding such multiple subsets of features that will appropriately promote disagreement among base classifiers, thus fulfilling the requirement of diversity in the ensemble [53]. Of course this is only one of the possible usages of the idea of ensembles of feature subsets. As an example, in [54] it is proposed to consider such ensembles in order to eventually build a single, more robust feature subset, used later to train a single decision model. However, in this chapter we focus on EFS understood as outputting multiple subsets, further referred to as base feature subsets, by analogy to base classifiers and as the actual means for constructing base classifiers in the combined decision model. A simplified scheme of such approach is illustrated by Fig. 4.

There are numerous methods of searching for ensembles of feature subsets such as random subspace techniques [55], multi-objective genetic algorithms [56], or, e.g. combinations of bagging and traditional FSS [57]. In order to construct a good ensemble, most of those methods take into account various diversity aspects when defining constraints or optimization principles. We refer the reader to [58, 59] for a more detailed discussion on diversity and disagreement measures.

Diversity based on the differentiation of feature subsets enables us to increase the knowledge representation power of decision models. One might assume that this type of diversity does not necessarily lead to increasing the corresponding classifier ensemble's diversity with respect to the outputs of its particular components. However, if appropriately handled, searching for ensembles of minimally overlapping base feature subsets may lead to the construction of base classifiers as being complementary to each other by means of correct analysis of different instance subspaces [51].

As an illustration, let us consider a group of strongly correlated features. In the case of traditional FSS, one might expect only one representative of that group to be present in the resulting feature subset. It may occur that some of the features preferred by domain experts are not included. Adding preferred features would then

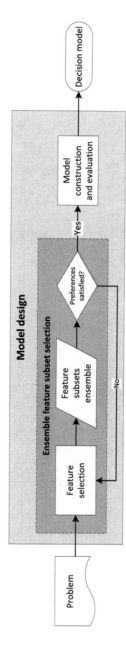

Fig. 4 Decision model design based on ensembles of feature subsets

Fig. 5 A data set with nine
features and exactly three
decision reducts: R1, R2 and
R3. For permutation-based
algorithm proposed in [18,
27], almost 43% out of 11!
feature permutations result
with R1, while slightly over
28.5% of permutations result
with each of R2 and R3

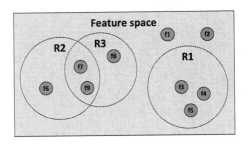

lead to redundancy and, as a consequence, to an increased risk of overfitting. When it
comes to ensembles, strongly correlated features can be split among different feature
subsets, with a higher probability of having each of the preferred features in some of
the subsets. It may be regarded as a consensus between avoiding redundancy at the
level of each of separate base feature subsets and the fact that in some applications
it is truly worth operating with more features than it might seem at a first glance.

5 Ensembles of Decision Reducts

Let us now explain how rough sets can be used as the EFS method. First of all, rough
set techniques allow the production of many feature subsets in the form of decision
reducts, which determine predefined decision classes according to some specified
criteria. This assures the quality of feature subsets used as inputs in further learning
process. Strongly correlated features are then expected to occur exchangeably in the
discovered decision reducts. The same situation takes place for subsets of features
that enable analyzing decisions from different angles. This results in the ensembles
consisting of complementary yet simple feature subset based classifiers.

As mentioned in Section 4, the extraction of the most interesting decision reducts
from data is not easy. There is a number of theoretical results emphasizing the complexity of search for minimal (optimal) or generating all (almost all) decision reducts
(see e.g. [14, 17]). From the perspective of the DSS model design, we should also
remember that it may be reasonable to work with relatively low numbers of different decision reducts because overcomplicated feature subset ensembles could be
too difficult to handle for people. In [18, 27], in order to search for decision reducts
ensembles, we used a heuristic algorithm based on randomly generated permutations of features. For each tested permutation, the procedure analogous to well-
known backward feature elimination (see e.g. [21]) was applied to construct the
corresponding decision reduct. Features were tested in reversed order of appearance
in permutation, with (approximate) decision determination criteria examined every
time.

Figure 5 shows the potential of the above technique to promote ensembles with
high input diversity according to the subsets of features. It illustrates a data set with
only three existing decision reducts (R1, R2, R3). As R1 and R2 are overlapping, it
should be preferred to include either R1 and R3, or R2 and R3 into the ensemble.

It turns out that such combinations of decision reducts are indeed more likely to be discovered while searching through the space of feature permutations and memorizing the best obtained results. The discovery process can be further optimized by more intelligent search operators (see e.g. [24]) or adding optimization criteria reflecting other types of ensemble diversity (see e.g. [60]).

Feature permutation based methodology can be also generalized onto discovery of other forms of data based knowledge representation, such as approximate functional dependencies [18] or already mentioned decision bireducts [51] that can be, actually, treated as a rough set inspired adaptation of the ideas of bagging and boosting. Another important aspect of using a generic mechanism based on permutations is its ability to take into account domain expert preferences. Let us note that features occurring in front of a permutation are more likely to get included into the resulting decision reduct. Thus, human preferences can be translated into feature weights or rankings applied during random generation of permutations. The above technique does not require advanced algorithmic modifications. It influences only the input permutations. This way, domain experts may interact with the EFS framework fully iteratively.

6 Conclusions

In machine learning, models based on symbolic methods allow expressing discovered knowledge in domain terms and presenting it to people in easy to interpret forms, such as decision rules or trees. On the other hand, even if non-symbolic approaches are more adequate for a given data problem, some symbolic techniques can be used as a prior step in order to support domain experts interested in tuning the model and, this way, expressing their experience. From this perspective, FSS is surely a good phase to interact with people. It plays a very important role in the construction of decision models. It enables us to simplify them, which is essential for efficiency and interpretability of the learning algorithms.

Rough set methods can be applied in the FSS process or used explicitly to build symbolic classifiers. Rough set based decision reducts can be therefore considered in various general scenarios of FSS. By definition, decision reducts provide the same or similar level of decision determination as the whole set of features. Thus, the use of decision reducts allows eliminating redundancies and giving domain experts clearer means to interact with DSS models by adding or removing features.

Rough set based algorithms can be also employed to produce multiple decision reducts, which is important for the EFS methodologies. The use of ensembles gives a better multi-perspective view of dependencies discovered in the data. It is worth working with base feature subsets that are substantially different from each other. In this case, feature subsets in the ensembles can be kept relatively smaller than in a single feature subset approach to the DSS design. From this perspective, it may be useful to leverage various types of approximate decision reducts ensembles that are aimed at inexact, mutually complementary determination of decisions.

Ensembles of feature subsets provide one more layer of model interpretability. They allow creating models based on simpler classifiers. However, the use of ensembles requires an additional mechanism of combining base classifier predictions, which might be difficult to follow by decision-makers. Moreover, decision-makers may find it hard to operate with too many feature subsets. Such issues need to be further investigated with respect to both prediction and representation characteristics of the ensemble based DSSs. Nevertheless, the ability to learn and interact at the level of multiple feature subsets seems to provide more advantages than disadvantages.

Acknowledgements The second author was supported by the grant N N516 077837 from the Ministry of Science and Higher Education of the Republic of Poland and by the National Centre for Research and Development (NCBiR) under the grant SP/I/1/77065/10 by the strategic scientific research and experimental development program: "Interdisciplinary System for Interactive Scientific and Scientific-Technical Information".

References

1. Kivijärvi, H., Tuominen, M.: A decision support system for evaluating intangible investments. Comput. Ind. Eng. **25**(1–4), 353–356 (1993)
2. Januszewski, A.: The model and tools for creating a decision support system with the application of activity based costing (ABC-DSS). In: Proc. of the 6th Int. Conf. on Business Information Systems, Colorado Springs, USA (2003)
3. Tan, D., Sim, Y., Yeoh, W.: Applying feature selection methods to improve the predictive model of a direct marketing problem. In: Proc. of the 2nd International Conference on Software Engineering and Computer Systems (ICSECS), pp. 155–167. Springer, Berlin (2011)
4. Wauters, T., Verbeeck, K., Verstraete, P., Vanden Berghe, G., De Causmaecker, P.: Real-world production scheduling for the food industry: an integrated approach. Eng. Appl. Artif. Intell. (2011). doi:10.1016/j.engappai.2011.05.002
5. Doyle, L.: Supply chain information systems and decision support. In: Adam, F., Humphreys, P. (eds.) Encyclopedia of Decision Making and Decision Support Technologies. Information Science Reference, pp. 814–821. IGI Global, Hershey (2008)
6. Burstein, F., Holsapple, C.W.: Handbook on Decision Support Systems, Parts 1 & 2, 1st edn. Springer, Berlin (2008)
7. Klösgen, W., Żytkow, J.M. (eds.): Handbook of Data Mining and Knowledge Discovery. Oxford University Press, London (2002)
8. Kovalerchuk, B., Vityaev, E., Yupusov, H.: Symbolic methodology in numeric data mining: relational techniques for financial applications. Comput. Engin. Finance Sci. J. (2002)
9. Agrawal, R., Imieliński, T., Swami, A.: Mining association rules between sets of items in large databases. In: Proc. of the 1993 ACM SIGMOD Int. Conf. on Management of Data. ACM, New York (1993)
10. Nair, B.B., Mohandas, V.P., Sakthivel, N.R.: A decision tree—rough set hybrid system for stock market trend prediction. Int. J. Comput. Appl. **6**(9), 1–6 (2010)
11. Hung, Y.H.: A neural network classifier with rough set-based feature selection to classify multiclass IC package products. Adv. Eng. Inform. **23**(3), 348–357 (2009)
12. Lingras, P., Butz, C., Bhalchandra, P.: Financial series forecasting using dual rough support vector regression. In: Peters, G., Lingras, P., Ślęzak, D., Yao, Y. (eds.) Rough Sets: Selected Methods and Applications in Management and Engineering. Springer, Berlin (2012)
13. Pawlak, Z.: Rough Sets: Theoretical Aspects of Reasoning About Data. Kluwer Academic, Dordrecht (1991)
14. Pawlak, Z., Skowron, A.: Rudiments of rough sets. Inf. Sci. **177**(1), 3–27 (2007)

15. Banka, H., Mitra, S.: Feature selection, classification and rule generation using rough sets. In: Peters, G., Lingras, P., Ślęzak, D., Yao, Y. (eds.) Rough Sets: Selected Methods and Applications in Management and Engineering. Springer, Berlin (2012)
16. Świniarski, R.W., Skowron, A.: Rough set methods in feature selection and recognition. Pattern Recognit. Lett. **24**(6), 833–849 (2003)
17. Moshkov, M., Piliszczuk, M., Zielosko, B.: Partial Covers, Reducts and Decision Rules in Rough Sets. Springer, Berlin (2010)
18. Ślęzak, D.: Rough sets and functional dependencies in data: foundations of association reducts. In: Transactions on Computational Science 5. LNCS, vol. 5540, pp. 182–205. Springer, Berlin (2009)
19. Jensen, R., Shen, Q.: Computational Intelligence and Feature Selection: Rough and Fuzzy Approaches. Wiley, Hoboken (2008)
20. Yao, Y., Zhao, Y., Wang, J.: On reduct construction algorithms. In: Transactions on Computational Science 2. LNCS, vol. 5150, pp. 100–117. Springer, Berlin (2008)
21. Guyon, I., Elisseeff, A.: An introduction to variable and feature selection. J. Mach. Learn. Res. **3**, 1157–1182 (2003)
22. Kohavi, R., Sommerfeld, D.: Feature subset selection using the wrapper method: overfitting and dynamic search space topology. In: Proc. of KDD 1995, pp. 192–197 (1995)
23. Bazan, J.G., Nguyen, H.S., Nguyen, S.H., Synak, P., Wróblewski, J.: Rough set algorithms in classification problem. In: Polkowski, L., Tsumoto, S., Lin, T.Y. (eds.) New Developments in Knowledge Discovery in Information Systems, pp. 49–88. Physica-Verlag, Heidelberg (2000)
24. Wróblewski, J.: Adaptive aspects of combining approximation spaces. In: Pal, S.K., Polkowski, L., Skowron, A. (eds.) Rough-Neural Computing, pp. 139–156. Springer, Berlin (2004)
25. Breiman, L.: Bagging predictors. Mach. Learn. **24**(2), 123–140 (1996)
26. Kuncheva, L.I.: Combining Pattern Classifiers: Methods and Algorithms. Wiley, New York (2004)
27. Ślęzak, D., Widz, S.: Rough-set-inspired feature subset selection, classifier construction, and rule aggregation. In: Proc. of RSKT. LNCS, vol. 6954, pp. 81–88. Springer, Berlin (2011)
28. Lim, A.H.L., Lee, C.: Processing online analytics with classification and association rule mining. Knowl.-Based Syst. **23**(3), 248–255 (2010)
29. Bao, Y., Zhang, L.: Decision support system based on data warehouse. World Acad. Sci. Eng. Technol. **71**, 172–176 (2010)
30. Jukic, N., Jukic, B., Malliaris, M.: Online analytical processing (OLAP) for decision support. In: Handbook on Decision Support Systems 1. Int. Handbooks on Information Systems (2008)
31. Panchal, H.M.: Online analytical mining: architecture and challenges. IUP J. Syst. Manag. **8**(2), 40–45 (2010)
32. Holsapple, C.W., Sena, M.P.: The decision-support characteristics of ERP systems. Int. J. Hum.-Comput. Interact. **16**(1), 101–123 (2003)
33. Liu, B.C., Tzeng, G.H., Hsieh, C.T.: Energy planning and environmental quality management: a decision support system approach. Energy Econ. **14**(4), 302–307 (1992)
34. Sprague, R.H., Watson, H.J.: Decision Support for Management. Prentice-Hall, Englewood Cliffs (1996)
35. Mora, M., Forgionne, G., Gupta, J.N.D. (eds.): Decision Making Support Systems: Achievements and Challenges for the New Decade. Idea Group Publishing, Hershey (2003)
36. Averweg, U.R.: Decision support systems and decision-making processes. In: Adam, F., Humphreys, P. (eds.) Encyclopedia of Decision Making and Decision Support Technologies. Information Science Reference, pp. 218–224. IGI Global, Hershey (2008)
37. Paprika, Z.Z.: Analysis and intuition in strategic decision making: the case of California. In: Adam, F., Humphreys, P. (eds.) Encyclopedia of Decision Making and Decision Support Technologies. Information Science Reference, pp. 20–28. IGI Global, Hershey (2008)
38. Han, J., Kamber, M.: Data Mining: Concepts and Techniques, 2nd edn. Morgan Kaufmann, San Mateo (2006)
39. Blum, A., Langley, P.: Selection of relevant features and examples in machine learning. Artif. Intell. **97**, 245–271 (1997)

40. Kohavi, R., John, G.H.: Wrappers for feature subset selection. Artif. Intell. J. **97**(1–2), 273–324 (1997)
41. Lal, T., Chapelle, O., Weston, J., Elisseeff, A.: Embedded methods. In: Guyon, I., Gunn, S., Nikravesh, M., Zadeh, L. (eds.) Feature Extraction, Foundations and Applications. Springer, Berlin (2005)
42. Janusz, A., Stawicki, S.: Applications of approximate reducts to the feature selection problem. In: Proc. of RSKT. LNCS, vol. 6954, pp. 45–50. Springer, Berlin (2011)
43. Grzymała-Busse, J.W., Ziarko, W.: Rough sets and data mining. In: Wang, J. (ed.) Encyclopedia of Data Warehousing and Mining, 2nd edn., pp. 1696–1701. IGI Global, Hershey (2009)
44. Yao, Y.: Three-way decisions using rough sets. In: Peters, G., Lingras, P., Ślęzak, D., Yao, Y. (eds.) Rough Sets: Selected Methods and Applications in Management and Engineering. Springer, Berlin (2012)
45. Dietterich, T.G.: Ensemble methods in machine learning. In: Proc. of Int. Workshop on Multiple Classifier Systems (MCS). LNCS, vol. 1857, pp. 1–15. Springer, Berlin (2000)
46. Polikar, R.: Ensemble based systems in decision making. IEEE Circuits Syst. Mag. **6**, 21–45 (2006)
47. Kuncheva, L.I., Whitaker, C.: Measures of diversity in classifier ensembles. Mach. Learn. **51**, 181–207 (2003)
48. Sollich, P., Krogh, A.: Learning with ensembles: how overfitting can be useful. In: Touretzky, D., Mozer, M., Hasselmo, M. (eds.) Advances in Neural Information Processing Systems, vol. 8, pp. 190–196. MIT Press, Cambridge (1996)
49. Dietterich, T.G., Bakiri, G.: Solving multiclass learning problems via error-correcting output codes. J. Artif. Intell. Res. **2**, 263–286 (1995)
50. Nguyen, S.H., Bazan, J.G., Skowron, A., Nguyen, H.S.: Layered learning for concept synthesis. In: Transactions on Rough Sets I. LNCS, vol. 3100, pp. 187–208. Springer, Berlin (2004)
51. Ślęzak, D., Janusz, A.: Ensembles of bireducts: towards robust classification and simple representation. In: Proc. of Int. Conf. on Future Generation of Information Technology (FGIT). LNCS, vol. 7105. Springer, Berlin (2011)
52. Freund, Y.: Boosting a weak learning algorithm by majority. Inf. Comput. **121**(2), 256–285 (1995)
53. Kuncheva, L.I., Whitaker, C.: Feature subsets for classifier combination. An enumerative experiment. In: Multiple Classifier Systems. Proc. of the 2nd Int. Workshop MSC 2001. LNCS, vol. 2096, pp. 228–237. Springer, Berlin (2001)
54. Saeys, Y., Abeel, T., Van de Peer, Y.: Robust feature selection using ensemble feature selection techniques. In: Proc. of ECML PKDD 2008, Part II. LNAI, vol. 5212, pp. 313–325. Springer, Berlin (2008)
55. Ho, T.K.: The random subspace method for constructing decision forests. IEEE Trans. Pattern Anal. Mach. Intell. **20**(8), 832–844 (1998)
56. Oliveira, L.S., Morita, M., Sabourin, R.: Feature selection for ensembles using the multi-objective optimization approach. Stud. Comput. Intell. **16**, 49–74 (2006)
57. Stefanowski, J.: An experimental study of methods combining multiple classifiers—diversified both by feature selection and bootstrap sampling. In: Atanassov, T.K., Kacprzyk, J., Krawczak, M., Szmidt, E. (eds.) Issues in the Representation and Processing of Uncertain and Imprecise Information, pp. 337–354. Akademicka Oficyna Wydawnicza EXIT, Warsaw (2005)
58. Tang, E.K., Suganthan, P.N., Yao, X.: An analysis of diversity measures. Mach. Learn. **65**(1), 247–271 (2006)
59. Tsymbal, A., Pechenizkiy, M., Cunningham, P.: Diversity in search strategies for ensemble feature selection. Inf. Fusion **6**(1), 83–98 (2005)
60. Ślęzak, D., Widz, S.: Evolutionary inspired optimization of feature subset ensembles. In: Proc. of NaBIC, pp. 437–442 (2010)

Part IV
Methods and Applications in Management

Financial Series Forecasting Using Dual Rough Support Vector Regression

Pawan Lingras, Cory Butz, and Parag Bhalchandra

Abstract   This chapter uses the concept of lower and upper bounds of a real-valued variable to model daily low and high values of a stock market index. A trader would like to buy a stock at the lowest value of the day and sell at the highest possible value. The conservative traders will look for low and high values that are guaranteed within a tolerance. The aggressive traders may want to know how low and high can a stock go in a day to formulate their trading strategies. The dual rough support vector modeling described in this chapter can cater to both conservative and aggressive traders.

1 Introduction

Pawlak [1] broadened the notion of rough set by proposing rough real functions. A variation of the rough real functions using rough patterns can be seen in rough neural networks proposed by [2, 3]. A similar body of work can also be seen within fuzzy set theory from [4]. The topic continues to attract research interest as seen in recent publications by [5–13].

We will describe this extension of rough set theory using the notion of rough patterns. A rough pattern consisting of rough values has several semantic and computational advantages in many analytical applications. Some examples of rough values are stock values expressed in terms of daily highs and lows; daily temperatures

P. Lingras (✉)
Department of Mathematics and Computer Science, Saint Mary's University, Halifax, Canada
e-mail: pawan.lingras@smu.ca

P. Lingras · P. Bhalchandra
School of Computational Sciences, Swami Ramanand Teerth Marathwada University, Nanded, India

P. Bhalchandra
e-mail: srtmun.parag@gmail.com

C. Butz
Department of Computer Science, University of Regina, Regina, Saskatchewan, S4S 0A2, Canada
e-mail: butz@cs.uregina.ca

G. Peters et al. (eds.), *Rough Sets: Selected Methods and Applications in Management and Engineering*, Advanced Information and Knowledge Processing,
DOI 10.1007/978-1-4471-2760-4_7, © Springer-Verlag London Limited 2012

expressed as daily highs and lows; rainfall for a region expressed as high and low values. Any computation done using rough values can be reformulated in terms of conventional numbers. However, the use of rough values provides a better semantic interpretation of results in terms of upper and lower bounds. Moreover, some of the numeric computations cannot be conceptualized without explicitly discussing the upper and lower bound framework. The notion of intervals and rough values is one of the significant components of granular computing as evidenced in some of the recent work [14–18].

Single layer perceptrons [19, 20] model linearly separable classification problems. Support vector machines (SVMs) extend single layer perceptrons by using non-linear transformations for separating objects [21–23]. The non-linear transformation in SVMs is instituted with the use of kernel functions [23]. *Support vector regression* (SVR) extends the traditional linear regression by introducing non-linearity using kernel functions [24, 25]. The ϵ-SVR adds the notion of tolerance margin. As long as the actual data values are within ϵ distance from the predicted values, it is assumed that there is no prediction error. Therefore, the predictions from an ϵ-SVR can be looked at as an ϵ-tube instead of a curve. This chapter describes two approaches for the modeling of rough values with *support vector regression* (SVR). One approach, by attempting to ensure that the predicted high value is not greater than the upper bound and that the predicted low value is not less than the lower bound, is *conservative* in nature. On the contrary, an *aggressive* approach seeks a predicted high which is not less than the upper bound and a predicted low which is not greater than the lower bound. The usefulness of this dual philosophy is demonstrated by modeling the rough pattern of a stock market index, and can be taken advantage of by conservative and aggressive traders.

2 Dual Rough Support Vector Regression

Support vector machines (SVMs), proposed by Vapnik [23, 26–28], are used for creating functions from a set of labeled training data [29]. The function can be a classification function with binary outputs or it can be a general regression function. For classification, SVMs operate by attempting to find a hypersurface in the space of possible inputs that splits the positive examples from the negative examples. The split will be chosen to have the largest distance from the hypersurface to the nearest of the positive and negative examples. Intuitively, this makes the classification correct for testing data that is near, but not identical, to the training data. The linear separability restriction in perceptron is overcome by the use of a non-linear transformation Φ as shown in Fig. 1. Support vector machines use kernel functions to avoid the explicit non-linear transformations.

In addition to using the kernel functions for non-linear modeling, support vector regression (SVR) employs the margin concept for the regression problem with the help of ϵ-insensitive loss functions [27, 30]. SVR has been found especially useful in time series predictions [24, 25, 31, 32].

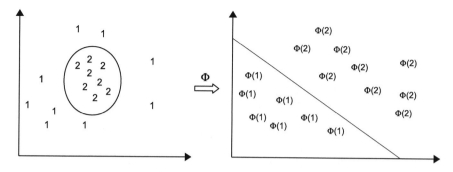

Fig. 1 Support vector machine transformation to linearly separable space

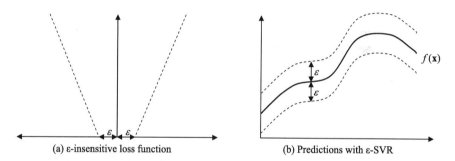

(a) ε-insensitive loss function   (b) Predictions with ε-SVR

Fig. 2 Support vector regression

Vapnik [27] proposed an ϵ-insensitive loss function:

$$l_\epsilon(f(\mathbf{x}), y) = \max(0, |y - f(\mathbf{x})| - \epsilon) \tag{1}$$

shown in Fig. 2(a). The vertical axis denotes the loss. The horizontal axis corresponds to the value of $f(\mathbf{x})$. The two axes meet at $f(\mathbf{x}) = y$. If the predicted value is within $\pm\epsilon$ of the actual value, the prediction is considered lossless. Fig. 2(b) shows how the actual values in the margin around the predicted function are considered acceptable or error-free. Increasing the ϵ value, reduces the number of support vectors. A large enough value of ϵ will lead to a constant regression function. The ϵ-insensitive loss function is ideally suited for modeling rough values as can be seen by the ϵ-tube around the prediction function in Fig. 2(b).

The corresponding SVR is called an ϵ-SVR. In addition to using the ϵ-loss function, ϵ-SVR also uses the kernel functions for non-linear modeling. The details of the formulation can be found in [24, 25]. Lingras and Butz [33] proposed dual extensions of SVR for modeling the rough patterns.

3 Rough Patterns

Pawlak proposed the concept of rough real functions which can be useful for rough controllers [1]. The notion of rough real functions was defined as an approximate value in case exact values cannot be represented by the given set of values. However, the notion can be used in a broader context. Lingras [34] used the rough values to develop supervised and unsupervised neural networks [35, 36] and genetic algorithms [37]. This section describes rough values and patterns.

In some cases, a precise value of an entity may not be available. For example, one may estimate the current temperature to be between 20 and 25°C. In other cases, it may not even be possible to state a precise value. Many spatial (rainfall in Nova Scotia) or temporal (daily temperature) variables fall in this category. We cannot associate a precise value for daily temperature, only a range of value using the highest and lowest temperatures recorded on that day. We use rough or interval values to measure such quantities. For continuous variables, rough values are special cases of intervals as they focus on the end points. However, unlike intervals, rough values can also be used to represent a set of discrete values using the minimum and maximum values in the set. Let $Y = \{y_1, y_2, \ldots, y_n\}$ be a set of values collected for a variable such as daily temperature or stock market index. Each *rough value y* is denoted by a pair $(\underline{y}, \overline{y})$: $\underline{y} = \inf\{y \in Y\}$, and $\overline{y} = \sup\{y \in Y\}$. Here, sup is defined as the maximum value from the set, while inf corresponds to the minimum value. The definitions of inf and sup can be modified to exclude the outliers. For example, one could use the bottom 5th percentile value for $\underline{y}$ and top 5th percentile value for $\overline{y}$. The above definition by Pawlak accommodates sets with continuous as well as discrete values. If the values are continuous, the set will be infinite and the resulting rough values correspond to the conventional notion of interval. *Rough patterns* are sequences of rough or interval values [34]. We will look at a real world example of a rough pattern using a stock market index.

3.1 Rough Patterns in Financial Time Series

The Dow Jones Industrial Average (DJIA) is an index based on stock prices of the 30 most prominent companies listed on U.S. stock exchanges such as NYSE and NASDAQ. It is one of the most closely watched stock market indices in the world. The data used in this study was obtained from Yahoo! (www.yahoo.com). It consisted of the date, opening value, closing value, high and low values, as well as the number of shares traded on the exchange. Data is only available for the trading days, i.e., when the New York stock exchange was open. For example, in the ten years from May 21st, 1997 to May 20th, 2007 there were 2514 trading days.

Most of the prediction models are based on the closing values. The closing value of a stock or stock market index has impact on secondary investment instruments, such as mutual fund values and overseas markets. However, the traders on the New York stock exchange are reacting to minute by minute changes to stock prices, in

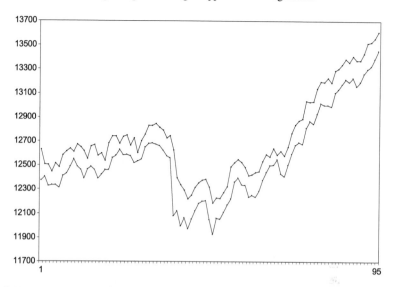

Fig. 3 Dow Jones Industrial Average (DJIA) for early 2007

addition to key indices like the DJIA. The stock exchanges are open from 10 a.m. to 3:30 p.m. from Monday through Friday with the exception of holidays. During these five and a half hours, one can get minute-by-minute updates on the values of DJIA. That will mean a total of 330 values per day. It will be difficult to manage such a large amount of data in any financial modeling. It is neither possible nor necessary to model/predict minute-by-minute values of the index. The traders however are interested in knowing how high or low a stock or index may go on a given day. For example, a trader who is looking to sell a stock or DJIA based financial derivative may wait until the high for the day is reached. Conversely, a trader who is looking to buy a stock or DJIA based financial derivative may wait until the low for the day is reached. Therefore, accurate prediction of trading range given by the rough pattern for a stock or stock index is an important part of stock market analysis.

Figure 3 shows the rough pattern for the daily values of the DJIA from January 1st to May 20th, 2007. The DJIA rough pattern consists of two curves. The top curve corresponds to the daily high's and the bottom one corresponds to the daily low values.

It is important to realize that there can be a considerable variation in the difference between high and low values, even though the general trend of the high and low values is essentially the same. Analysis of ten years of data from May 21st, 1997 to May 20th, 2007 shows the minimum difference to be 34.42, with a maximum value of 848.52. Figure 4 shows the distribution of differences between highs and lows to be more or less normal. The average of the difference is 232, which is close to the median and mode values. This analysis suggests that the high and low values should be separately analyzed.

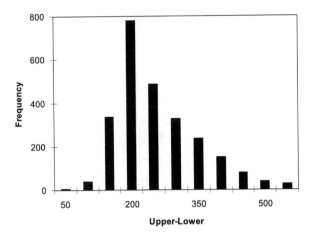

Fig. 4 Dow Jones Industrial Average (DJIA) for early 2007

4 Conservative and Aggressive Modeling of Rough Patterns

The formulation of rough ϵ-SVR to model rough patterns needs a definition of $\pm$ in the context of rough values. Let us assume that y is a rough value given by $(\underline{y}, \overline{y})$. Lingras and Butz [33] described dual approaches termed as conservative and aggressive. In the conservative approach, the tube of predicted values will be tucked inside the tube of actual values. That is, the actual lower value $\underline{y}$ will not be higher than $\underline{f}(\mathbf{x})$ and the actual upper value $\overline{y}$ will not be lower than $\overline{f}(\mathbf{x})$. Let $fc(\mathbf{x}) = (\underline{f}c(\mathbf{x}), \overline{f}c(\mathbf{x}))$ be the conservative prediction of y such that

$$y = (\underline{f}c(\mathbf{x}) - \epsilon, \overline{f}c(\mathbf{x}) + \epsilon). \tag{2}$$

The aggressive model, on the other hand, will tell us how low the lower value can drop and how high the upper value can rise. The *aggressive* prediction, denoted fa, for a rough value $fa(\mathbf{x}) = (\underline{f}a(\mathbf{x}), \overline{f}a(\mathbf{x}))$ is more formally described as:

$$fa(\mathbf{x}) = (\underline{y} - \epsilon, \overline{y} + \epsilon). \tag{3}$$

Equation (3) indicates that the actual lower value $\underline{y}$ will be equal or higher than $\underline{f}a(\mathbf{x})$ and the actual upper value $\overline{y}$ will be equal or lower than $\overline{f}a(\mathbf{x})$.

The conservative Rough ϵ-insensitive loss function, $lc_{r\epsilon}$, is shown in Fig. 5(a), which illustrates that we need to have an ϵ margin only on the outer side of the lower and upper prediction functions. The aggressive rough ϵ-insensitive loss function, $la_{r\epsilon}$, is illustrated in Fig. 5(b). As can be seen, we need only to have an ϵ margin on the inner side of the lower and upper prediction functions.

The conservative modeling of rough patterns is depicted in Fig. 6(a). As can be seen, the predicted rough pattern will be inside the actual rough values of the variables as suggested by Eq. (2). Figure 6(b) depicts the aggressive modeling of rough patterns. As suggested by Eq. (3), it can be observed that the predicted rough pattern will be outside the actual rough values of the variables.

The objective of conservative modeling is to construct a $fc(\mathbf{x})$ such that $lc_{r\epsilon}$ is minimized. Aggressive modeling, on the other hand, attempts to minimize $la_{r\epsilon}$.

Fig. 5 Conservative and
aggressive rough
ϵ-insensitive loss functions

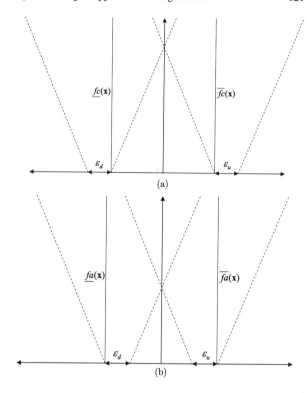

Lingras and Butz [33] describe the optimization process for both of these modeling
approaches.

5 Experimental Analysis of Dual RSVR

The study data used in Lingras and Butz's [33] experiments consisted of the daily
high and low values of the DJIA from May 21st to May 20th, 2007. There were a
total of 250 trading days during the study period.

Conservative and aggressive RSVR described in the previous section were applied to model the DJIA rough pattern. The input vector consisted of the previous
ten days high's and low's. Therefore, the model was applied to $250 - 10 = 240$ days.
The output was the rough value for the next day.

Lingras and Butz [33] experimented with linear and polynomial Kernels and different values of $\epsilon = 150, 75, 50$. The results seemed to significantly improve when
ϵ was reduced from 150 to 75. The performance gain was not obvious when ϵ was
further reduced to 50.

Error distribution for the two models is shown in Fig. 7. The error is calculated
as $actual - predicted$. That means negative errors correspond to over-prediction and
positive errors correspond to under-prediction. Figure 7(a) shows the frequency of

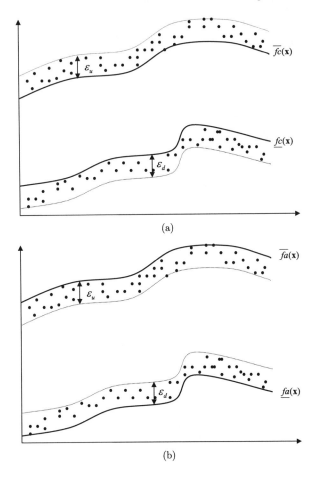

(a)

(b)

errors using three types of bars for conservative modeling. The hollow bars for the
lower prediction means that the actual value is less than 75 points (the value of ϵ_d)
below the predicted value for the conservative model, and hence is acceptable according to the loss function $lc_{r\epsilon}$. The striped bars for lower predictions mean that
the values are over-predicted leading to a lower loss (because ϵ_d will be deducted
for over-predictions of lower values). The solid bars indicate under-prediction of
lower values. The reverse is true for upper predictions, i.e., solid bars indicate over-
prediction, striped bars are under-predictions leading to lower loss (ϵ_u will be deducted for under prediction of upper values), and hollow bars are under-predictions
by less than 75 points (the value of ϵ_u) leading to zero loss. Based on Eq. (2) and
the loss function $lc_{r\epsilon}$, hollow bars are the most desirable, followed by striped bars,
while the solid bars are least desirable.

Figure 7(b) also shows the frequency of errors using three types of bars for aggressive modeling. However, the meaning of the bars for the aggressive modeling is
a mirror image of that for the conservative modeling. The hollow bars for the lower
prediction means that the actual value is less than 75 points (the value of ϵ_d) above

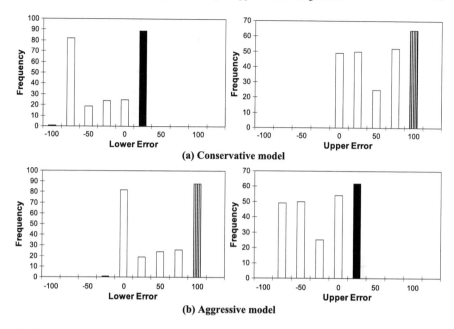

Fig. 7 Error distribution for conservative (*top*) and aggressive (*bottom*) rough ϵ-SVR modeling of rough DJIA pattern with $\epsilon = 75$

the predicted value for the conservative model, and hence is acceptable according to the loss function $la_{r\epsilon}$. The striped bars for lower predictions mean that the values are under-predicted leading to a lower loss (because ϵ_d will be deducted for under-predictions of lower values). The solid bars indicate over-prediction of lower values. The opposite is true for upper predictions, i.e., solid bars indicate under-prediction, striped bars are over-predictions leading to lower loss (as ϵ_u will be deducted for over prediction of upper values), and hollow bars are over-predictions by less than 75 points (the value of ϵ_u) leading to zero loss. Similar to conservative modeling, based on Eq. (3) and the loss function $la_{r\epsilon}$, the hollow bars are the most desirable, followed by striped bars, leaving solid bars serving as least desirable.

The abundance of hollow and striped bars, for both conservative and aggressive models, means that both approaches performed as expected. The errors for conservative modeling are on the outer sides of 0 (negative for lower values and positive for upper values), while they are on the inner side of 0 (positive for lower values and negative for upper values) for aggressive modeling. This observation clearly underscores the difference between the two philosophies. One can also notice a similarity between Fig. 7(a) and the conservative loss function $lc_{r\epsilon}$ given in Fig. 5(a). Similar correspondence can be drawn between Fig. 7(b) and the aggressive loss function $la_{r\epsilon}$ given in Fig. 5(b).

Figures 8 and 9 show a comparison of predicted and actual values for both models. In order to have an amplified picture of the comparisons, we focus on the volatile days between February 6, 2007 and April 9, 2007. It can be seen that the two models provide a very good similarity between the actual and predicted curves. Figure 8

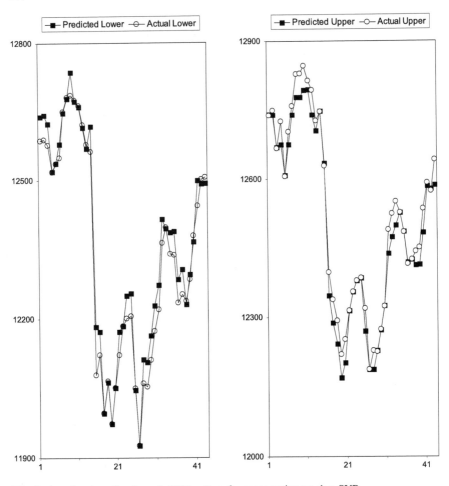

Fig. 8 Actual and predicted rough DJIA pattern for conservative rough ϵ-SVR

shows that the conservative rough ϵ-SVR model almost never over-predicts the upper values. However, there are some under-predictions of lower values. Since drops in stock markets tend to be more dramatic than rises, a certain amount of uncertainty in the prediction of lower values should be tolerated. Thus, modeling provided by conservative rough ϵ-SVR follows the philosophy suggested by Eq. (2). Similarity between the objective of conservative modeling given by Fig. 6(a) and the results of our formulation shown in Fig. 8 lend further credence to our approach. The conservative rough ϵ-SVR will give the users of the information a certain amount of trust in the fact that the actual upper values will not be lower than the predicted values and the actual lower values will not be higher than the predicted ones. This knowledge can be helpful in practical applications such as formulating conservative trading strategies. On the other hand, Fig. 9 shows that the aggressive rough ϵ-SVR model almost never under-predicts the upper values. However, similar to conserva-

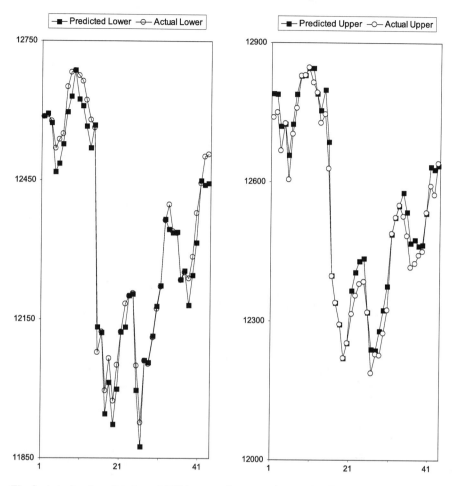

Fig. 9 Actual and predicted rough DJIA pattern for aggressive rough ϵ-SVR

tive modeling, there are some over-predictions of lower values due to dramatic drops in stockmarkets. Thus, the modeling provided by aggressive rough ϵ-SVR follows the philosophy suggested by Eq. (3). Once again, the correspondence between the objective of aggressive modeling given by Fig. 6(b) and the results of our formulation shown in Fig. 9 further support our approach. The aggressive rough ϵ-SVR will give users a certain amount of confidence that the actual upper values will not be higher than the predicted values and the actual lower values will not be lower than the predicted ones. This knowledge can be helpful in practical applications like designing aggressive trading strategies.

The accuracy of the two models for the most volatile period is very encouraging. It should be noted that the large stock market fluctuations are affected by many external factors. For example, the major dip at the end of February shown in Figs. 8 and 9 was precipitated by a large drop on Shanghai stock exchange. Our models did not take into account the large Shanghai drop. As such, training for larger time period and incorporating external factors, coupled with thorough testing, will be necessary before these models should be used in practice.

6 Conclusions

This chapter used the concept of lower and upper bounds for describing real-valued variables such as a stock market index. Explicit modeling of low and high values in a stock market is necessary because lows and highs can fluctuate individually, while still following the same overall trend. Moreover, the methods presented here can play an integral part in developing conservative and aggressive trading strategies. While we have presented this work in terms of the highs and lows of a stock market index (Dow Jones Industrial Average), the techniques described here are applicable to any application where the domain must necessarily be represented with rough values.

References

1. Pawlak, Z.: Rough real functions. http://citeseer.ist.psu.edu/105864.html (1994)
2. Lingras, P.: Rough neural networks. In: Proc. the International Conference on Information Processing and Management of Uncertainty in Knowledge-based Systems (IPMU'96), pp. 1445–1450 (1996)
3. Lingras, P.: Unsupervised learning using rough Kohonen neural network classifiers. In: Proc. Symposium on Modelling, Analysis and Simulation, CESA'96 IMACS Multiconference, pp. 753–757 (1996)
4. Tanaka, H., Lee, H.: Interval regression analysis by quadratic programming approach. IEEE Trans. Fuzzy Syst. **6**, 473–481 (1998)
5. Chuang, C.-C.: Extended support vector interval regression networks for interval input–output data. Inf. Sci. **178**, 871–891 (2008)
6. Guo, P., Tanaka, H.: Dual models for possibilistic regression analysis. Comput. Stat. Data Anal. **51**, 253–266 (2006)
7. Hong, D.H., Hwang, C.: Support vector fuzzy regression machines. Fuzzy Sets Syst. **138**, 271–281 (2003)
8. Hong, D.H., Yi, H.C.: A note on fuzzy regression model with fuzzy input and output data for manpower forecasting. Fuzzy Sets Syst. **138**, 271–281 (2003)
9. Hong, D.H., Hwang, C.: Extended fuzzy regression models using regularization method. Inf. Sci. **164**, 31–46 (2004)
10. Hong, D.H., Hwang, C.: Interval regression analysis using quadratic loss support vector machine. IEEE Trans. Fuzzy Syst. **13**, 229–237 (2005)
11. Hong, D.H., Hwang, C.: Support vector interval regression machine for crisp input and output data. Fuzzy Sets Syst. **157**, 1114–1125 (2006)
12. Jeng, J.T., Chuang, C.C., Su, S.F.: Support vector interval regression networks for interval regression analysis. Fuzzy Sets Syst. **138**, 283–300 (2003)
13. Shivaswamy, P.K., Chu, W., Jansche, M.: A support vector approach to censored targets. In: Proc. Seventh IEEE International Conference on Data Mining, pp. 555–560 (2007)
14. Greco, S., Matazarro, B., Slowinski, R.: Parameterized rough set model using rough membership and Bayesian confirmation measures. Int. J. Approx. Reason. **49**, 285–300 (2008)

15. Kreinovich, V.: Interval Computation as an important part of granular computing: an introduction. In: Handbook of Granular Computing, pp. 3–31. Wiley, New York (2008)
16. Pedrycz, W., Skowron, A., Kreinovich, V.: Handbook of Granular Computing. Wiley, New York (2008)
17. Slezak, D., Wroblewski, J., Eastwood, V., Synak, P.: Brighthouse: an analytic data warehouse for ad-hoc queries. PVLDB 1(2), 1337–1345 (2008)
18. Slezak, D., Wroblewski, J., Eastwood, V., Synak, P.: Rough sets in data warehousing. RSCTC, 505–507 (2008)
19. Minsky, M.L., Papert, S.A.: Perceptrons. MIT Press, Cambridge (1969)
20. Rosenblatt, F.: The perceptron: a perceiving and recognizing automaton. Project PARA, Cornell Aeronautical Lab (1957)
21. Casey, K., Garrett, A., Gay, J., Montgomery, L., Dozier, G.: An evolutionary approach for achieving scalability with general regression neural networks. Nat. Comput. 8, 133–148 (2009)
22. Chen, M., Hariharaputran, S., Hofestadt, R., Kormeier, B., Spangardt, S.: Petri net models for the semi-automatic construction of large scale biological networks. Nat. Comput. 10, 1077–1097 (2011)
23. Vapnik, V.: Statistical Learning Theory. Wiley, New York (1998)
24. Yang, H., Chan, L., King, I.: Support vector machine regression for volatile stock market prediction. In: Yin, H., Allinson, N., Freeman, R., Keane, J., Hubbard, S. (eds.) Intelligent Data Engineering and Automated Learning—IDEAL 2002. LNCS, vol. 2412, pp. 391–396. Springer, Berlin (2002)
25. Yang, H.: Margin variations in support vector regression for the stock market prediction. M.Phil. dissertation, Department of Computer Science and Engineering, The Chinese University of Hong Kong (2003). http://www.svms.org/finance/Yang2003.pdf
26. Vapnik, V.: Estimation of Dependencies Based on Empirical Data. Nauka, Moscow (1979)
27. Vapnik, V.: The Nature of Statistical Learning Theory. Springer, New York (1995)
28. Vapnik, V.N., Golowich, S., Smola, A.: Support vector method for function approximation, regression estimation and signal processing. Adv. Neural Inf. Process. Syst. 9, 281–287 (1997)
29. Platt, J.C.: Support vector machines. http://research.microsoft.com/users/jplatt/svm.html (2003)
30. Smola, A., Scholkopf, B.: A tutorial on support vector regression. In: NeuroCOLT2 (1998)
31. Mukherjee, S., Osuna, E., Girosi, F.: Nonlinear prediction of chaotic time series using support vector machines. In: Principe, J., Gile, L., Morgan, N., Wilson, E. (eds.) IEEE Workshop on Neural Networks for Signal Process VII, pp. 511–519. IEEE Press, New York (1997)
32. Muller, K.R., Smola, A., Ratsch, G., Scholkopf, B., Kohlmorgen, J., Vapnik, V.: Predicting time series with support vector machines. ICANN, 999–1004 (1997)
33. Lingras, P., Butz, C.J.: Conservative and aggressive rough svr modeling. Theor. Comput. Sci. 412, 5885–5901 (2011)
34. Lingras, P.: Applications of rough patterns. In: Rough Sets in Data Mining and Knowledge Discovery 2, pp. 369–384. Springer, Berlin (1998)
35. Lingras, P.: Fuzzy-rough and rough-fuzzy serial combinations in neurocomputing. Neurocomputing 36, 29–44 (2001)
36. Peters, J.F., Han, L., Ramanna, S.: Rough neural computing in signal analysis. Comput. Intell. 17, 493–513 (2001)
37. Lingras, P., Davies, C.: Applications of rough genetic algorithms. Comput. Intell. 17, 435–445 (2001)

Grounding Information Technology Project Critical Success Factors Within the Organization

Applying Rough Sets

M. Gordon Hunter and Georg Peters

Abstract   This chapter presents the idea of employing Rough Set Theory to assess risk and assist in reducing the complexity of managing IT-projects. There are many generic lists of critical success factors. Initially, these factors should be grounded within the specific organization. Then an early warning system, proposed here, may be employed based upon Rough Set Theory to assess the risk of specific IT-projects. The identification of risk will lead the project manager to focus on specific issues that must be resolved in order to contribute to the success of the project. We also show how DRSA-Dominance based Rough Set Approach can be utilized to analyze IT-projects.

1 Introduction

Shore [1] suggests that managing IT-projects is a difficult endeavor. Often these projects lead to disappointing results. There are implementation delays and cost over runs, sometimes resulting in complete project failure [2]. Indeed, Kaufman and Korrapati [3] determined that information technology project success rate was approximately 30%. This statistic supports earlier findings. For instance, Cunningham [4] reported on an investigation of 7,400 IT-projects. The results indicated that 34% were over budget and behind schedule; 31% were either abandoned or modified; and 24% were actually completed within budget and as scheduled.

A common aspect which contributes to information technology project failure is the lack of risk management [5–7]. Thus, it is incumbent upon organizations to consider alternatives to manage the risk involved in IT-projects [6–8]. The challenge for project managers is to identify the risks and then to take appropriate action [9].

M.G. Hunter (✉)
Faculty of Management, University of Lethbridge, Lethbridge, Alberta T1K 3M4, Canada
e-mail: ghunter@uleth.ca

G. Peters
Department of Computer Science and Mathematics, Munich University of Applied Sciences, 80335 Munich, Germany
e-mail: georg.peters@cs.hm.edu

G. Peters et al. (eds.), *Rough Sets: Selected Methods and Applications in Management and Engineering*, Advanced Information and Knowledge Processing,
DOI 10.1007/978-1-4471-2760-4_8, © Springer-Verlag London Limited 2012

This chapter proposes employing Rough Set Theory to assess risk and assist in reducing complexity in managing IT-projects. The next section reviews the many generic critical success factor lists. Then, the contention is proffered that the critical success factors list should be grounded in the specific organization. Once the critical success factor list is grounded the concepts of Rough Set Theory may be employed. The description of Rough Set Theory employs an analogy related to a "traffic light" warning system. Furthermore we discuss how DRSA—Dominance based Rough Set Approach can support the analysis of IT-projects data. Finally, conclusions are presented regarding the use of Rough Set Theory in the management of IT-projects.

2 Plethora of Critical Success Factors

There are many lists of critical success factors. They vary depending upon the type of information technology project. A review of the available literature identified a number of these critical success factors lists, which relate to IT-projects. The remainder of this section presents a description of the critical success factors lists. They have been categorized by types of IT-projects which relate to Enterprise Resource Planning projects, Business Intelligence projects, Off-shore projects, and Public Sector projects.

2.1 Enterprise Resource Planning Projects

One area where a number of research projects have been conducted recently involves the implementation of Enterprise Resource Planning (ERP) projects. These systems are renowned for integrating all of the cross-functional information needs of an organization. However, these projects are also notorious for cost over runs and implementation delays [10]. As suggested by Francoise et al. [11] managers of ERP projects must be able to deal with a vast array of issues related to technical, organizational, and human considerations. They must also master change management and the promotion of user involvement.

Francoise et al. [11] identified the essential activities for managing ERP implementation projects. They developed a list of thirteen critical success factors as shown in Table 1. This list is based upon a number of previous investigations [12–21].

This list was developed using a Delphi survey of twelve professional experts. The list of thirteen critical success factors was expanded to incorporate 107 difficult issues which outlined typical traps.

Nah et al. [20] investigated ERP implementation in multi-national manufacturing companies. They administered a survey to management and non-management staff in multi-national companies. After conducting a survey of previously generated critical success factors lists [22, 23] they focused on four important factors. Those are top management support, teamwork and composition, enterprise-wide communication, and project management program. While their conclusion is, not surprisingly,

Table 1 Critical success factors in implementing ERP systems [11]

• Project teamwork and composition	• Software development, testing and troubleshooting
• Organizational culture & change mgt.	• Monitoring and evaluation of performance
• Top management support	• Project champion
• Business plan and long-term vision	• Organizational structure
• BPR and customization	• End-user involvement
• Effective communication	• Knowledge management
• Project management	

Table 2 Twenty-two critical success factors model [23]

• Top Management Support	• Dedicated Resources
• Project Team Competence	• Use of Steering Committee
• Interdepartmental Cooperation	• User Training on Software
• Clear Goals and Objectives	• Edu. on New Business Processes
• Project Management	• Business Process Re-Engineering
• Interdepartmental Comm.	• Minimal Customization
• Management of Expectations	• Architecture Choices
• Project Champion	• Change Management
• Vendor Support	• Partnership with Vendor
• Careful Package Selection	• Use of Vendors' Tools
• Data Analysis and Conversion	• Use of Consultants

that all are important, they also suggest that the traditional approach to change management may not be the best approach for a successful ERP implementation. They suggest that a further emphasis should be placed upon communication and a formal project management approach.

Somers and Nelson [23] developed a model of twenty-two critical success factors which is included here as Table 2.

A unified critical success factors model was developed by Esteves and Pastor [22]. The factors are classified by strategic and tactical factors within an organizational and technological perspective. Their model is included here as Table 3.

Plant and Willcocks [24] extended the work of Somers and Nelson [23] by examining the perceptions of project managers of critical success factors at different stages of ERP implementations. They grounded their investigation in specific companies.

Remus [25] investigated the critical success factors for implementing enterprise portals. He interviewed 15 portal integrators who identified twenty one critical success factors as listed in Table 4 (# = Rank).

One of the interesting aspects of Remus' [25] analysis of critical success factors is his presentation of results organized by stages of projects. Thus, he presented the top five critical success factors based upon the stages of analysis, design, implementation, introduction, and evaluation.

Table 3 Unified (organizational) critical success factors model [22]

Strategic	Tactical
Organizational	
• Sustained management support	• Dedicated staff and consultants
• Effective organizational change mgt.	• Strong comm. in- & outward
• Good project scope management	• Formalized project plan/schedule
• Adequate project team composition	• Adequate training program
• Comprehensive BPR	• Preventive troubleshooting
• Adequate project champion role	• Appropriate usage of consultants
• User involvement and participation	• Empowered decision-makers
• Trust between partners	
Technological	
• Adequate ERP strategy	• Adequate software configuration
• Avoid customization	• Legacy systems knowledge
• Adequate ERP version	

Table 4 Critical success factors for enterprise portal projects [25]

#	Critical success factor	#	Critical success factor
1	User acceptance	12	User training and education
2	Selection of appropriate portal package	13	Defining the portal architecture
3	Top management support	14	Dedicated resources
4	Requirements analysis	15	Business process reengineering
5	Project management	16	Clear goals and objectives
6	Strong communication in- & outward	17	Portal engineering roadmap
7	Process and application integration	18	Portal strategy
8	Prototyping	19	Project monitoring & controlling
9	Portal design	20	Flexible project structure
10	Change management	21	Organizational culture
11	Team competencies and skills		

2.2 Business Intelligence Projects

Business intelligence systems attempt to improve the timeliness and quality of data employed in the decision making process. Negash [26] suggests that business intelligence systems involve gathering and storing data and then applying knowledge management tools in order to develop and provide planners and decision makers with information to support activities related to gaining or attaining competitive advantage.

Table 5 Critical success factors for business intelligence systems [27]

#	Critical success factor
1	Committed management support and sponsorship
2	Business user-oriented change management
3	Clear business vision and well-established case
4	Business-driven methodology and project management
5	Business-centric championship and balanced project team composition
6	Strategic and extensible technical framework
7	Sustainable data quality and governance framework

Employing a panel of fifteen experts Yeoh et al. [27] through a Delphi technique developed a list of seven critical success factors as shown in Table 5.

2.3 Off-Shore Projects

Offshore software development has been mainly driven as a way to address the Y2K issue [28] and the high demand for web-based systems [29]. Remus and Wiener [30] interviewed twenty-two experts who had experience administering offshore software development projects. They identified twenty nine critical success factors as shown in Table 6.

It is interesting that they make the following comment about their results: "... we see these 29 factors as potential critical success factors, which might become critical success factors depending on situational and contextual factors" [30]. This comment is further supported by others who contend that contextual factors must also be taken into consideration when employing critical success factors to assist in managing software development projects [31, 32].

Remus and Wiener [30] do provide a further analytical breakdown of various criteria for the top five critical success factors. They provide the breakdown from both a company and project perspective.

2.4 Public Sector Projects

The order of importance of critical success factors for public sector software development projects differs from those identified for private sector projects [33]. They suggest that this difference is related to the goals and objectives of government entities, which involve unbiased execution of policy and stability of administration [34]. This approach inhibits change and creates a risk averse environment through managerial control structures that restrict consideration of options [35]. Rosaker and Olson [33] surveyed 149 IT-project managers in sixteen states in USA. Their findings supported previous research by Pinto and Prescott [36] which identified ten

Table 6 General critical success factor ranking [30]

#	Critical success factor	#	Critical success factor
1	Definition of clear project goals	17	Definition of an accurate contract
2	Continuous controlling of project results	18	Legal and political stability in the offshore country
3	Ensuring a continuous communication flow	19	Face-to-face meetings with the offshore provider on a regular basis
4	High quality of offshore employees	20	Selection of a suitable software component
5	Good language abilities of offshore employees	21	Efficient internal organizational structure
6	Composition of an appropriate project team	22	Creation of a cultural sensitivity among employees
7	Preparation of a detailed project specification	23	Comprehensive industry knowledge of the offshore provider
8	Creation of a partnership-like relationship	24	Appropriate internal technical knowledge
9	Sustained management support	25	Development of a comprehensive business case
10	Establishment of an efficient IT infrastructure	26	Suitable company size of the offshore provider
11	Ensuring bilateral knowledge transfer	27	Comprehensive experience with IT outsourcing projects
12	Definition of project standards	28	International corporate culture
13	Financial stability of the offshore provider	29	Geographical closeness of the offshore provider
14	Early internal change management		
15	Standardized and documented processes		
16	Standardized and documented processes on provider side		

critical success factors as shown in Table 7. However, they also determined that the relative importance for the critical success factors differed from that of private sector investigations. This lends further support to the contention that context is important in managing software development projects and employing critical success factors.

Rosaker and Olson [33] conclude by suggesting, "... choices must be made as to where to concentrate attention or resources".

In summary, many of the investigations described above included broad surveys or panels of experts. Nah et al. [37] conducted a survey of management and non-management in various multi-national companies. Rosaker and Olson [33] surveyed 149 information technology project managers in a number of states in USA. Yeoh et

Table 7 Public sector critical success factors [36]

#	Critical success factor	#	Critical success factor
1	Mission	6	Technical tasks
2	Top management support	7	Client acceptance
3	Project schedules/planning	8	Monitoring and feedback
4	Client consultation	9	Communication
5	Personnel	10	Trouble-shooting

al. [27] employed a panel of fifteen experts. Francoise et al. [11] conducted a Delphi survey of twelve professional experts.

Some of the investigations were conducted with somewhat of a more focused approach. Plant and Willcocks [24] grounded their investigation in specific companies. Remus [25] organized his results by project stages. Remus and Wiener [30] employed twenty-two experts. However, they suggested that situational and contextual factors be incorporated in the development of a critical success factors list. It is these latter projects that lead to the idea of grounding the development of a critical success factors list within the organization and by project stages. This idea is developed further in the following two sections.

Also, it is unfortunate that many of the critical success factors lists described above include factors which are generic in nature. While a specific list may relate to a certain type of information technology project, they do not necessarily identify specific actions that a project manager should take. What is needed is a guide upon which a project manager may focus. This guide should be grounded within an organization and it should consider the specific aspects of the stages of an information technology project. The idea occurs that by looking at specific companies and stages in implementation this might be the start of a way of grounding the critical success factors in a manageable process. This idea is further expounded upon in the following two sections.

3 Grounding

As suggested above, the development of an appropriate critical success factors list should be grounded within a specific organization. Grounded Theory [38] suggests the gathering of data from those who have experience relative to the research question. These first-hand organization-relevant recollections are clearly remembered [39, 40]. More specifically, Narrative Inquiry [41] facilitates recording personal accounts of first-hand experiences [42].

The above approach will locate the development of a critical success factors list within the organization. As suggested by Remus [25] consideration should also be given to the differences in emphasis of critical success factors across the different stages of an information technology project. Also project managers must remain cognizant of the ever changing contextual and situational environment of an organization [30]. Thus, it would be prudent to establish a program of identifying a revised critical success factors list on a regular basis. The organizational environment will inevitably change.

Individuals within the organization will learn from their past experiences with information technology implementation projects. This learning may lead to revised critical success factors lists. Further, individuals who are hired by the organization or consultants may bring a new perspective to the development of an organization-relevant critical success factors list.

4 Rough Sets

4.1 Traffic Light Warning System

Rough Set Theory [43–45] incorporates the ability to discern objects of interest. Basically, Rough Set Theory may be employed to define a set of objects by two approximations. The term "lower approximation" describes the set which contains only objects which are unambiguous members of the set. Thus, these unambiguous members of the set are discernable from objects which do not belong to the set. However, if it is not clear that an object is a member of the set (i.e. the object's membership in the set is ambiguous) it will be assigned to a set which is termed the "upper approximation". The contention here is that these concepts of ROUGH SET THEORY may be applied to the management of information technology implementation projects in order to assist project managers to place their emphasis on the "important" aspects of the project. Within the application of Rough Set Theory these important aspects would be those objects which would be assigned to the lower approximation set of objects. The following paragraphs further develop this idea.

The following analogy is employed to describe how the project manager would develop a critical success factors list which incorporates the emphasis of a specific organization. The analogy involves the use of Rough Set Theory to develop a "traffic light" warning system for information technology project management [46].

Thus, the overall status of an information technology project may be determined, relative to the "traffic light" warning system as follows:

- *Red*: the project is currently at risk
- *Yellow*: the status of the project risk is currently unclear, so further investigations should be conducted to assess potential risk
- *Green*: the project is currently not at risk

In relation to Rough Set Theory, this "traffic light" warning system results in the establishment of two sets of objects—*red* set and a *green* set. Thus, if an information technology project can be assigned to the lower approximation of one of these sets the project's membership is unambiguous and may be defined as follows:

Fig. 1 Two stage approach of
the rough set theory analysis

- *Red* set: IT-projects assigned to the lower approximation of this *red* set are currently at risk. Immediate project management action will be necessary
- *Green* set: IT-projects assigned to the lower approximation of this *green* set are currently not at risk. The projects are proceeding well, thus normal project management attention will be acceptable

There will be IT-projects which do not belong to the lower approximation of either the *red* set of the *green* set. The status of these IT-projects is ambiguous according to Rough Set Theory. Thus, in the terminology of Rough Set Theory these IT-projects are simultaneously members of the upper approximations of both the *red* set and the *green* set.

With reference to the "traffic light" warning system these ambiguous IT-projects are assigned to a new set referred to as the *yellow* set. Further investigation will be required of these ambiguous IT-projects to clarify their status, assess the risk, and to decide on a course of action.

The development of the "traffic light" warning system involves a two stage approach consisting of a "classifier design" and the "classifications". This approach is depicted in Fig. 1.

- Classifier Design: In this first stage a decision table is defined. This definition is based upon the critical success factors list that has been determined to be the most appropriate for the organization at the current time. This approach was explained in the previous section on Grounding.
- Classifications: Based upon the decision table defined in the first stage IT-projects may be analyzed by the critical success factors list. The result will be the assignment of the IT-projects to one of the project status alternatives.

Classifier Design   In this stage the decision table is created. A small sample decision table is shown in Table 8.

The projects #2 and #4 are definite members of the *red* set while the projects #3 and #6 undoubtedly belong to the *green* set. However, the projects #1 and #5 have identical attribute values average, high, extensive, no but lead to contradicting decisions, *red* for project #1 and *green* for project #5. So, their membership in one of these sets is not clearly defined. In rough set terminology these projects are coevally assigned to the upper approximations of the *red* as well as the *green* set.

Classifications   The decision table may be employed to determine the status of IT-projects. This requires an evaluation of each information technology project regarding the specific critical success factors list. By combining the results of each critical success factors evaluation a determination may be made about the status of each information technology project. Consequently, based upon the classifier design, an IT-project may be assigned to one of the "traffic light" warning system categories as shown in Fig. 2.

Table 8 Sample decision table of critical success factors [46]

Project	Critical Success Factors*				Status	Issue
	TMS	PTC	UTS	UOC		
1	Average	High	Extensive	No	Red	Ambiguous
2	Low	Weak	Moderate	Yes	Red	
3	High	High	Moderate	Yes	Green	
4	Average	Weak	Low	No	Red	
5	Average	High	Extensive	No	Green	Ambiguous
6	Average	High	Extensive	Yes	Green	

*TMS = Top Management Support, PTC = Project Team Competence, UTS = User Training on Software, UOC = Use of Consultants

Fig. 2 Traffic light-like warning system for IT-projects

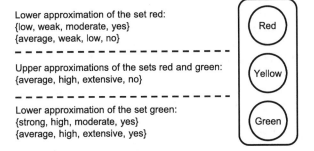

As described above, IT-projects assigned to the *red* set are currently, at risk; those assigned to the *yellow* set require further investigation; and those assigned to the *green* set are currently not at risk. It is interesting to note that the classification process may also be employed to focus the attention of the project managers on specific critical success factor for those information projects which are assigned to the *yellow* set.

Also, it is incumbent upon the organization to regularly review the established decision table. As the organization's environment changes and internal learning takes place the critical success factors list may change. This regular review activity will serve to ensure the process of information technology project review is current and grounded within the specific environment of the organization.

4.2 Dominance Based Rough Sets Approach

When the collected data on IT-projects are of ordinal nature Dominance based Rough Sets Approach (DRSA) [47] can be applied.

DRSA has gained intensive attention recently and has already been applied to a wide range of applications. For example, it has been applied to customer relationship management [48], customer satisfaction analysis [49, 50], the analysis of the

Table 9 Evaluation of an IT project

Project	Critical Success Factors[*]			Project performance
	TMS	PTC	UTS	
1	High	Average	Low	Poor
2	Average	Average	Low	Average
3	Average	Average	Moderate	Average
4	High	High	Moderate	Sound
5	High	Average	Extensive	Sound
6	High	High	Extensive	Sound
7	Low	Weak	Low	Poor
8	Low	Weak	Moderate	Poor

[*]TMS = Top Management Support, PTC = Project Team Competence, UTS = User Training on Software

advantages of firms [51], and the technical diagnostic of a fleet of vehicles [52] and many more. In these applications Variable-Consistency DRSA (VC-DRSA) [53] is of special importance.

We briefly discuss its potential for the research of critical success factors in IT project management. For example, consider the projects as depicted in Table 9.[1] All data are of ordinal nature:

- TMS (Top Management Support): *high ≻ average ≻ low*
- PTC (Project Team Competence): *high ≻ average ≻ weak*
- UTS (User Training on Software): *extensive ≻ moderate ≻ low*
- Project Performance: *sound ≻ average ≻ poor*

Then decision rules like:

- R01: IF [PTC $\succeq$ average] $\wedge$ [UTS $\succeq$ moderate]
        THEN [Project Performance $\succeq$ average]
- R02: IF [PTC $\preceq$ average] $\wedge$ [UTS $\preceq$ low]
        THEN [Project Performance $\preceq$ average]
- R03: ...

can be induced.

Rule R01 leads to a *Project Performance ≽ average* while rule R02 leads to a *Project Performance ≼ average*.

Obviously rule R01 shows a *Threats for Deterioration* [55] since it requires certain minimum levels of fulfillment of the critical success factors PTC and UTS to hold.

In contrast to this rule R02 shows *Opportunities for Improving* [55] since advancements of the critical success factors PTC and UTS can possibly improve the

---

[1]The structure of the example has been adapted from the college student example presented by Greco et al. [54].

project performance. Parameters for evaluation the attractiveness of the rules, like the *support*, the *strength* and the *certainty* have been adapted by Słowiński and Greco [55] from association rule mining [56].

5 Conclusion

This chapter has presented the idea of employing Rough Set Theory to assist in reducing the complexity of managing IT-projects. Depending upon the type of information technology project there are many generic critical success factor lists. The proposal outlined in this chapter was to first ground the list in relation to the type of information technology project and, more importantly, within the current environment of the organization.

Then Rough Set Theory may be applied to the organization-specific critical success factor list. The techniques of Rough Set Theory, through the incorporation of the "traffic light" warning system analogy, will facilitate the analysis and categorization of projects. This categorization will direct the project manager toward those projects which are currently at risk. Further, it will be incumbent upon the organization to ensure that the critical success factor list remains current relative to the environment of the organization.

This chapter also shows the great potential of Dominance based Rough Set Approach for the analysis of ordinal data in the field of IT project management. The induced rules disclose hidden characteristics and my enrich the analysis of IT-projects.

There are many factors and issues that project managers must be cognizant of in managing IT-projects. If there is a way to address the plethora of complex tasks then project managers will be able to more effectively perform their activities. The proposal outlined in this chapter is meant to address this issue.

References

1. Shore, B.: Failure rates in global is projects and the leadership challenge. J. Glob. Inf. Technol. Manag. **8**(3), 1–5 (2005)
2. Scott, J.E., Vessey, I.: Managing risks in enterprise integration systems implementations. Commun. ACM **45**(4), 74–81 (2002)
3. Kaufman, C., Korrapati, R.B.: A project management office (pmo) framework for successful implementation of information technology projects. Proc. Acad. Inf. Manag. Sci. **11**(1), 1–6 (2007)
4. Cunningham, M.: It's all about the business. Inform **13**(3), 83 (1999)
5. Hedelin, L., Allwood, C.M.: It and strategic decision-making. Ind. Manag. Data Syst. **102**(3), 125–139 (2002)
6. Jiang, J.J., Klein, G.: Software project risks and development focus. Proj. Manag. J. **32**(1), 3–9 (2001)
7. Willcocks, L., Graeser, J.: Delivering It and E-business Value. Computer Weekly Series. Butterworth and Heinemann, Oxford (2001)
8. Hartman, F., Ashrafi, R.A.: Project management in the information systems and information technologies industries. Proj. Manag. J. **33**(3), 4–14 (2002)

9. Baccarini, D., Salm, G., Love, P.E.D.: Management of risks in information technology projects. Ind. Manag. Data Syst. **104**(3/4), 286–295 (2004)
10. Wang, E., Chou, H.W., Jiang, J.: The impacts of charismatic leadership style on team cohesiveness and overall performance during erp implementation. Int. J. Proj. Manag. **23**(3), 173–180 (2005)
11. Francoise, O., Bourgault, M., Pellerin, R.: Erp implementation through critical success factors' management. Bus. Process. Manag. J. **15**(3), 371–394 (2009)
12. Bradford, M., Florin, J.: Examining the role of innovation diffusion factors on the implementation success of enterprise resource planning systems. Int. J. Account. Inf. Syst. **4**(3), 205–225 (2003)
13. Cantu, R.: A framework for implementing enterprise resource planning systems in small manufacturing companies. Master's thesis, St. Mary's University, San Antonio, TX (1999)
14. Chang, S.I.: ERP life cycle implementation, management and support: implications for practice and research. In: Proceedings of the 37th Hawaii International Conference on Systems Sciences, Big Island, HI, pp. 3579–3588. IEEE Computer Society, Los Alamitos (2004)
15. Esteves, J., Pastor, J., Casanovas, J.: A framework proposal for monitoring and evaluating training in erp implementation projects. Technical research report, Universidad Politecnica Catalunya, Barcelona, Spain (2002)
16. Gargeya, V.B., Brady, C.: Success and failure factors of adopting SAP in ERP system implementation. Bus. Process. Manag. J. **11**(5), 501–516 (2005)
17. Holland, C.P., Light, B.: Critical success factors model for erp implementation. IEEE Softw. **16**(3), 30–36 (1999)
18. Huang, S.M., Chang, I.C., Li, S.H., Lin, M.T.: Assessing risk in ERP projects: identify and prioritize the factors. Ind. Manag. Data Syst. **104**(8), 681–688 (2004)
19. Kanjanasanpetch, P., Igel, B.: Managing knowledge in enterprise resource planning (ERP) implementation. In: Engineering Management Conference, 2003. IEMC'03. Managing Technologically Driven Organizations: the Human Side of Innovation and Change, Albany, NY, pp. 30–35 (2003)
20. Nah, F.H., Lau, L.S., Kuang, J.: Critical factors for successful implementation of enterprise resource systems. Bus. Process. Manag. J. **7**(3), 285–296 (2001)
21. Sun, A., Yazdani, A., Overend, J.D.: Achievement assessment for enterprise resource planning (ERP) system implementations based on critical success factors (CSF). Int. J. Prod. Econ. **98**, 189–203 (2005)
22. Esteves, J., Pastor, J.: Towards the unification of critical success factors for ERP implementation. In: Proceedings of the 10th Annual BIT Conference, Manchester, UK, pp. 60–69 (2000)
23. Somers, T., Nelson, K.: The impact of critical success factors across the stages of enterprise resource planning implementations. In: Proceedings HICSS 2001—34th Hawaii International Conference on System Sciences, Maui, Hawaii (2001)
24. Plant, R., Willcocks, L.: Critical success factors in international ERP implementations: a case research approach. J. Comput. Inf. Syst. **47**(3), 60–70 (2007)
25. Remus, U.: Critical success factors for implementing enterprise portals: a comparison with ERP implementations. Bus. Process. Manag. J. **13**(4), 538–552 (2007)
26. Negash, S.: Business intelligence. Commun. Assoc. Inf. Syst. **13**, 177–195 (2004)
27. Yeoh, W., Koronios, A., Gao, J.: Managing the implementation of business intelligence systems: a critical success factors framework. Int. J. Enterp. Inf. Syst. **4**(3), 79–94 (2008)
28. Amoribieta, I., Bhaumik, K., Kanaamedala, K., Parkhe, A.D.: Programmers abroad: a primer on offshore software development. McKinsey Q. **2**, 129 (2001)
29. Adelakun, O., Jennex, M.E.: Success factors for offshore information system development. J. Inf. Technol. Cases Appl. **5**(3), 12–29 (2003)
30. Remus, U., Wiener, M.: Critical success factors for managing offshore software development projects. J. Glob. Inf. Technol. Manag. **12**(1), 6–29 (2009)
31. Kieser, A., Nicolai, A.: Success factor research: overcoming the trade-off between rigor and relevance? J. Manag. Inq. **14**(3), 275–279 (2005)
32. March, J.G., Sutton, R.I.: Organizational performance as a dependent variable. Organ. Sci. **6**, 698–706 (1997)

33. Rosaker, K.M., Olson, D.L.: Public sector information system critical success factors. Transform. Gov. People Process Policy **2**(1), 60–70 (2008)
34. Holmes, D.: Egov: Ebusiness Strategies for Government. Nicholas Brealey, Naperville (2001)
35. Garson, D.: Public Information Technology: Policy and Management Issues. Idea Group Publishing, Hershey (2003)
36. Pinto, J.K., Prescott, J.E.: Variations in critical success over the stages in the project life cycle. J. Manag. **14**(1), 5–18 (1998)
37. Nah, F.H., Islam, Z., Tan, M.: Empirical assessment of factors influencing success of enterprise resource planning implementations. J. Database Manag. **18**(4), 26–50 (2007)
38. Glaser, B.G., Strauss, A.L.: The Discovery of Grounded Theory: Strategies for Qualitative Research. Aldine DeGruyter, New York (1976)
39. Swap, W., Leonard, D., Shields, M., Abrams, L.: Using mentoring and storytelling to transfer knowledge in the workplace. J. Manag. Inf. Syst. **18**(1), 95–114 (2001)
40. Tulving, E.: Organization of Memory. Academic Press, New York (1972)
41. Scholes, R.: Language, narrative, and anti-narrative. In: Mitchell, W. (ed.) On Narrativity, pp. 200–208. University of Chicago Press, Chicago (1981)
42. Bruner, J.: Acts of Meaning. Harvard University Press, Cambridge (1990)
43. Pawlak, Z.: Classification of objects by means of attributes. Technical Report 429, Institute for Computer Science, Polish Academy of Sciences (1981)
44. Pawlak, Z.: Rough sets. Int. J. Comput. Inf. Sci. **11**, 341–356 (1982)
45. Pawlak, Z.: Rough Sets: Theoretical Aspects of Reasoning About Data. Kluwer Academic, Dordrecht (1991)
46. Peters, G., Poon, S., Hunter, M.G.: Analysing qualitative interviews in information systems research—complexity reduction by the application of rough concepts. In: Proceedings ACIS 2009—20th Australasian Conference on Information Systems, pp. 994–1001 (2009)
47. Greco, S., Matarazzo, B., Slowinski, R.: Rough sets theory for multicriteria decision analysis. Eur. J. Oper. Res. **129**(1), 1–47 (2001)
48. Liou, J.J.H.: A novel decision rules approach for customer relationship management of the airline market. Expert Syst. Appl. **36**(3), 4374–4381 (2009)
49. Greco, S., Matarazzo, B., Slowinsk, R.: Rough set approach to customer satisfaction analysis. In: Rough Sets and Current Trends in Computing (RSCTC 2006). LNAI, vol. 4259, pp. 284–295. Springer, Berlin (2006)
50. Greco, S., Matarazzo, B., Slowinski, R.: Customer satisfaction analysis based on rough set approach. Z. Betriebswirtsch. **16**(3), 325–339 (2007)
51. Li, Y., Liao, X., Zhao, W.: A rough set approach to knowledge discovery in analyzing competitive advantages of firms. Ann. Oper. Res. **168**(1), 205–223 (2009)
52. Sawicki, P., Zak, J.: Technical diagnostic of a fleet of vehicles using rough set theory. Eur. J. Oper. Res. **193**(3), 891–903 (2009)
53. Dembczynski, K., Greco, S., Kotłowski, W., Slowinski, R.: Statistical model for rough set approach to multicriteria classification. In: Knowledge Discovery in Database (PKDD 2007). LNCS, vol. 4702, pp. 164–175. Springer, Berlin (2007)
54. Greco, S., Matarazzo, B., Slowinski, R.: Decision rule approach. In: Figueira, J., Greco, S., Ehrgott, M. (eds.) Multiple Criteria Decision Analysis: State of the Art Surveys. International Series in Operations Research & Management Science, vol. 78, pp. 507–555. Springer, Berlin (2005)
55. Slowinski, R., Greco, S.: Measuring attractiveness of rules from the viewpoint of knowledge representation, prediction and efficiency of intervention. In: Advances in Web Intelligence (AWIC 2005). LNAI, vol. 3528, pp. 11–22 (2005)
56. Agrawal, R., Imielinski, T., Swami, A.: Mining association rules between sets of items in large databases. In: Proceedings SIGMOD 1993—ACM Special Interest Group on Management of Data Conference, pp. 207–216 (1993)

Workflow Management Supported by Rough Set Concepts

Georg Peters and Roger Tagg

Abstract Workflow systems have gained increasing importance in recent decades. Some of the most important drivers for this rising interest have been the shifts within organizations, first in the mid-1990s from function structures to business processes, then more recently toward service oriented architectures. Today workflow systems support a wide range of processes, from the highly standardized to the relatively flexible. The efficient management of workflow is of great importance for the performance of any organization, but it still remains a challenge in dynamic and often unpredictable environments. Methods of dealing with such challenges include dynamic instance adaptation, partial completion, case handling and even manual overriding in the case of exceptions. Besides classic approaches that utilize stochastic methods, soft computing concepts have been proposed in order to improve the management of workflows; one example is the use of fuzzy Petri nets. In this chapter, we discuss the further potential of soft computing concepts, in particular rough set theory, for supporting the management of workflow systems. We show how rough sets can support the design of lean workflow systems, particularly lean decision rules at decision gate (in particular OR-splits), by detecting excessive and redundant information. Furthermore, we discuss how rough sets can be utilized to disclose missing information in a workflow system. We also discuss where the accountability lies for resolving missing information, and assign the responsibility to either the workflow design or the monitoring phase. Finally, we demonstrate how rough sets help predict the routing of a process within a workflow system. Early information about the routing of a process helps to efficiently allocate the resources of an organization.

G. Peters (✉)
Department of Computer Science and Mathematics, Munich University of Applied Sciences, 80335 Munich, Germany
e-mail: georg.peters@cs.hm.edu

R. Tagg
School of Computer and Information Science, University of South Australia, Adelaide SA 5000, Australia
e-mail: roger.tagg@unisa.edu.au

G. Peters et al. (eds.), *Rough Sets: Selected Methods and Applications in Management and Engineering*, Advanced Information and Knowledge Processing,
DOI 10.1007/978-1-4471-2760-4_9, © Springer-Verlag London Limited 2012

1 Introduction

Triggered by Hammer and Champy's seminal book "Reengineering the Corporation" [1] business process management has become a core strategy for organizations to maintain and optimize their performance. Originally focusing on business process reengineering (BPR) Hammer and Champy [1] define it as "Fundamental rethinking and radical redesign of business processes to achieve dramatic improvements in critical, contemporary measures of performance, such as cost, quality, service, and speed".

For several centuries process design has been a well established approach in disciplines like engineering; any construction plan can be regarded as a process map, whether it is for building a house or developing a technical product like a camera or a car. For example, the conveyor belt has become one of the symbols for effective and efficient process-based manufacturing. So, while the ideas were not new for many manufacturing and technical companies, Hammer and Champy's book was instrumental in extending the process design view to the more information and service oriented parts of business. This also reflects the shift, in most mature economies today, from manufacturing to service industries.

While business processes are defined independently of any implementation platform, workflow systems are often related to the implementation of business processes on the basis of information technology.[1] Therefore, workflow systems can be considered as analogous to a conveyor belt for business and service processes.

For some years, business process management and workflow systems have gained even more importance due to a technological change in IT from large monolithic architectures toward small specialized software objects, such as in SOA (Service Oriented Architecture) [3], that can be easier managed. Monolithic IT architectures integrate business functions and processes in a way which makes them complex and inflexible in the face of changes.

In contrast, in these new IT architectures business functions and processes have been separated. Basically, the idea of SOA is to design small self-contained software objects that can be quickly and easily combined to support the business processes of an organization. In this context, workflow systems have regained attention as a central layer to glue these software objects together.

The objective of this chapter is to discuss the potential of selected methods of rough set theory to support the design and the management of workflow systems, especially in environments of uncertainty and change.

The chapter is organized as follows. In the next section we discuss some fundamentals of workflow systems. In Sect. 3 we present the fundamental idea behind rough sets. Section 4 discusses how rough sets can support the design of lean workflow systems. In Sect. 5 we utilize rough sets to disclose missing information in workflows. In Sect. 6 we show how rough sets can be used to predict case routes. The chapter concludes with a summary.

---

[1] However, see van der Aalst and van Hee [2] who use the terms "business process" and "workflow" interchangeably.

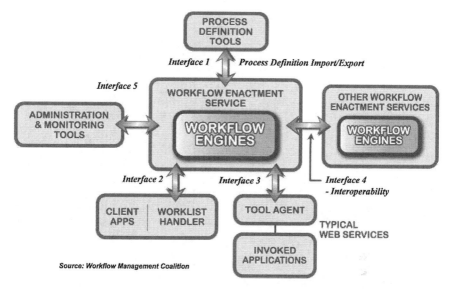

Fig. 1 Workflow reference model of the WfMC[2]

2 Some Fundamentals of Workflow Systems

2.1 Workflow Architectures and Perspectives

Workflow Architecture Frameworks   The Workflow Management Coalition[3] (WfMC) developed a Workflow Reference Model [4] to define a common frame for the components and linking interfaces of a workflow system (see Fig. 1).

In the context of our chapter we will discuss selected potentials of rough set methods to support

1. the definition, particularly lean workflow design (Sect. 4)
2. the administration and monitoring, especially to give early alerts about missing information (Sect. 5) and predicted case routes (Sect. 6)

of workflows.

Perspectives of Workflow Management   In the management of workflow systems, the control view (i.e. what tasks can follow other tasks) often seems to dominate. However, as Jablonski and Bussler [5] point out, workflow management in practice also includes consideration of data, time and resources. Hence, a holistic view of workflow management is characterized by the following perspectives:

1. *Control*, concerned with the status and routing in a workflow system.

---

[2]©WfMC (http://www.wfmc.org/images/stories/workflow_web.jpg, retrieved 30.12.2010).
[3]http://www.wfmc.org.

Fig. 2 Classifying
workflows [6]

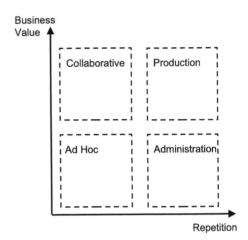

2. *Data*, namely what information needs to be maintained for each business case, particularly in order to resolve OR-split decisions and termination of repeating loops.
3. *Time*, concerned with the duration of task execution times, delays and deadlines.
4. *Resources*, concerned with the availability of humans, equipment and materials to carry out tasks.

One perspective cannot be totally decoupled from the other perspectives; they are not disjunctive but overlap to certain extents. For example, the control perspective requires data in order to monitor the status of the workflow and to perform routing tasks.

The main concerns of our work are with control flow and data perspectives, especially regarding their interaction. Further, we show that rough set methods can also be used to support the resource management perspective.

2.2 Flexibility in Workflow Systems

Workflow Systems can be regarded as one component part of CSCW ("Computer Supported Cooperative Work"), in that it is an interdisciplinary area of research addressing the support and management of cooperative work. In this context workflow systems represent standardized, repetitive practices; this is in contrast to groupware systems which are designed for processes with low or even non-existent rates of repetition, which reflect high flexibility requirements.

In an approach to defining workflows (Fig. 2) developed by the GIGA Information Group [6], groupware systems address the processes with low repetition rates (e.g. collaborative and ad hoc processes), while classic workflow systems support highly repetitive processes that are commonly observed in production and administration.

Bridging the gap between groupware and workflow systems remains a challenging task. The need for flexibility in workflows arises because the assumptions that underly the existence of an ideal (and unalterable) business process sometimes fail to hold true. Taking the data perspective, the data needed—both to make the workflow routing decisions and to do the tasks themselves—is often missing, conflicting or late. Resource perspective situations can include the unavailability of qualified humans, or shortages or even total lack of other resources. Time pressures include the existence of impending deadlines, especially where the tasks in a process that still have to be completed are expected to take more time than remains to complete the whole business case. Such time pressures may be caused by the inability to finish individual tasks within the expected timescale. Finally, it often happens that the business process itself is required to change—often because of a changing business environment, competitive pressure, unfavorable customer service feedback etc.

Theoretical approaches to providing flexibility have included Exceptions [7], Dynamic Instance Adaptation [8], Partial Completion [9, 10] and Case Handling [11]. Examples of dynamic instance adaptation could include skipping one or more tasks, changing the sequence of tasks, declaring a task sufficiently completed, or relaxing the task dependency rules.

In Case Handling, proposed by van der Aalst et al. [12] the approach is to reduce the number of inter-task dependency rules and let things happen when the data to carry out the tasks, or to resolve any OR conditions, is available. Certain human participants can also have special privileges to skip or re-do tasks.

Mixed-initiative Management, as proposed by Rubinstein and Corkill [13] specifically brings in temporal and resource perspectives. As with the suggestion that we propose later in Sect. 6, the style of their solution is to give early warning to the process owner of possible delays or missed deadlines.

The emphasis in the two last approaches is on addressing the "non control flow" perspectives (such as data and resource availability) for performing tasks and for completing cases in a timely manner. It is an interesting issue as to whether flexibility built into a workflow model can ever be good enough to cover most situations (including emergency handling), or whether the task of adapting instances is really a job best left to human judgment.

2.3 Intelligent Approaches to Workflow Management

A main challenge in workflow management is to handle the reality of open systems, which are characterized by constant changes as well as vague and uncertain information. To deal with such situations, several concepts to describe uncertainty and vagueness have been suggested. The most established and oldest is probability theory, which goes back to the 17th and 18th century when it was introduced by Bernoulli, Laplace, Pascal and others. In 1965 probability theory was joined by fuzzy set theory [14, 15]. Recently, Zadeh [16] has been promoting a general theory of uncertainty that provides a holistic framework to describe any kind of uncertainty.

In the workflow management literature, there has been some movement toward addressing the problems of handling the variability of individual process instances or business cases, but rough set concepts have not generally been considered to date.

However, there have been several studies based on the application of intelligent concepts such as soft computing methods [17, 18], including fuzzy sets [14, 15], neural nets [19, 20] and genetic algorithms [21]. Although our approach is primarily based on rough sets, some brief comment on these other methods, in particular fuzzy sets, is appropriate at this point.

Zirpins et al. [22] concentrate on fuzzy conditions in workflows, particularly where the condition is a compound one, with simple conditions connected by AND. These authors have attempted to incorporate measures of probability together with the fuzziness. They also use process mining as a means of deriving the workflow models.

Fuzzy business process engineering has been introduced by Huesselmann [23] who suggested a fuzzified eEPC (extended Event-driven Process Chains) [24]. Fuzzy workflows have been proposed by Adam et al. [25] in conjunction with the modeling of workflows using eEPC. An enhanced "fuzzy operator" for the exclusive OR operator is introduced, which uses a min-max inference mechanism.

Wang et al. [26] also apply fuzzy reasoning to a workflow model, with a view to matching changed versions of a model. Chan and Zhang [27] have applied fuzzy workflow nets (a variant of Petri nets) in an emergency control application, where dynamic instance adaptation is an essential feature of the application.

2.4 Modeling Notations for Workflows

In the practice of designing workflow systems, several different notations have been proposed that are in use presently. Popular notations include BPMN (Business Process Modeling Notation) [28, 29],[4] eEPC (extended Event-Driven-Process Chain) [30] and UML Activity Diagrams [31].[5]

A more formal concept with strong mathematical foundations is Petri Net theory [32, 33], which has up to now been primarily used in technical applications. However, the potential of Petri Nets for business and workflow modeling has been recognized [2], especially since it allows rigid formal analysis of its properties. With some enhancements, Petri Nets are used as the basic modeling notation for some commercial workflow management systems (WfMS), e.g. COSA.

We will therefore use Petri Nets throughout this chapter to illustrate our proposed concepts (for an excellent and comprehensive introduction to Petri Nets the reader is referred to the paper of Murata [34]).

---

[4]http://www.bpmn.org.

[5]http://www.uml.org/.

Fig. 3 Lower and upper
approximations

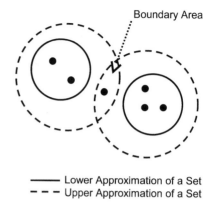

Boundary Area

——— Lower Approximation of a Set
– – – Upper Approximation of a Set

3 Some Fundamentals of Rough Sets

To make this chapter self-contained we briefly discuss some of the relevant basic
properties of rough sets.

3.1 Basic Properties of Rough Sets

Rough sets were introduced by Pawlak [35, 36] in 1982. Since then they have gained
increasing attention in research and real life applications. The fundamental idea of
rough sets is to classify objects into three disjunctive categories.

An object

1. surely belongs
2. surely does not belong
3. possibly belongs

to a set.

To obtain these categories Pawlak suggested to describe a set by two approximations, a *lower approximation* and a *boundary*[6] (see Fig. 3). Objects belonging to
the lower approximation surely belong to the set. To indicate the notion of 'sure'
membership the lower approximation is also called the *positive region*.

Objects within the boundary *may possibly* belong to the corresponding set. Note,
the join of the lower approximation and the boundary is called the *upper approximation* of the set, thus subsuming both the sure and possible members of the set.

Hence, objects not belonging to the upper approximation are *surely not* members
of the corresponding set. To indicate this, this zone is called the *negative region*.

This leads to the three fundamental properties of rough sets:

1. An object can be a member of one lower approximation at most.

---

[6]Note, the boundary is not a geometric region in the spatial sense, but a set.

2. An object that is a member of the lower approximation of a set is also member of the upper approximation of the same set.
3. An object that does not belong to any lower approximation must be a member of at least two upper approximations.

Many advances have been made in rough set theory over the last decades. However, we limit our presentation to these three fundamentals of rough sets. For an introduction to the fundamental idea of rough set theory see Pawlak et al. [37] and for a more extended presentation of its basic principles, Grzymala-Busse [38]. Detailed surveys, especially on its mathematical foundations, can be found for example in Komorowski et al. [39] or Polkowski [40].

It should be noted that the original rough set theory is purely set-based. However, a new interval-based approach has recently been proposed, e.g. Yao et al. [41]. Applications of interval-based rough set theory are in the field of cluster analysis [42, 43] and others. However, in this chapter we limit our proposals to the set-based version of rough set theory.

3.2 Rough Petri Nets

The potential of rough set theory to Petri Nets has already been investigated by J.F. Peters et al. who suggested rough Petri Nets [44–47], where the *transitions* function as rough gates. In their example application, Peters et al. applied this idea to sensor and filter models.

4 Lean Workflow Design

4.1 Reducts in Rough Set Theory

A widely used method of rough set theory is based on the concept of reducts. Consider Table 1 which shows observed decisions about the acceptance of orders received by a reselling company. Three features have been identified as important:

- *Customer Classification* rates customers into three categories, ranging from A=important to C=low-value customers
- *Credit Rating* classifies customers into two groups, customers with good and weak credit ratings
- *Stock Availability* indicates whether the product the customer wants to buy is on stock or has to be ordered by the reseller.

The reseller wants to develop a rule-based system to quickly decide whether a customer order should be accepted or declined. Obviously, the features *Customer Classification* and *Credit Rating* are sufficient to determine the decision; the attribute *Stock Availability* is redundant. In rough sets terms the reduced set of attributes

Table 1 Observed customer orders (version I)

#	Customer classification	Credit rating	Stock availability	Decision order =
1	B	good	available for order	accept
2	B	weak	available for order	decline
3	B	good	in stock	accept
4	C	weak	in stock	decline
5	C	good	available for order	decline

{*Customer Classification, Credit Rating*} is called a *Reduct*. We further see that in the reduced set two rules are identical, namely the rules pair (#1, #3) so that a set of four rules with two attributes is sufficient to represent the decision about customer orders.

Reducts are widely used for feature selection in data mining [48], e.g. in bioinformatics [49]. Several algorithms have been proposed to determine reducts (e.g. in [50, 51]) and software tools are available that support the identification of reducts (e.g. ROSE2,[7] Rosetta,[8] RSES[9]). Note the similarity of reducts to primary keys in database systems.

4.2 Detecting Excessive or Redundant Information at OR-Splits

In workflow nets the OR-splits are decision gates where the route of a case is determined. Hence, a decision table as depicted in Table 1 defines the routing at one such OR-split (see also Fig. 4). Note, that in Petri nets the cases are symbolized by tokens. In our example the cases (tokens) are the customer orders.

Obviously, the rough concept of reducts helps to design simple and efficient workflow systems by avoiding over-complex decision rules. In line with this terminology we call a place that has a decision rule based on a reduct a *Reduced Place*.

5 Disclosing Missing Routing Information

5.1 Discernibility and Indiscernibility in Rough Set Theory

To disclose missing information in workflows, we propose to apply the idea of discernible versus indiscernible objects from rough set theory.

---

[7]http://idss.cs.put.poznan.pl/site/rose.html, retrieved 04.01.2011.

[8]http://www.lcb.uu.se/tools/rosetta, retrieved 04.01.2011.

[9]http://logic.mimuw.edu.pl/~rses, retrieved 04.01.2011.

Fig. 4 OR-split and the corresponding set of decision rules

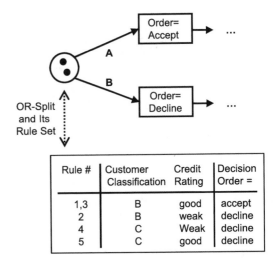

Rule #	Customer Classification	Credit Rating	Decision Order =
1,3	B	good	accept
2	B	weak	decline
4	C	Weak	decline
5	C	good	decline

Consider an extended variate of the decision table as introduced in Sect. 4.1 consisting of eight observed customer orders (Table 2). Four orders are accepted (decision {Order=accept}) while the remaining four are declined (decision {Order=decline}).

The pair of customer orders #4 and #5 on the one hand and the pair of customer orders #6 and #8 on the other hand share the same characteristics {B, weak, in stock} and {C, good, available for order} respectively. However, the decisions on these orders differ. So, applying these decision rules would lead to conflicting results.

Let us consider customer orders #4 and #5. While customer order #4 is accepted customer order #5 is declined although the customer orders are indiscernible with respect to their characteristics. Therefore, an order of a B-customer with a weak credit rating who wants to buy a product that is on stock may, in some cases be accepted and in other cases declined. Hence, this may be considered a "borderline" order that needs further processing before a final decision can be taken.

Table 2 Observed customer orders (version II)

#	Customer classification	Credit rating	Stock availability	Decision order =
1	B	good	available for order	accept
2	A	good	in stock	accept
3	B	weak	available for order	decline
4	B	weak	in stock	accept
5	B	weak	in stock	decline
6	C	good	available for order	decline
7	C	weak	in stock	decline
8	C	good	available for order	accept

Table 3 Firing rules and rough approximations

Order characteristics	Firing	Rough approximation(s)
{B, good, available for order} {A, good, in stock}	Order=accept	Lower Approximation of set {Order=accept}
{B, weak, available for order} {C, weak, in stock}	Order=decline	Lower Approximation of set {Order=decline}
{B, weak, in stock} {C, good, available for order}	no firing	Upper Approximations of sets {Order=accept}, {Order=decline}

Fig. 5 A place in two upper approximations

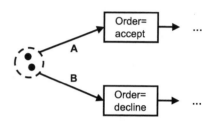

As already discussed in Sect. 3 this order is therefore assigned to the upper approximations of both the sets {Order=accept} and {Order=decline}. The same applies to the pair of customer orders #6 and #8.

Fortunately the remaining customer orders lead to clear decisions. While customer orders #1 and #2 are indubitably acceptable, #3 and #7 have to be declined. So #1 and #2 belong to the lower approximation of the set {Order=accept} while the customer orders #3 and #7 are members of the lower approximation of the set {Order=decline}.

The implication for the treatment of new customer orders is straightforward; new customer orders with case variables equal to those of #1, #2, #3 and #7 can be treated immediately, while customer orders that have the characteristics {B, weak, in stock} and {C, good, available for order} need some more detailed examination.

The firing rules for the transitions and the related assignment of tokens (customer orders) to the rough approximations are depicted in Table 3.

5.2 Incomplete Information at OR-Splits

Rough Places Obviously the set of firing rules as depicted in Table 3 is insufficient to deal with all eight customer orders (tokens). Some tokens get stuck on the input place of the OR-split. To indicate this we say that the place belongs to the upper approximations of both sets {Order=accept} and {Order=accept}. We indicate this by a "dashed circle" place notation as depicted in Fig. 5.

Application of Rough Places to Workflows: Incomplete Decision Rules The appearance of incomplete decision rules (*rough places*) may arise for two reasons.

Fig. 6 Tokens in lower and
upper approximations

Token in the upper approximations
of the sets {Order=accept} and
{Order=decline} ,
e.g. {?, good, available for order}

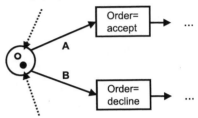

Token in one lower approximation
(set {Order=accept}),
e.g. {B, good, available for order}
or {C, good, available for order}

First, an incomplete decision rule, indicated by the appearance of places in upper approximations of both sets {fire=yes} and {fire=no}, can be interpreted as a poorly designed workflow system. The system has to be improved to run properly without any further interruption. Second, a decision rule might intentionally be designed incomplete. Then, for example, the normal cases would pass the decision gate (OR-split) undisturbed. The exceptions would intentionally be "caught" in the upper approximation of a place and presented to the end user for further special treatment.

5.3 Incomplete Case Information

Rough Tokens   Consider an order of a new customer. Information on the credit rating of the new customer can be provided by a rating agency and the stock availability can be checked. Let us assume that the customer has a good credit rating and that the ordered product is not on stock.

However, classification of the customer is not possible since information on her/his shopping frequencies, average order sizes etc. have not yet been obtained. So, formally, the assessable information can be represented as: {?, good, available for order}. Since information is missing, the order cannot be processed. However an order of a B-customer would be accepted, while orders of customers belonging to category C would require further special treatment in any case.

In such a case we call the token *rough token* and assign it to the upper approximation. To graphically distinguish between tokens (customer orders) belonging to lower or upper approximations we suggest their representation as shown in Fig. 6, namely a "hollow" token for those in the upper approximation.

Application of Rough Tokens to Workflows: Incomplete Case Information
This example is concerned with the information carried by the token (concept of *rough tokens*). A possible area of application of the proposed method is to provide

early warning of potential delays within a workflow system that could be caused by incomplete information in certain business cases. The aim would be to get the workflow system to alert the end user when a choice is waiting on more information. If only the immediate decision is considered, the next transition will be held up. If the complete process including all potential downstream activities is considered, the alert is a warning that further down the track, a transition may be held up.

Ideally, the workflow system should monitor the arrival of the required extra data, so that transitions can be automatically enabled without user intervention. This may well involve facilities to set up software agents that can talk to the applications that manage this data. If, however, it can be seen in advance that certain combinations of case attributes mean that a choice cannot be resolved, the workflow template should probably be altered to allow for a "don't know" branch. The process owner would need to define how long cases can be left in this state, and what should happen to them when time runs out.

5.4 Rough Places Versus Rough Tokens

The main difference between *rough places* and *rough tokens* is related to who is responsible when a token gets stuck at an OR-split.

– In the first case discussed above, the token carries all the required information, but the firing rules at the OR-split are insufficient to take a decision. Therefore, the responsibility is at the OR-split and hence related to the *design* of the workflow system.
– In the second case, the token cannot provide the requested information. Therefore, the token is accountable for its inability to proceed further. Hence, the *monitoring system* is responsible for solving this problem.

6 Prediction of Case Routes

In the following section we utilize the concepts introduced so far, and propose *rough transitions* to predict case routes in Petri Nets.[10]

---

[10]In Petri Net theory *places* are passive elements storing tokens. Transitions are active elements since they can change the state of the net when they "fire". Hence, transitions are the only elements in a Petri Net that have the capability to make decisions. In the following sections we do not question this concept. However, we graphically mark input places and/or tokens on input places to indicate whether one or more corresponding transitions can fire or not. The decision rules still remain in the only active elements of the Petri Net, the transitions.

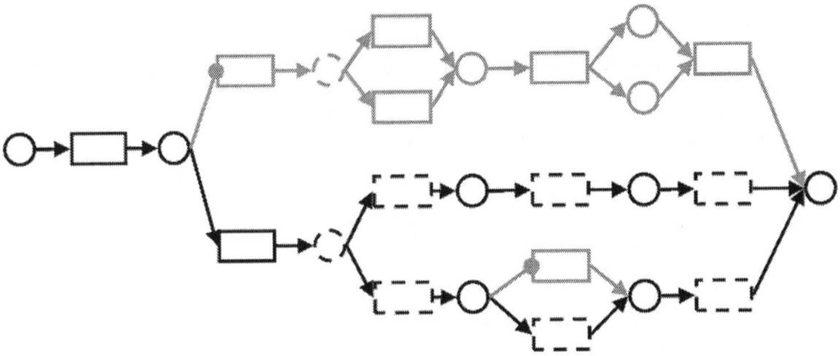

Fig. 7 Rough transitions

6.1 Rough Transitions

A token can only proceed when both the token as well as the place the token is assigned to belong to lower approximations. In such a case the decision rule at the OR-split has sufficient information and a transition is enabled to fire.

However, when a token belongs to an upper approximation and/or the place belongs to an upper approximation then the token gets stuck. It is not defined which of the transitions may fire. This leads to the concept of rough transitions.

Let us define the following decision sets {fire=yes} and {fire=no}. Transitions which will surely fire belong to the lower approximation of the set {fire=yes} while transitions that will definitely not fire belong to the lower approximation of the set {fire=no}. The remaining transitions belong to the upper approximations of both sets {fire=yes} and {fire=no}.

As an example, consider the Petri Net given in Fig. 7.[11] Black solid-lined transitions will surely fire. Therefore, they belong to the lower approximation of the set {fire=yes}. The gray transitions will definitely not fire,[12] consequently they belong to the lower approximation of the set {fire=no}. The status of remaining dashed transition is unclear; they may or may not fire. So they belong to both upper approximations of the sets {fire=yes} and {fire=no}.

Please note, that rough transitions, like rough places, depend on the cases (tokens). Therefore, they are dynamic properties of Petri Nets.

---

[11]Since the effects on the capability of making a decision are the same for both rough tokens and places (in both cases a token cannot proceed) we will, for simplicity, only display rough places in the example.

[12]The selected path is indicated by a normal arrowhead while the path that is not selected is indicated by a dot in Fig. 7.

6.2 Application of Rough Transitions to Workflows: Incomplete Path Information

Resource management is a crucial task in any company. The concept of *rough transitions* supports more efficient management of resources in the following way. As depicted in Fig. 7 there are three categories of transition:[13] (i) transitions that will be performed surely, (ii) transitions that will not be performed and (iii) transitions that may be performed. While in the first case resources have to be allocated to the transitions, in the second case any allocated resources can be released. Uncertainty is reduced to the third case in which it is unclear whether resources are needed to perform the transitions or not.

An example of a user-friendly graphical presentation that could support rough transitions is offered by the WFMS named Chameleon developed by a group based at the University of Queensland, Australia [52]. In the user's view of the process instance, color coding is used to indicate paths that are able to be followed at a given point in time. As this WFMS stands currently, colors can only represent states that follow deterministically from the control flow rules, can't be done yet (e.g. yellow), waiting for synchronization (e.g. green), ready to be done (e.g. blue) and already done (e.g. red). There is not yet any consideration of data or resource availability, incomplete rules etc. However, it seems relatively simple to extend this color scheme to include the equivalent of the black, gray and dashed routes in Fig. 7.

7 Conclusion

In this chapter we have presented some ways in which workflow management can be supported by rough set approaches. In particular, we introduced reduced places, rough places, rough tokens and rough transitions. Reduced places provide lean decision rules at OR-splits in process models. Rough places, rough tokens and rough transitions reveal three different kinds of incomplete information in a process: (i) incomplete decision rules, (ii) incomplete case information and (iii) incomplete path information. The immediate disclosure of these different kinds of incomplete information can function as an early warning system in workflow management. It helps to optimize the allocation of resources and may avoid unnecessary process delays. Since rough set theory is a well developed mathematical concept it provides easy accessible and rich methods to efficiently handle information needs in workflow management. Hence, rough sets can support the management of workflow systems by ensuring that just the right amount of information is provided and that resources are allocated efficiently.

---

[13]In Petri Nets transitions are only regarded as active entities in the sense that they can change the state of the net. So, generally, business activities can be mapped to transitions and places as well. However, in our context we follow the conventions of leading business process notations, like EPC [30], where business activities can only be assigned to active entities ("functions").

References

1. Hammer, M., Champy, J.A.: Reengineering the Corporation: a Manifesto for Business Revolution. Harper Business Books, New York (1993)
2. van der Aalst, W., Hee, K.: Workflow Management—Models, Methods, and Systems. MIT Press, Cambridge (2002)
3. Rosen, M., Balcer, M., Smith, K., Lublinsky, B.: Applied SOA: Service-oriented Architecture and Design Strategies. Wiley, New York (2008)
4. Hollingsworth, D.: Workflow management coalition—the workflow reference model. Technical Report Document Number TC00-1003, Workflow Management Coalition (1995)
5. Jablonski, S., Bussler, C.: Workflow-management. International Thomson Publishing, Bonn (1995)
6. Leymann, F., Roller, D.: Production Workflow: Concepts and Techniques. Prentice Hall, Upper Saddle River (2000)
7. Klein, M., Dellarocas, C.: A knowledge-based approach to handling exceptions in workflow systems. J. Comput. Support. Collab. Work **9**, 399–412 (2000)
8. Horn, S., Jablonski, S.: An approach to dynamic instance adaption in workflow management applications. In: Proceed. Workshop "Towards Adaptive Workflow Systems", ACM 1998 Conference on Computer Supported Cooperative Work, Seattle, WA, USA. ACM, New York (1998)
9. Lin, J., Orlowska, M.: Partial completion of activity in business process specification. In: Proceed. IRMA Conference, San Diego, CA, USA, pp. 186–189 (2005)
10. Peters, G., Tagg, R.: Dimensions of partial completion of activities in workflow management. In: Proceed. Australian Conference on Information Systems, Sydney, Australia (2005)
11. van der Aalst, W., Weske, M., Grünbauer, D.: Case handling: a new paradigm for business process support. Data Knowl. Eng. **53**(2), 129–162 (2005)
12. van der Aalst, W., Berens, P.: Beyond workflow management: product-driven case handling. In: Proceed. 2001 International ACM SIGGROUP Conference on Supporting Group Work, Boulder, Colorado, USA, pp. 42–51. ACM, New York (2001)
13. Rubinstein, Z.B., Corkill, D.D.: Mixed-initiative management of dynamic business processes. In: Proceedings 2003 IEEE International Workshop on Soft Computing in Industrial Applications, Binghamton, New York, USA, pp. 39–44 (2003)
14. Zadeh, L.: Fuzzy sets. Inf. Control **8**, 338–353 (1965)
15. Zimmermann, H.J.: Fuzzy Set Theory and Its Applications, 4th edn. Kluwer Academic, Boston (2001)
16. Zadeh, L.: Toward a generalized theory of uncertainty (GTU) an outline. Inf. Sci. **172**, 1–40 (2005)
17. Mitra, S., Acharya, T.: Data Mining: Multimedia, Soft Computing, and Bioinformatics. Wiley, New York (2003)
18. Maimon, O., Rokach, L. (eds.): Soft Computing for Knowledge Discovery and Data Mining. Springer, Berlin (2007)
19. Haykin, S.: Neural Networks: a Comprehensive Foundation, 2nd edn. Prentice Hall, Upper Saddle River (1998)
20. de Wilde, P.: Neural Network Models. Theory and Projects, 2nd edn. Springer, Berlin (1997)
21. Goldberg, D.E.: Genetic Algorithms in Search, Optimization, and Machine Learning. Addison-Wesley, Boston (1989)
22. Zirpins, C., Schütt, K., Piccinelli, G.: Flexible workflow description with fuzzy conditions. In: LCS2002—London Communications Symposium, University College London, London, UK (2002)
23. Huesselmann, C.: Fuzzy-geschäftsprozessmanagement. Josef Eul Verlag, Lohmar (2003)
24. Keller, G., Nüttgens, M., Scheer, A.: Semantische Prozessmodellierung auf der Grundlage Ereignisgesteuerter Prozeßketten (EPK). Technical report, Universitaet des Saarlandes, Saarbruecken, Germany (1992)

25. Adam, O., Thomas, O., Martin, G.: Fuzzy workflows—enhancing workflow management with vagueness. In: Joint International Meeting EURO/INFORMS, Istanbul, Turkey (2003)

26. Wang, R., Yan, X., Wang, D., Zhao, Q.: Flexible workflow autonomic object intelligence algorithm based on extensible Mamdani fuzzy reasoning system. In: Global Design to Gain a Competitive Edge, pp. 251–260. Springer, London (2008)

27. Chan, H., Zhang, K.: Application of fuzzy workflow nets in web-based emergency command system. In: Proceed. 2nd IASTED International Conference on Web Technologies, Applications and Services (WTAS 2006), Calgary, Canada, pp. 67–71 (2006)

28. Briol, P.: BPMN—the Business Process Modeling Notation Pocket Handbook. Lulu Press, Morrisville (2008)

29. White, S., Miers, D.: BPMN Modeling and Reference Guide Understanding and Using BPMN. Future Strategies Inc., Lighthouse Pt (2008)

30. Scheer, A.W.: ARIS—Business Process Modeling. Springer, Berlin (2000)

31. Fowler, M.: UML Distilled: a Brief Guide to the Standard Object Modeling Language. Addison-Wesley, Boston (2003)

32. Petri, C.: Kommunikation mit Automaten. Schriften IIM 2, University of Bonn, Institut für Instrumentelle Mathematik, Bonn (1962)

33. Girault, C., Valk, R.: Petri Nets for Systems Engineering. Springer, Berlin (2002)

34. Murata, T.: Petri nets: properties, analysis and applications. Proc. IEEE **77**(4), 541–580 (1989)

35. Pawlak, Z.: Rough sets. Int. J. Comput. Inf. Sci. **11**, 341–356 (1982)

36. Pawlak, Z.: Rough Sets: Theoretical Aspects of Reasoning About Data. Kluwer Academic, Dordrecht (1992)

37. Pawlak, Z., Grzymala-Busse, J., Slowinski, R., Ziarko, W.: Rough sets. Commun. ACM **38**(11), 89–95 (1995)

38. Grzymala-Busse, J.W.: Rough set theory with applications to data mining. In: Negoita, M.G., Reusch, B. (eds.) Real World Applications of Computational Intelligence. StudFuzz, vol. 179, pp. 221–244. Springer, Berlin (2005)

39. Komorowski, J., Pawlak, Z., Polkowski, L., Skowron, A.: Rough sets: a tutorial. In: Pal, S.K., Skowron, A. (eds.) Rough-fuzzy Hybridization: a New Trend in Decision Making, pp. 3–98. Springer, Singapore (1999)

40. Polkowski, L.: Rough Sets. Physica-Verlag, Heidelberg (2003)

41. Yao, Y.Y., Li, X., Lin, T.Y., Liu, Q.: Representation and classification of rough set models. In: Proceedings Third International Workshop on Rough Sets and Soft Computing, San Jose, CA, USA, pp. 630–637 (1994)

42. Lingras, P., West, C.: Interval set clustering of web users with rough k-means. J. Intell. Inf. Syst. **23**, 5–16 (2004)

43. Peters, G.: Some refinements of rough k-means. Pattern Recognit. **39**, 1481–1491 (2006)

44. Peters, J.F., Skowron, A., Suraj, Z., Ramanna, S., Paryzek, A.: Modeling real-time decision-making systems with rough fuzzy Petri Nets. In: Proceed. EUFIT98—6th European Congress on Intelligent Techniques & Soft Computing, pp. 985–989 (1998)

45. Peters, J.F., Skowron, A., Suraj, Z., Ramanna, S.: Guarded transitions in rough Petri Nets. In: Proceedings EUFIT99—7th European Congress on Intelligent Systems & Soft Computing (1999). Abstract p. 171, paper on CD

46. Peters, J.F., Skowron, A., Suray, Z., Ramanna, S.: Sensor and filter models with rough Petri Nets. In: Burkhard, H.D., Czaja, L., Skowron, A., Starke, P. (eds.) Proceedings of the Workshop on Concurrency, Specification and Programming, Humboldt-University, Berlin, Germany, pp. 203–211 (2000)

47. Peters, J.F., Ramanna, S., Suraj, Z., Borkowski, M.: Rough neurons: Petri Net models and applications. In: Pal, S.K., Polkowski, L., Skowron, A. (eds.) Rough-neuro Computing, pp. 472–491. Springer, Berlin (2003)

48. Swiniarski, R.W., Skowron, A.: Rough set methods in feature selection and recognition. Pattern Recognit. Lett. **24**, 833–849 (2003)

49. Mitra, S.: Computational intelligence in bioinformatics. Trans. Rough Sets **III**, 134–152 (2005)

50. Starzyk, J.A., Nelson, D.E., Sturtz, K.: A mathematical foundation for improved reduct generation in information systems. Knowl. Inf. Syst. **2**, 131–146 (2000)
51. Kryszkiewicz, M., Cichon, K.: Toward scalable algorithms for discovering rough set reducts. Trans. Rough Sets **I**, 120–143 (2004)
52. Shelomanov, N.: Validation and optimisation of workflow processes. Technical report, University of Queensland, St Lucia, Queensland, Australia (2003)

Part V
Methods and Applications in Engineering

Rough Natural Hazards Monitoring

Marek Sikora and Beata Sikora

Abstract An example of rough sets application in a forecasting module of natural hazards monitoring systems in hard-coal mines is presented in this paper. Rough sets are applied for reduction a number of variables used during the hazard assessment, checking the variables significance and defining decision rules. Obtained decision rules are the ground for developing a system forecasting hazardous states. Tasks of hazards monitoring systems and an architecture of the forecasting module that is the component of the monitoring system are presented in the paper. Examples of two practical applications illustrate the described module. The first one concerns microseismic hazards forecasting, the second is connected with gaseous hazards forecasting.

1 Introduction

Natural hazards are one of the most frequent reasons of accidents and disasters in mining industry. This concerns in particular underground mining in which upsetting stability of rock mass (so-called microseismic hazards) and risks connected with concentration of dangerous gases in mine undergrounds are the most serious and frequent hazards. These hazards are monitored by equipment placed in mine undergrounds and visualized by surface monitoring systems. Moreover, the monitoring systems estimate hazards by so-called expert assessment methods [1]. Based on information delivered by the system a dispatcher, if necessary, makes a decision concerning: switching-off the power in a given area of the mine; evacuation of the

M. Sikora (✉)
Institute of Innovative Technologies EMAG, Katowice, Poland
e-mail: msikora@emag.pl

M. Sikora
Institute of Informatics, Silesian University of Technology, Gliwice, Poland
e-mail: Marek.Sikora@polsl.pl

B. Sikora
Institute of Mathematics, Silesian University of Technology, Gliwice, Poland
e-mail: Beata.Sikora@polsl.pl

G. Peters et al. (eds.), *Rough Sets: Selected Methods and Applications in Management and Engineering*, Advanced Information and Knowledge Processing,
DOI 10.1007/978-1-4471-2760-4_10, © Springer-Verlag London Limited 2012

crew from endangered zones; temporal stop of mining and taking preventives that are meant to lower the degree of hazard (for example: executing relieving shooting or slowing down the mining process in order to lower concentration of dangerous gases). The dispatcher decisions are meant to minimize the risk of disaster dangerous for crew and mining machinery as well as to keep current the production process.

Expert methods of hazard assessment are based on processed measurement data. For microseismic hazards information coming from seismometers and geophones are the basis of assessments. Analyzing microseismic energy and activity, expert methods (we distinguish two methods: seismologic and seismoacoustic [1]) classify hazards as one of the following states: safe, low risk, high risk, hazardous. In the case of methane hazards, maximal concentration level for selected group of methanemeters is analyzed.

By dint of high non-precision of expert methods research on new algorithms of hazard assessment are carried on all the time [2, 3]. In particular, methods of linear prognosis [4] and artificial neural networks [5, 6] were tried to be applied for assessment of microseismic hazards purposes. Moreover, examples of application a special kind of rule classifier for the problem of microseismic hazards assessment are presented in papers by Sikora and Wróbel [7] and by Sikora [8]. In the paper [9] Sikora and Sikora present the application of so-called regression rules to forecast methane concentration in mining excavation.

A forecasting module applying methods of machine learning to forecast microseismic and methane hazards is presented in this chapter. The module realizes functions of: data cleaning and preparation, evaluating data quality, hazards forecasting and monitoring a quality of generated forecasts. To evaluate data quality and to develop the forecasting model rough sets were used. Rough sets proposed by Pawlak [10] has found many practical applications in various domains of human activity. In industrial applications rough sets were used, among others, for diagnostic models developing [11–13] and control algorithms defining [14–16].

In dominant majority of cases rough sets are exerted to approximate describing of concepts by minimizing a set of variables necessary to define the description. Moreover, rough set provides tools for searching an influence of a given variable on possibility of a given concept defining. Generating a set of rules that classify objects to appropriate concepts is also possible by means of rough sets [17–19]. Very important is that methodology offered by rough set is a source of interpretable knowledge about analyzed data. Such knowledge can be compared with expert knowledge or beliefs before application of the forecasting system in industry.

2 Natural Hazards Monitoring Systems

Two main groups of natural hazards monitoring systems in hard-coal mines are distinguished: seismic systems (divided into seismoacoustic and microseismic systems) and methane-fire systems. Measurement data are transmitted to surface measuring stations and than stored in databases (Fig. 1, upper part). It is also possible

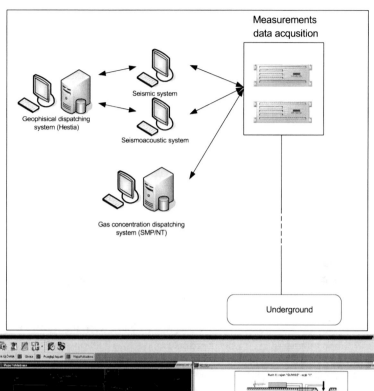

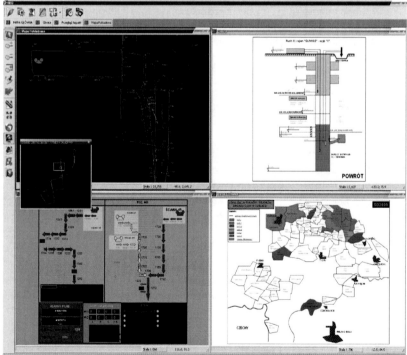

Fig. 1 Hazards monitoring systems: data flow scheme (*upper figure*), data visualization on maps and graphic charts (*lower figure*)

to send control signals to underground equipment through the surface measuring stations. Monitoring systems transfer converted data to so-called disposal systems which aim is security and production complex monitoring apart from monitoring a concrete hazard. The most popular disposal monitoring systems in Polish coal mines are Hestia [8, 20] and SMP-NT [21]. Hestia monitors seismic hazards and SMP NT monitors gas-fire ones. Both the systems have over 50 applications in Polish, Eastern European (Ukraine, Russia) and Asian (China) coal mines.

The disposal system goal is to present actual measurement data and hazard evaluation by expert methods (if the assessment hasn't been made by specialist system before). By dint of the layout of autonomous and configurable windows (Fig. 1, lower part), the disposal system is adapted to preferences of each dispatcher.

3 Architecture of the Forecasting Module

The forecasting module is autonomous software integrated with the disposal system on database level. Through the database data are downloaded and forecast results are transmitted to the disposal system. The forecasting module executes functions concerning measurement data aggregation and preparation, training and validation sets based on which forecasting models are created. Moreover, the forecasting module controls the quality of generated forecasts and sends an appropriate message to an operator in the case of deterioration of the quality. The data analysis itself is made without the module. Obtained results of the analysis are transferred to the module in the form of a set of parameters that enable it to make forecasts on hazards for coming new measurement data. Figure 2 presents the module architecture.

Since measurement data are collected with various frequency, it is necessary to aggregate the gathered data so that a single record will describe a situation in monitored area of the coal mine that took place for specified time period (e.g. for 1 minute). Therefore, consecutive records of aggregated data can be treated as a sequence of time windows. Each window is described by some vector of features (field of the record), each feature reflects aggregated values of a variable for aggregation period. Such functions as minimum, maximum, average, range, difference, sum, among others are applied for the aggregation. Data aggregation consists also in defining new variables to reflect changes dynamics between consecutive time windows. The dynamics can be expressed by means of differences and increments. Data prepared in such way are uploaded to two places. Firstly, if the system works in forecasting mode, then each new aggregated record of data is transferred to the forecasting model and a new hazard forecast is generated. Secondly, aggregated data land in the archive, and based on archival data an analyst creates the forecasting model. During downloading data for analysis, the analyst defines additionally a dependent variable and forecast horizon.

We will illustrate the above description with an example. Let be given T aggregated records containing information about n variables. This means that for each $t \in T$ we have a realization of multidimensional time series $\mathbf{x}_t = (x_1, x_2, \ldots, x_n)_t$. Appropriate configuration of aggregating functions enables us

Fig. 2 The forecasting
module architecture

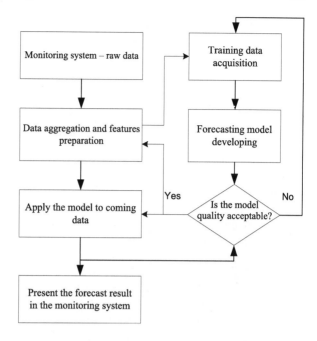

to obtain a vector of data that is increased by any delay of any variable e.g. $((x_1)_{t-1}, (x_1)_{t-2}, (x_2)_{t-2}, (x_1, x_2, \ldots, x_n)_t)$ and to add information about dynamics of changes of variables values in consecutive time windows, for example $((x_1)_{t-1}, (x_1)_{t-2}, (x_2)_{t-2}, (x_1, x_2, \ldots, x_n)_t, ((x_1)_t - (x_1)_{t-1}))$. Adding a dependent variable y_t denotes selection one of present variables as the dependent variable and determination the forecast horizon. This means that there is $x_i \in \{x_1, x_2, \ldots, x_n\}$ such that $y_t = (x_i)_{t+h}$.

The configuration of data aggregation process depends on a configuration defined by a user. Choice of a subset of archival data that will be analyzed and the analysis process itself are made by the analyst. It is worth mentioning that the aggregation process includes also data cleaning, so substituting missing values and data smoothing. Details concerning all functions connected with data cleaning and aggregation that are realized by the forecasting module are described in [22].

As it has been already noted, the analysis results are implemented in the module in the form of the set of parameters describing decision rules used during the forecasting. It is worth noting that the forecasting module enables us to make use of both rules obtained by rules induction algorithm and rules defined by a domain expert.

In the forecasting module a user determines also which parameters describing the model quality should be monitored. If the module realizes the classification task, the parameter is a number of errors of the classifier, and two errors *false positive* and *false negative* are distinguished in each decision class. If values of the parameters (the number of *false positive* errors and number of *false negative* errors) exceed certain threshold levels, then appropriate message is generated. Generation of the message about decrease of forecasts accuracy means that repeat analysis taking into account latest of collected data should be carried out. The forecasting module has own database in which aggregated data, forecasts results, and models (sets of rules) used for the forecasting in a given time period are saved.

4 Rough Sets and Descriptive Data Analysis

Rough sets enable descriptive data analysis for defining accurate or approximate descriptions of concepts. It is also possible to verify which of features used for description are redundant, and which are needful to obtain good description. Being consistent with terminology formerly applied let us assume that a set U of records (objects) described by a vector A of features (attributes) is given. Attributes belonging to A can be of symbolic or real type. Moreover, let a variable $d \notin A$ of symbolic type which is called the decision attribute be distinguished. Then we can define a decision table $\mathbf{DT} = (U, A \cup d)$. The notation $a(x) = v$ means that the value of the attribute a for the object x is equal to v. It can be easily noticed that for the given $\mathbf{DT}$ all values of any attribute $a \in A \cup d$ in the considered table can be determined. This set is called the set of values of a and is denoted by Va. The decision class we called a set of objects belonging to U with the same values of the decision attribute. Hence there exists the decision class $X_v = \{u \in U : d(u) = v\}$ for each value $v \in Vd$.

A standard rough sets model [10] assumes that numeric attributes were put to discretization before the analysis [23]. This means that the set of values Va of the numeric attribute has been divided into separable intervals $(Va = \bigcup_{i=0}^{k_a} \langle c_i^a, c_{i+1}^a \rangle)$. Boundary points c_i of the intervals can be defined by a domain expert or automatically by means of one of many discretization algorithms [23–25]. These algorithms are implemented in various data mining packages such as Weka [26] or RSES [27].

In the standard rough sets model a indiscernibility relation can be connected with each set $B \subseteq A$, defined on $U \times U$ by the formula (1):

$$\text{IND}(B) = \{(x, y) \in U \times U : \forall_{a \in B} a(x) = a(y)\}. \tag{1}$$

In special causes the set B can be a singleton or $B = A$. The relation $\text{IND}(B)$ is reflexive, symmetric and transitive, therefore is an equivalence relation. To equivalence classes of the relation belong these object from U that are indiscernible with respect to attributes included in B. Equivalence classes of the relation $\text{IND}(B)$ make it possible to define an accurate or, if it is not possible, approximate (rough) description of decision classes. Defining such description consists in finding B-lower and B-upper approximation of a class and determining a boundary region [10, 19].

$$\underline{B}X_v = \{x : [x]_{\text{IND}(B)} \subseteq X_v\}, \qquad \overline{B}X_v = \{x : [x]_{\text{IND}(B)} \cap X_v \neq \emptyset\},$$
$$BNX_v = \overline{B}X_v - \underline{B}X_v.$$

To the lower approximation belong these objects that we can unambiguously and doubtlessly assign to a given decision class based on information about values of attributes from the set B. To the upper approximation belong objects about which we are not sure whether they are representatives of the given decision class or not. A positive region of the decision table (denoted by $POS_{DT}(B)$) is the sum of lower approximations of decision classes. Therefore in the set $POS_{DT}(B)$ all objects that we can unambiguously assign to corresponding decision classes are included. In terms of the description of data included in the decision table particularly interesting is whether some attributes are redundant from the decision classes approximation viewpoint. This is associated with a definition of relative reduct [10, 19]. Any subset $B \subseteq A$ is called the relative reduct in the decision table **DT** if and only if it satisfies two conditions. The first one is $POS_{DT}(B) = POS_{DT}(A)$. The second tells that no set $C \subseteq A$ such that $C \subset B$ satisfies the first condition. For the given decision table many relative reducts can exist, attributes belonging to each of them create so-called core. The problem of determining all relative reducts in a given decision table is NP-hard [19]. However, many heuristics and algorithms enabling reducts calculation for large data sets have been proposed [28, 29]. Implementations of selected algorithms of relative reducts calculations are included, among others, in the RSESlib library and the RSES program [27]. Rough sets provides also coefficients that enable it to characterize numerically the attribute set significance. The coefficient (2) is called the classification quality coefficient, (3) is called the attribute significance coefficient. Both the coefficients are the gain type criterion. This means that the higher value of the coefficients the stronger influence of the set B of attributes (or of the attribute a for formula (3)) on decision classes approximation abilities. Both the coefficients take values from the set $\langle 0, 1 \rangle$.

$$\gamma_{DT}(B) = \frac{card(POS_{DT}(B))}{card(U)} \qquad (2)$$

$$\sigma_{DT}(a) = \gamma_{DT}(A) - \gamma_{DT}(A \setminus \{a\}) \qquad (3)$$

5 Induction of Decision Rules and Evaluation the Rule-Based Classifier Quality

Descriptions of decision classes can be applied for defining a classification system that classifies new unknown objects to decision classes [17]. The ground for developing such system are decision rules which can be obtained from relative reducts found for the whole **DT** or for each object separately (these are so-called objects-related relative reducts [19]). A disadvantage of these solutions is very big number of obtained rules which are too much matched to training data. The most frequent solution of this problem is to generate only a certain limited number of rules [17]. Such rules are created based on a set of attributes which is the subset of a set of attributes forming the relative reducts [18]. Another approach is to use rough sets for reduction a set of attributes only, and then apply some of popular sequential covering rules induction algorithms [30, 31]. In research described here the RMatrix algorithm was used for rules induction [18]. The RMatrix algorithm generates decision rules in the form "**if** Conditions **then** decision". More precisely these are rules of the form (4):

$$\textbf{if } w_1 \textbf{ and } w_2 \textbf{ and} \ldots \textbf{and } w_k \textbf{ then } d = v. \qquad (4)$$

The conjunction of elementary conditions w_i occurs in the rule premise. Any elementary condition is the expression of the form $w_i \equiv a_i = Z_i$, where a_i is the name of the conditional attribute, Z_i is the value of a symbolic attribute or one of intervals obtained after numeric attributes discretization (e.g. risk = low; concentration_methane = $\langle 0, 0.8 \rangle$). An expression pointing to assignment of an example satisfying the premise to the particular decision class is found in the conclusion. For the rule (4) positive examples we call objects belonging to the decision class X_v, all other objects we call negative examples. Let p denote a set of positive examples covered by a rule r (P stands for all positive examples), and n denote a set of negative examples covered the rule r (N stands for all positive examples). Basic quality measures defined for the rule are the precision $p/(p+n)$ and coverage p/P. We aim at inducing rules characterized by maximal accuracy and maximal coverage. Depending on the quality measure used during rules induction various results can be obtained [18, 32, 33]. In the version of RMatrix presented here the RSS (Rule Specificity and Sensitivity) measure (5) was used for created rules quality evaluation:

$$\text{RSS}(r) = \frac{p}{P} - \frac{n}{N}. \tag{5}$$

RMatrix creates one rule for each object x occurring in a decision table. Elementary conditions of the form $a = Z$, are added to the rule premise in turn. If a is the symbolic attribute, then $Z = a(x)$, otherwise Z is one of intervals get after discretization such that $a(x) \in Z$. The best elementary condition $a = Z$ is the one which enables distinguishing as much positive examples from negative ones as possible. After adding the next condition the quality of partial rule created in such way is evaluated. The adding of elementary conditions is finished while all attributes $a \in A$ have been considered. The rules for which the highest value of the measure (5) was obtained is remembered as the output one. After the rules induction, a filtration phase is initialized. Firstly, all duplicates are removed from the set of rules. Secondly, from the set of rules these of rules are removed which are unnecessary in aspect of classifier optimization criterion. The process of removing unnecessary rules, called also the rule filtration, is done by the Forward algorithm. The Forward algorithm, starting with one-rule descriptions of each decision class, builds a classifier, and then in each iteration it successively adds a rule from the ranking list to the classifier provided that adding of this rule increases the quality (6) of classifier. Rules sorted decreasingly according to a value of the measure (5) create the ranking list. The detailed description of the Forward algorithm can be found in [18].

The quality of obtained rule-based classifier is usually measured by the classification accuracy. The accuracy of the classification may be however misleading in the case of unbalanced data distribution of decision classes [31, 34]. In this instance it is better to use sensitivity and specificity of the classifier [34, 35]. The classification accuracy for smaller decision class (called primary class or minority class) can be evaluated on the basis of so-called classification confusion matrix (Fig. 3).

The all of correctly classified cases (examples) from the primary class are called true-positives (*TP*); incorrectly classified primary cases are called false-negatives

Fig. 3 Classification
confusion matrix

		actual class	
		primary	secondary
predicted	primary	TP	FP
class	secondary	FN	TN

(*FN*); correctly classified cases from the secondary class are called true-negatives (*TN*), and incorrectly classified secondary cases are called false-positives (*FP*). Two measures are usually used for evaluation of the classifier quality: *sensitivity* = $TP/(TP+FN)$ (i.e. conditional probability of true positives of a given primary class) and *specificity* = $TN/(TN+FP)$ (i.e. conditional probability of true-negatives of a given secondary class). High values of the sensitivity and specificity are desirable for the classification task but unfortunately there is usually a trade-off between each measure. This trade-off can be represented graphically by using a ROC curve [34]. The criterion which optimizes sensitivity and specificity of the classifier is called the Class-gain (6) measure [31, 35].

$$Class\text{-}gain = Specificity + Sensitivity - 1 \qquad (6)$$

The measure (6) enables it to find a good balance between capabilities of hazards identification (true-positives) and minimization of false alarms (false-positives). During the classification the voting mechanics is applied. The aim of the classification process is to assign an example (particularly a test example) $t \in T$ to a corresponding decision class. If the example t is covered by several rules which assign it to different decision classes, we deal with ambiguous assignment problem. This ambiguity is resolved with a rule voting process [17]. The strength of each voting rule depends on its RSS (5) value evaluated on the training set or so-called tuning set. For each decision class the sum of votes of rules covering the given example t is calculated. The example t is assigned to the class for which the sum of votes is the largest.

6 Seismic Hazards Forecasting

The first example of the presented methodology application is connected with microseismic hazards assessment. Data were gathered form the Hestia system and came from the longwall 508 in the hard-coal mine "Wesoła" in Mysłowice. The analysis aimed at defining a system that classifies seismic hazards with the eight-hour forecast horizon.

Data were aggregated in eight-hour (shift) time windows. Value of conditional attributes contained the following information: results of seismic hazard assessment for nearest eight hours obtained by expert methods—seismological and seismoacoustic; information about whether the shift is mining or maintenance; maximal and average energy (in joules), and maximal and average seismic activity (expressed in number of impulses) registered by geophones deployed around the monitored excavation (the geophone that registers maximal energy we denote by GMax); deviations of energy and activity expressing dynamism of changes of monitored values during consecutive time windows (the method of the deviations calculation in accordance with the expert seismoacoustic method [1]); a number of seismic phenomena registered in time windows; a number of seismic phenomena in respective energetic groups (the groups 10^2 J, 10^3 J, ..., 10^7 J, 10^8-10^9 J were distinguished); a summary energy of seismic phenomena registered in time windows and a maximal energy of seismic phenomena registered. Values of assessments obtained by expert methods had the following meaning: a—safe state, b—low risk, c—high risk, d—hazardous state.

The decision variable contained information about whether during consecutive shift the seismic energy that is the sum of registered tremors energy and microseismic energy registered by the geophone GMax exceeds the value $5 \cdot 10^5$ J. As research shows [2, 3, 5], exceeding the level of energy associates with increase of high-energy tremor hazard. There are 576 examples in the training set which corresponds with 192 days of the longwall monitoring. In the testing set 288 examples corresponding with 96 days of the monitoring were included. In the training set 65 examples represented the state "hazardous", in the testing set it was 32 such examples.

The first part of the analysis consisted in discretization of the training set, and then in discretization the testing set based on established set of cuts. After the discretization each numerical attribute was divided into three subsets on average. The attribute informing about average aberration of energy registered by geophones was divided into the biggest number of intervals, five ones. After the discretization the classification quality coefficient DT was equal to 1 for whole set of conditional attributes. This means that there is no inconsistencies in the data set. Then, relative reducts were determined. Two relative records were in the set, both were composed of 11 attributes which means that the reduction enables limitation of the set of attributes size from 23 to 11. Analyzing attributes creating both the reducts, attributes contained in no reduct were removed from the training set. These attributes were: results of expert seismological assessment; information about whether a shift is mining; information about summary energy of phenomena in the following energetic groups 10^4 J, 10^5 J, 10^6 J, 10^7 J and 10^8-10^9 J. The set of attributes reduced in such way was a superset of each reduct and, during further analysis, was called the quasi-reduct. From among of attributes chosen to the quasi-reduct only attributes keeping results of expert seismoacoustic assessment and the average energy measured by geophones did not occur in both determined relative reducts. This means that all selected attributes besides those ones are very relevant for description of decision classes defining "hazardous state" and "safe state". Removing whichever of them would cause the coefficient γ_{DT} decrease. More precise analysis of attributes significance that consists in calculation values of attributes significance coefficient σ_{DT} makes it possible to establish a ranking of attributes significance. Six the most significant attributes together with the significance coefficient value are presented in Table 1.

Values of the coefficient are low which means that no attribute having explicit influence on possibility of distinguishing between hazardous sates and safe states can be indicated.

Table 1 Microseismic data—attributes significance analysis

Attribute	σ_{DT}
Number of impulses registered by the geophone GMax	0.035
Number of phenomena registered from the energy interval 10^2 J	0.029
Energy registered by the geophone GMax	0.021
Maximal energy of the registered seismic phenomena	0.016
Value of the average deviation of changes of energy registered by geophones	0.009
Value of the average deviation of changes of impulses registered by geophones	0.009

Table 2 Microseismic data—results of the test data classification

Set of attributes	Overall classification accuracy	Accuracy of the class "hazardous state"	Accuracy of the class "safe state"	Class-gain	Number of rules
All	78.8	72.2	79.6	0.515	21
Quasi-reduct	76.8	72.2	77.4	0.492	16

The second part of the analysis consisted in determining decision rules and classifying the testing set in which examples had been omitted during descriptive analysis occurred. The classification results are presented in the second table. The results are given for a classifier get based on all attributes and based on reduced set of attributes. The overall classification accuracy and accuracy of each decision class expressing the accuracy with which we are able to forecast hazardous and safe states are shown in the table. The results are given in percentages, 100% means that all testing examples were assigned to corresponding decision classes. Moreover, values of the Class-gain measure and the number of determined rules are presented in the table.

As Table 2 shows, the classifier enables forecasting hazardous states with the accuracy of 75% on average. The reduced set of attributes leads to slightly worse results. Since the size of analyzed data set is not large, the process of whole data set aggregation and preparing is not a big computational problem. A model get on the whole data set can be sent to the forecasting module. Is the model worth applying yet? Results of hazards forecasting by the complex method [1, 8] which is a combination of results of seismic and seismoacoustic hazards assessment methods are helpful in answering the question. For our forecast task this method is characterized by the accuracy of 79% (thus higher than the classifier) for the "safe state", and the accuracy only of 44% for the "hazardous state" (much lower than the classifier). Thereby Class-gain for the expert method is merely equal to 0.23. This means that the classifier forecasts better the hazardous state defined by us than the expert method does.

Approval for application the method of hazard assessment causes necessity of presentation the assessment algorithm to a group of experts. For the rule classifier this boils down to presenting a set of rules and a classification algorithm. It is worth mentioning that a number of rules obtained is small and can be simply interpreted by experts for the sake of applied filtration algorithm. By dint of application the measure RSS during induction, generated rules consist of small number of elementary conditions. For the decision class corresponding with the "hazardous state" rules are not 100% accurate (which means that a certain number of negative examples covers them, too). Examples of two the best rules for each decision class are presented below, with the rules their accuracy is presented, too. Is the accuracy of the second rule too low? Considering a distribution of examples in the training set ("hazardous"—65, "safe"—511) we can calculate that probability of drawing an example representing the class "hazardous" is here equal to $65/(65 + 511) = 0.11$. A rule indicating the decision class "hazardous" with the accuracy of 0.57 should be considered well condensing the probability of drawing an example from the class "hazardous". Results obtained by the classifier support the thesis.

If the average number of registered impulses < 1515 **and** the maximal energy of registered seismic phenomena $< 2.5 \cdot 10^3$ J **then** the "safe state" (Precision 0.979)

If the average seismic energy registered by geophones $> 1.2 \cdot 10^5$ J **and** the average deviation of seismic energy registered by geophones $> 378\%$ **then** the "hazardous state" (Precision 0.57)

7 Methane Hazard Forecasting

The second example of application of the forecasting module concerns monitoring methane concentration in mine excavation. A source of data is the methane-fire disposal system SMP/NT [21]. Research were carried out based on data receipted from the hard-coal mine "Wesoła" in Mysłowice. The aim of analysis was verifying whether a forecast of methane concentration registered by the sensor M32 placed on the top end of the longwall face is possible. Values of conditional attributes contained earlier readings from methanemeters M32, M31 and the anemometer AN31. Additionally, information about whether mining works are carried out is available. Measurement data were aggregated to ten-minute periods. Each aggregated record reflected maximal values registered by individual sensors in consecutive ten-minute periods. The forecast horizon amounted to 1 which mean that an attempt at prediction maximal methane concentration is made ten minutes ahead. Five succeeding delays of each conditional attribute were considered as supplementary conditional attributes. As an example, for the sensor M32 we have at our disposal not only maximal concentration of CH_4 registered in the most actual time window t, but also maximal concentrations registered in preceding time windows $M32_{t-1}, \ldots, M32_{t-5}$. Moreover, to reflect dynamics of changes of measured quantities in consecutive time

Table 3 Methane
data—attributes significance
analysis

Attribute	σ_{DT}
$M32_t$	0.080
$AN31_t - AN32_{t-2}$	0.042
$AN32_t - AN32_{t-2}$	0.024
$M32_t - M32_{t-2}$	0.021
$AN32_{t-2}$	0.018
$AN31_t - AN32_{t-1}$	0.015

windows the difference between actual and previously measured value was also calculated for each conditional attribute (e.g. $M32_{t-1} - M32_{t-2}$). Values of a decision attribute represented three hazard states connected with methane emission: the concentration less then 0.8% equated with a safe state, concentrations from the interval $\langle 0.8, 1.5 \rangle$ indicate an acceptable state, concentrations over 1.5% denote a hazardous state. Since methane emission on the longwall face is characterized by one week periodicity, the training set is composed of data registered Monday through Thursday, data registered on Friday and Saturday were testing data. The distribution of examples between respective states were the following: 32% examples represented the safe state, 60.7% the admissible state, 7.3% the hazardous state.

The first part of the analysis consisted in the training set discretization, and then the testing set discretization based on an established set of cuttings. After the discretization each numerical attribute was divided into two subsets on average. The attribute M32 informing about actual methane concentration registered by the methanemeter M32 was divided into the biggest number of intervals, four ones. After the discretization the classification quality coefficient γ_{DT} was equal to 1 for whole set of conditional attributes. This means that there is no inconsistencies in the data set. One relative reducts was determined. It was composed of the following 12 attributes: $MM32_t$, $AN31_t$, $Output_t$, $AN31_{t-5}$, $AN32_{t-2}$, $AN32_{t-3}$, $AN32_{t-4}$, $AN32_t - AN32_{t-2}$, $AN32_t - AN32_{t-1}$, $AN32_t - AN32_{t-2}$, $M32_t - M32_{t-1}$, $M32_t - M32_{t-2}$. The reduction enables reducing the set of attributes from 35 to 12. Significance coefficients for six the most significant attributes are presented in Table 3.

The most significant for methane concentration forecasting is the information about current methane concentration, dynamics of changes of this concentration, and about dynamics of changes of the quantity of air flowing through the excavation. It is also possible to draw a conclusion, based on an analysis of attributes occurring in the relative reduct, that readings not older than $t - 2$ aggregation period have essential meaning for assumed forecast period.

The second part of the analysis consisted in decision rules induction and classifying the testing set (Table 4).

The accuracy obtained by the classifier is good, and is equal to almost 90%. The classifier obtained for the set of attributes reduced to the reduct is characterized by great ability of hazardous states forecasting. This happens at the cost of generation

Table 4 Methane data—results of the test data classification

Set of attributes	Overall classification accuracy	Accuracy of the class "hazardous state"	Accuracy of the class "safe state"	Class-gain	Number of rules
All	88.0	94.6	85.0	85.0	13
Reduct	86.4	93.3	82.7	90.0	12

Table 5 The classifier confusion matrix

		Forecasting		
		Safe	Admissible	Hazardous
Real	Safe	209	12	3
	Admissible	36	360	39
	Hazardous	0	2	18

higher number of so-called false alarms, i.e. the hazardous state is forecasted while another state is observed in reality.

An analyst should decide based on the classification confusion matrix which classifier is better. In particular, the Class-gain value calculated for the case of more then two decision classes may be helpful [36]. The confusion matrix for the classifier determined for the reduced data set is presented in Table 5.

For methane hazards no advanced hazard expert assessments exist, therefore the methane hazard assessment in mining practice bases on forecasts accuracy and a number of false alarms. However, information interesting for persons responsible for correctness of the process of mining can be found in determined rules. Among rules determined for considered excavation the following rule occurred:

If mining is conducted **and** airflow registered by AN32 > 1.55 **then** the "hazardous state" (Precision 0.289 with a priori precision of the decision class "hazardous state" amounted to 0.029)

This rule is unexpected because tells that while mining is conducted and an excavation is intensively aired the methane concentration on a longwall face increases. Intuitively the more intensive airing should be predicted on pushing methane outside the excavation, nevertheless the rule shows the opposite dependency. An analysis of maps that illustrate sensors placing showed that the anemometer AN32 is placed in top end of the face. Intensive ventilation of the tail gate causes gases flowing back to the longwall face and increase of methane concentration. Therefore, to maintain an admissible methane concentration the drift should not be ventilated too intensively during mining works. The presented example is pertinent illustration of the fact that obtained rules may include information interesting for a user.

8 Conclusions

The example of application of rough sets in the forecasting module being an extension of natural hazards monitoring systems in hard-coal mines has been presented in the chapter. Presented practical examples of data analysis coming from these systems show that rough sets can be a source of knowledge about data collected by the systems. Based on attributes building object-related relative reducts rule-based classifier systems forecasting hazardous states with high accuracy can be created. Moreover, presented examples of application show that fully automatic configuration of the forecasting module that requires no intervention of an analyst is at present impossible.

The analyst task is selection of initial list of conditional attributes, determining intervals of data aggregation and defining attributes that reflect dynamics of changes of monitored values. The analyst is also intended to evaluate the quality of created forecasting models and to choose the most adequate model, testing many forecast models to be required. In this chapter results obtained based on rough sets are presented, but rule classifiers can be also obtained using sequential covering rules induction algorithms [30, 31].

The presented methodology assumes that there is available a training set based on which a forecasting model is determined. In considered domain of applications this causes that at the beginning of a longwall face exploitation the forecasting module collects only measurement data. Therefore there arises a question of when should be recognized that sufficient set of training data is collected. The data set giving a forecasting model characterized by the forecast quality better than expert methods do, should be find sufficient one. The choice of indices that will be used for the forecast quality evaluation depends also on a data analyst. In this chapter the following indices were used: classification accuracy, accuracy of decision classes, class-gain. In practice, the analyst liaising with dispatcher responsible for monitoring a given hazard should decide about approval for use a forecasting model.

In experimental research conducted with seismic data coming from two longwalls sufficient quality of forecasts was obtained after 10% of planned exploitation of the longwalls on time. The analysis of data coming from 30% of planned exploitation of the longwalls on time helped to obtain even better forecasting model [8]. Results of the research show that it is worth checking periodically whether increasing the training data set a better forecasting model can be obtained.

We should remember that verification of the model quality has to be done based on a testing data set not influenced by the training set. The train-and-test method, in which an available set of historical data is divided into two training and testing parts, was used for verification of the forecasting models quality in this chapter. Other methods, particularly the cross-validation [37], enables us to evaluate better the model quality in special cases.

The forecasting module described in this chapter makes also possible realization of regression tasks that consist in forecasting a precise value of the dependent variable [9, 22]. However, that subject matter exceeds this study.

References

1. Barański, A., Drzewiecki, J., Kabiesz, J., Konopko, W., Kornowski, J., Krzyżowski, A., Mutke, G.: Rules of application of the comprehensive and detailed rockburst hazard assessment methods in hard-coal mines. Instruction 20, Central Mining Institute, Katowice, Poland (2007) (in Polish)
2. Lasocki, S.: Probabilistic analysis of seismic hazard posed by mining induced events. In: Proceedings of the Sixth International Symposium on Rockburst and Seismicity in Mines, Australian Centre for Geomechanics, Western Australia, pp. 151–156 (2005)
3. Leśniak, A., Isakow, Z.: Space-time clustering of seismic events and hazard assessment in the Zabrze-Bielszowice coal mine. Int. J. Rock Mech. Min. Sci. **46**, 918–928 (2009)
4. Kornowski, J.: Linear prediction of aggregated seismic and seismoacustic energy emitted from a mining longwall. Acta Mont. **22**(129), 4–14 (2003)
5. Kabiesz, J.: Effect of the form of data on the quality of mine tremors hazard forecasting using neural networks. Geotech. Geolog. Eng. **24**(5), 1131–1147 (2005)
6. Rudajev, V., Ciz, R.: Estimation of mining tremor occurrence by using neural networks. Pure Appl. Geophys. **154**(1), 57–72 (1999)
7. Sikora, M., Wróbel, Ł.: Application of rule induction algorithms for analysis of data collected by seismic hazard monitoring systems in coal mines. Arch. Min. Sci. **55**(1), 91–114 (2010)
8. Sikora, M.: Induction and pruning of classification rules for prediction of microseismic hazard in coal mines. Expert Syst. Appl. **38**(6), 6748–6758 (2011)
9. Sikora, M., Sikora, B.: Application of machine learning for prediction a methane concentration in a coal-mine. Arch. Min. Sci. **51**(4), 475–492 (2006)
10. Pawlak, Z.: Rough Sets: Theoretical Aspects of Reasoning About Data. Kluwer Academic, Dordrecht (1991)
11. Nowicki, R., Słowiński, R., Stefanowski, J.: Evaluation of vibroacoustic symptoms by means of the rough sets theory. Comput. Ind. **20**, 141–152 (1992)
12. Rebolledo, M.R.: Integrating rough sets and situation-based qualitative models for processes monitoring considering vagueness and uncertainty. Eng. Appl. Artif. Intell. **18**, 617–632 (2005)
13. Sikora, M.: Application of machine learning and soft computing techniques in monitoring systems' data analysis by example of dewater pumps monitoring system. Arch. Control Sci. **17**(4), 369–391 (2007)
14. Mrózek, A.: Rough sets in computer implementation of rule-based control of industrial processes. In: Słowiński, R. (ed.) Intelligent Decision Support: Handbook of Applications and Advances of the Rough Sets Theory. Kluwer Academic, Dordrecht (1992)
15. Słowiński, R. (ed.): Intelligent Decision Support: Handbook of Applications and Advances of the Rough Sets Theory. Kluwer Academic, Dordrecht (1992)
16. Ziarko, W.P.: Acquisition of control algorithms for operation. In: Słowiński, R. (ed.) Intelligent Decision Support: Handbook of Applications and Advances of the Rough Sets Theory. Kluwer Academic, Dordrecht (1992)
17. Bazan, J.G., Nguyen, H.S., Nguyen, S.H., Synak, P., Wróblewski, J.: Rough set algorithms in classification problem. In: Polkowski, L., Tsumoto, S., Lin, T.Y. (eds.) New Developments in Knowledge Discovery in Information Systems, pp. 49–88. Physica-Verlag, Heidelberg (2000)
18. Sikora, M.: Decision rules based data models using TRS and NetTRS—methods and algorithms. Lect. Notes Comput. Sci. **5946**, 130–160 (2010)
19. Skowron, A., Rauszer, C.: The discernibility matrices and functions in information systems. In: Słowiński, R. (ed.) Intelligent Decision Support: Handbook of Applications and Advances of the Rough Sets Theory. Kluwer Academic, Dordrecht (1992)
20. Sikora, M., Mazik, P.: Towards the better assessment of a seismic hazard—the Hestia and Hestia map systems. Mech. Autom. Min. **3**(457), 5–12 (2009)
21. Krzystanek, Z., Dylong, A., Wojtas, P.: Monitoring of environmental parameters in coal mine—the SMP-NT system. Mech. Autom. Min. **9** (2004)

22. Sikora, M., Krzystanek, Z., Bojko, B., Śpiechowicz, K.: Hybrid adaptative system of gas concentration prediction in hard-coal mines. In: Proc. of XIX International Conference on Systems (ICSENG '08), pp. 19–21. IEEE Computer Society, Los Alamitos (2008)
23. Nguyen, H.S., Nguyen, S.H.: Discretization methods in data mining. In: Polkowski, L., Skowron, A. (eds.) Rough Sets in Knowledge Discovery, pp. 451–482. Physica-Verlag, Heidelberg (1998)
24. Fayyad, U.M., Irani, K.B.: Multi-interval discretization of continuous-valued attributes for classification learning. In: Proceedings of the 13th International Joint Conference on Artificial Intelligence, pp. 1022–1027. Morgan Kaufmann, San Mateo (1993)
25. Kerber, R.: Chimerge: discretization of numeric attributes. In: Proceedings of the Tenth National Conference on Artificial Intelligence, pp. 123–128. MIT Press, Cambridge (1992)
26. Witten, I.H., Frank, E.: Data Mining: Practical Machine Learning Tools and Techniques, 2nd edn. Morgan Kaufmann, San Mateo (2005)
27. Bazan, J., Szczuka, M., Wróblewski, J.: A new version of rough set exploration system. Lect. Notes Comput. Sci. 2475, 14–16 (2002)
28. Ślęzak, D.: Rough sets and functional dependencies in data: foundations of association reducts. Lect. Notes Comput. Sci. 5540, 182–205 (2009)
29. Yao, Y., Zhao, Y., Wang, J.: On reduct construction algorithms. Lect. Notes Comput. Sci. 5150, 100–117 (2008)
30. Furnkranz, J.: Separate-and-conquer rule learning. Artif. Intell. Rev. 13, 3–54 (1999)
31. Grzymala-Busse, J., Stefanowski, J., Wilk, S.: A comparison of two approaches to data mining from imbalanced data. J. Intell. Manuf. 16, 565–573 (2005)
32. Janssen, F., Furnkranz, J.: On the quest for optima rule learning heuristics. Mach. Learn. 78, 343–379 (2010)
33. Sikora, M., Wróbel, Ł.: Data-driven adaptive selection of rules quality measures for improving the rules induction algorithm. Lect. Notes Artif. Intell. 6743, 278–285 (2011)
34. Fawcett, T.: An introduction to ROC analysis. Pattern Recognit. Lett. 27, 861–874 (2006)
35. Bairagi, R., Suchindran, C.M.: An estimation of the cutoff point maximizing sum of sensitivity and specificity. Sankhya, Ser. B 51, 263–269 (1989)
36. Srinivasan, A.: Note on the location of optimal classifier in n-dimensional ROC space. Report PRG-TR-2-99, Oxford University Computing Laboratory (1999)
37. Kohavi, R.: A study of cross-validation and bootstrap for accuracy estimation and model selection. In: Proc. of the International Conference on Artificial Intelligence (IJCAI) (1995)

Nearness of Associated Rough Sets

Case Study in Image Analysis

Sheela Ramanna and James F. Peters

Abstract The focus of this chapter is on the nearness of associated sets and the answer to the question *Is a pair of sets sufficiently near to be considered similar?* In answering this question, we consider associated sets of a set. In particular, associated rough sets as well as associated near rough sets are introduced. A rough set X is associated with another set Y, provided that X is sufficiently near Y. In general, nonempty sets are sufficiently near, provided that the Čech distance between the sets is less than some number ε in the interval $(0, \infty]$. An application of the proposed approach is given in the context of image analysis with emphasis on detecting patterns in visual rough sets.

1 Introduction

This chapter introduces associated rough sets and associated near rough sets. Rough sets were introduced by Z. Pawlak [1–3] and elaborated in [4–7]. Near sets were introduced in [8–10], inspired by [11]. The study of associated sets of functions has a long history, starting in 1922 by A. Coble [12] and continuing to the present [13–17]. In this chapter, we consider the more general case of associated sets of a set. The basic idea with associated sets of a set is to define as well as characterise one set in terms of one or more other sets. An important advantage in considering associated rough sets is that by a characterising a rough set in terms of other rough sets, one can learn more about a particular rough set, i.e., the interpretation of a rough set relative to patterns in associated sets.

S. Ramanna (✉)
Department of Applied Computer Science, University of Winnipeg, Winnipeg, MB, Canada
e-mail: s.ramanna@uwinnipeg.ca

S. Ramanna · J.F. Peters
Computational Intelligence Laboratory, Department of Electrical and Computer Engineering, University of Manitoba, Winnipeg, MB, Canada

J.F. Peters
e-mail: jfpeters@ee.umanitoba.ca

G. Peters et al. (eds.), *Rough Sets: Selected Methods and Applications in Management and Engineering*, Advanced Information and Knowledge Processing,
DOI 10.1007/978-1-4471-2760-4_11, © Springer-Verlag London Limited 2012

The focus in this chapter is on visual rough sets, since there are many applications of associated visual rough sets i.e., the rough sets that are extracted from digital images. In particular, visual forms of tolerance rough sets provide a rich source of patterns. The study of tolerance rough sets is an active research area, beginning with [18, 19] and studied in the context of image analysis [20–24]. A tolerance relation defined in terms of descriptions of set members determines coverings on the sample sets that are rough sets.

A direct result of the proposed approach is its utility in a number of application areas such as visual surveillance [25], image authentication [26], trustworthiness of multimedia websites [27], content-based video detection in measuring (dis)similarity with a distance function in constructing associated visual sets [28], anomaly detection in image acquisition systems such as topographic satellites and airborne camera systems typically used in the inspection of power system equipment, terrain and city neighbourhoods, and detection of changes in vehicular traffic patterns from associated sets of intersection camera images. Typically, these applications involve either some form of similarity matching or image database classification. To measure similarity, a distance function is needed. A Čech distance between sets [29] is considered in this chapter. This form of distance between sets captures the greatest lower bound of the standard distances between pairs of set elements.

This chapter has the following organisation. The basics of rough sets, Čech distance between sets, and sufficiently near rough sets in Sect. 2. Associated rough sets are introduced in Sect. 3. A case study that brings together the ideas in this chapter is given in Sect. 4.

2 Preliminaries and Basic Ideas

This section briefly introduces the basic notions underlying the study of nearness of tolerance rough sets. We also introduce some basic terminology in Table 1 in the context of associated sets of sets.

2.1 Rough Set Basics

In a rough set approach to classifying sets of objects X, one considers the size of the boundary region in the approximation of X. In particular, assume that X is a nonempty set belonging to a universe U. Also, assume $\mathbb{F}$ is a set of partial functions representing object features. Let $\Phi \subset \mathbb{F}$. Then consider a partition of the universe determined by an equivalence relation $\sim_\Phi$ defined by

$$\sim_\Phi = \{(x, y) \in X \times X : \phi(x) = \phi(y), \text{ for all } \phi \in \Phi\}.$$

The notation $X_{/\sim_\Phi}$ denotes the set of all equivalence classes (quotient set) in the partition of X. Then, for $x \in X$, the notation $x_{/\sim_\Phi}$ denotes an equivalence class containing x, i.e., all elements $y \in x_{/\sim_\Phi}$ are indiscernible relative to the features

Table 1 Terminology

Term	Description
Associated set	Collection of sets associated with a set
Class	Set of objects determined by an equivalence or tolerance relation
Collection	Set of sets
Digital image	Set of points (i.e., set of pixels)
Object	Something describable
Pixel	Picture element
Pixel features	{colour, pixel gradient}
Point	Pixel
Rough set	Set with nonempty approximation boundary
Sufficiently near sets	Distance between sets less than some number ε in $(0, \infty]$

defined by $\phi \in \Phi$. The lower approximation of X relative to $\Phi \subset \mathbb{F}$ is denoted by $\Phi_*(X)$ and the upper approximation of X is denoted by $\Phi^*(X)$, where

$$\Phi_*(X) = \bigcup_{x_{/\sim_\Phi} \subseteq X} x_{/\sim_\Phi},$$

$$\Phi^*(X) = \bigcup_{x_{/\sim_\Phi} \cap X \neq \emptyset} x_{/\sim_\Phi}.$$

The Φ-boundary region of an approximation of a set X is denoted by $Bnd_\Phi(X)$, where

$$Bnd_\Phi(X) = \Phi^*(X) \backslash \Phi_*(X) = \{x \mid x \in \Phi^*(X) \text{ and } x \notin \Phi_*(X)\}.$$

Definition 1 (Rough set) A non-empty, finite set X is a rough set if, and only if, $|\Phi^*(X) - \Phi_*(X)| \neq 0$. That is, a set X is roughly classified whenever $Bnd_\Phi(X)$ is not empty.

2.2 Tolerance Rough Sets

In this chapter, the focus is on visual tolerance rough sets. But first we define tolerance rough sets in general. A nonempty set X is a rough set if, and only if the approximation boundary of X is nonempty. Rather than the usual partition of X with the indiscernibility relation introduced by Z. Pawlak [1, 2], set approximation is viewed in the context of a cover of X defined by a tolerance relation τ, where B is a set of features of objects $x \in X$ [18]. Let $A \subset X$ and let $\tau(x)$ denote a tolerance class containing the set of all objects $x \in A$, $y \in X$ such that $x \tau y$. The upper approximation of A is denoted by T^*A, the set of all such tolerance classes $\tau(x)$ that have

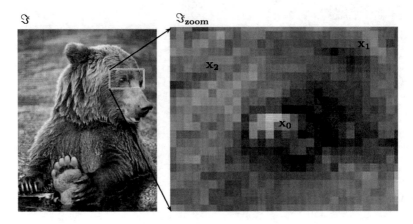

Fig. 1 Sample eye colour tolerance rough set zoomed ×1000

a nonempty intersection with A, i.e., $\tau(x) \cap A \neq \emptyset$. The lower approximation of A (denoted $T_* A$) is the set of all tolerance classes $\tau(x)$ contained in A, i.e., $\tau(x) \subset A$. A set $A \subset X$ is a *tolerance rough set* if, and only if the set $Bnd_\tau A = T_* A - T^* A$ (boundary of approximation of A) is nonempty.

Example 1 (Tolerance class in a digital image) A digital image is viewed as a set of points, where each point is a pixel (picture element). The pixels in the image of the Kodiak bear in Fig. 1 have been zoomed 1000 times so that they become visible, individually. For example, a selection of 4 pixels ▇ can be observed in the eye of the bear in Fig. 1. The colour of pixel ■ labelled x_0 in image $\Im_{zoom}$ in Fig. 1 is closely similar to the colour of pixels labelled x_1, x_2 in Fig. 1. The set of all pixels with the colour ■ is an example of a tolerance class, since the pixel colours are similar within some tolerance.

Example 2 (Discovering tolerance rough set in a digital image) To find tolerance rough sets (TRS) in this sample image, start by introducing one or more probe functions used to extract the feature values of the points. Pixel feature values are numbers in $[0, \infty]$, i.e., a pixel feature value is a real value representing the magnitude of a particular pixel feature such as grey level intensity, amount of red, green or blue, gradient of a pixel in relation to its neighbours. Let $\Im$ denote the set of pixels in the image of the bear in Fig. 1 and let $\Im_{zoom}$ denote the part of the head of the bear zoomed ×1000. In addition, let $x \in \Im_{zoom}$ denote a single image pixel. For simplicity, we consider only pixel colour (single colour that is a mixture of the primary colours) extracted with a single probe $\phi : \Im_{zoom} \to [0, \infty]$ defined by $\phi(x) =$ pixel colour. Define a tolerance relation τ_ϕ, where

$$\tau_\phi = \{(x, y) \in \Im_{zoom} \times \Im_{zoom} : |\phi(x) - \phi(y)| \leq \varepsilon\}$$

for $\varepsilon \in [0, 255]$ representing amounts of colour in the interval between 0 and 255. The set $\Im_{zoom}$ is an example of a tolerance rough set. This means, for instance, the

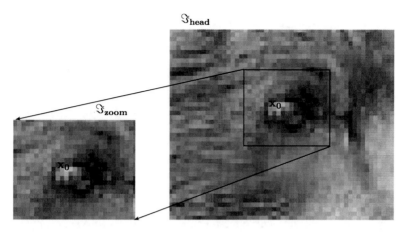

Fig. 2 Area containing tolerance rough set zoomed × 1000 from Fig. 1

Fig. 3 Another tolerance
rough set

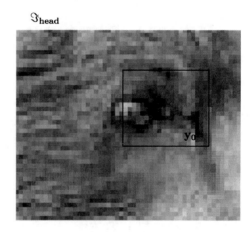

pixels with colour ■ in the tolerance class from Example 1 belong to a class in the upper approximation of $T^*\mathfrak{I}_{zoom}$ of the set named $\mathfrak{I}_{zoom}$ in Fig. 1, i.e., this class is partly in and partly outside the set $\mathfrak{I}_{zoom}$. This can be verified by looking at the border of $\mathfrak{I}_{zoom}$ in Fig. 1 as well as the border region $\mathfrak{I}_{head}$ containing the rough set (see Fig. 2).

Example 3 (Numerous tolerance rough sets) Numerous (in thousands) of tolerance rough sets can be found in $\mathfrak{I}_{head}$ in Fig. 2. To see this, view the box inside $\mathfrak{I}_{head}$ in Fig. 2 as a sliding window and move the box to a different position. For example, in Fig. 3, the sliding window has been moved to a new position (now the pixels in the tiny region labelled y_0 have descriptions that are quite similar (in some cases, identical) to the descriptions of the pixels in other parts of $\mathfrak{I}_{head}$.

2.3 Čech Distance Between Sets

This section briefly introduces the Čech distance between sets [29]. This form of distance between sets captures the greatest lower bound of the standard distances between pairs of set elements. A consideration of other forms of distance between sets[1] is outside the scope of this chapter. First, consider the Hausdorff lower distance between a point and a set used by E. Čech to compute the distance between two sets.

2.4 Distance Between a Point and a Set

Hausdorff [30, p. 128] introduced the function $D_\rho(x, B)$ to measure the distance a point x and a set of points B. Let $x \in X$, $B \subset \mathcal{P}(X)$ and let $\rho(x, y)$ is the standard distance between x and y, i.e., $\rho(x, y) = |x - y|$. The distance function $D_\rho : X \times \mathcal{P}(X) \to [0, \infty]$ is defined by

$$D_\rho(x, B) = \begin{cases} \inf\{\rho(x, b) : b \in B\}, & \text{if } B \text{ is not empty,} \\ \infty, & \text{if } B \text{ is empty,} \end{cases}$$

where ρ is a distance function.

Example 4 Assume $A = \left|\begin{smallmatrix} 1 & 2 \\ 3 & 4 \end{smallmatrix}\right|$, $B = \left|\begin{smallmatrix} 5 & 6 \\ 7 & 8 \end{smallmatrix}\right|$ denote intensities in a pair of greyscale images A, B.

$$D_\rho(1, B) = \inf\{4 = |1 - 5|, 5 = |1 - 6|, 6 = |1 - 7|, 7 = |1 - 8|\}$$
$$= 4.$$

2.5 Čech Distance Between Sets

The Čech distance between sets is obtained using the function $D_\rho : \mathcal{P}(X) \times \mathcal{P}(X) \to [0, \infty]$ defined by

$$D_\rho(A, B) = \begin{cases} \inf\{D_\rho(a, B) : a \in A, \\ \quad D_\rho(b, A) : b \in B\} & \text{if } A \text{ and } B \text{ are not empty,} \\ \infty, & \text{if } A \text{ or } B \text{ is empty.} \end{cases}$$

Then $D_\rho(A, B)$ measures the lower distance between the descriptions of objects in a pair of non-empty sets A, B.

Example 5 Assume $A = \left|\begin{smallmatrix} 1 & 2 \\ 3 & 4 \end{smallmatrix}\right|$, $B = \left|\begin{smallmatrix} 5 & 6 \\ 7 & 8 \end{smallmatrix}\right|$ denote intensities in three greyscale images A, B, C.

---

[1]See, e.g., [30].

Fig. 4 Taxicab

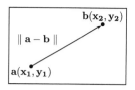

$$D_\rho(A, B) = \inf\{4 = |1 - 5|, 5 = |1 - 6|, 6 = |1 - 7|, 7 = |1 - 8|,$$
$$3 = |2 - 5|, 4 = |2 - 6|, 5 = |2 - 7|, 6 = |2 - 8|,$$
$$2 = |3 - 5|, 3 = |3 - 6|, 4 = |3 - 7|, 5 = |3 - 8|,$$
$$1 = |4 - 5|, 2 = |4 - 6|, 3 = |4 - 7|, 4 = |4 - 8|\}$$
$$= 1.$$

In most applications, one deals with sets of objects with descriptions (features). To compute the Čech distance between sets, what is known as the norm on tuples of real numbers is used. One of the simplest and most effective of such norms is known as the taxicab metric that we now briefly explain.

2.6 Taxicab Metric

The elements of an n-dimensional Euclidean space $\mathbb{R}^n$ are ordered n-tuples of real numbers $x = (x_1, \ldots, x_n)$. Assume, for example, $a, b \in \mathbb{R}^2$ with coordinates (x_1, y_1), (x_2, y_2), respectively (see Fig. 4). The norm on $\mathbb{R}^n$ is a distance function $\| \cdot \| : \mathbb{R}^2 \times \mathbb{R}^2 \to [0, \infty]$ (called the taxicab metric) is defined by

$$\|a - b\| = \sum_{i=1}^{2} |x_i - y_i|.$$

2.7 Standard Distance Between Descriptions of Points

The basic building block of the Hausdorff lower distance or the Čech distance is the distance between points. In this chapter, the focus is on the distance between descriptions of pixels (points) in a digital image. For example, a description of a pixel can be quite simply a value extracted the pixel by a single probe function. To see this, let $\Im$ denote a set of pixels in a digital image. Then let $\phi : X \to [0, \infty]$ be defined by $\phi(x) = $ intensity for $x \in \Im$. This is the situation for pixels a and b in sets A and B in Fig. 5. That is, $\phi(a)$ equals the intensity feature value of pixel a and $\phi(b)$ equals the intensity feature value of pixel b, i.e., $\phi(a)$ and $\phi(b)$ describe pixels a and b, respectively. Then the standard distance ρ between the descriptions is

$$\rho(\phi(a), \phi(b)) = |\phi(a) - \phi(b)|.$$

Fig. 5 Description distance
between pixels in A and B

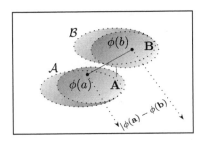

2.8 Čech Distance Between Descriptions of Sets

To measure the nearness of collections of rough sets, a norm version of the Čech distance is introduced [31, 32]. First, a distance function $\rho_{\|\cdot\|}$ is defined in the context of a normed space. Let X be a linear space over the reals with origin 0. A *norm* on X is a function $\|\cdot\| : X \to [0, \infty]$ satisfying several properties for a normed space [33]. Each norm on X induces a metric d on X defined by $d(x, y) = \|x - y\|$ for x, $y \in \mathbb{R}$ [34]. For example, let a, b denote a pair of n-dimensional vectors of numbers representing object feature values (e.g., positive real values representing intensities of light reflected from objects in a visual field), i.e., $a = (a_1, \ldots, a_i, \ldots, a_n)$, $b = (b_1, \ldots, b_i, \ldots, b_n)$ such that $a_i, b_i \in \mathbb{R}^{0+}$. Define a norm version of the Hausdorff lower distance [30, Sect. 22] in the following way.

$$D_{\rho_{\|\cdot\|}}(a, B) = \begin{cases} \inf\{\rho_{\|\cdot\|}(a, b) : b \in B\}, & \text{if } B \text{ is not empty,} \\ \infty, & \text{if } B \text{ is empty,} \end{cases}$$

where $\rho_{\|\cdot\|} : \mathbb{R}^n \times \mathbb{R}^n \to [0, \infty]$ is defined, e.g., by the $\|\cdot\|_1$ norm called the taxicab distance (see Sect. 2.6). Then, a norm Čech distance function $D_{\rho_{\|\cdot\|}} : \mathcal{P}(X) \times \mathcal{P}(X) \to [0, \infty]$ is defined by

$$D_{\rho_{\|\cdot\|}}(A, B) = \begin{cases} \inf\{D_{\rho_{\|\cdot\|}}(a, B) : a \in A, \\ \quad\quad D_{\rho_{\|\cdot\|}}(b, A) : b \in B\} & \text{if } A \text{ and } B \text{ are not empty,} \\ \infty, & \text{if } A \text{ or } B \text{ is empty.} \end{cases}$$

Then $D_{\rho_{\|\cdot\|}}(A, B)$ measures the lower distance between the descriptions of objects in a pair of non-empty sets A, B. Closer to home is the issue of finding the distance between pairs of tolerance rough sets. To do this, it helps computationally to view individual tolerance rough sets as collections of subsets.[2]

2.9 Čech Distance Between Collections of Subsets

The set of all subsets of a set X is denoted by $\mathcal{P}(X)$ (usually called the powerset of X). The set of all subsets of the powerset $\mathcal{P}(X)$ is denoted by $\mathcal{P}^2(X)$. A member

---

[2]Using this approach, one can introduce parallel computation as a means of finding the distance between large tolerance rough sets commonly found in digital images (see, e.g., [35]).

of $\mathcal{P}^2(X)$ are often denoted with a round capital letters such as $\mathcal{A}, \mathcal{B} \in \mathcal{P}^2(X)$ (as shown in Fig. 5).

Example 6 (Sample Čech distance between collections of subsets) Recall that pixel greyscale intensities are in the range from 0 to 255. In this example, we consider two very small 2×2 subimages (i.e., 4 pixels in each subimage). Assume $A = \begin{vmatrix} 1 & 2 \\ 3 & 4 \end{vmatrix}$, $B = \begin{vmatrix} 5 & 6 \\ 7 & 8 \end{vmatrix}$ denote intensities in two tiny greyscale subimages. The next step is to consider the subsets of a pair of collections.

$$\mathcal{A} = \{A_1, A_2\}, \qquad \mathcal{B} = \{B_1, B_2, B_3\}, \quad \text{where}$$
$$A_1 = \{1, 2\}, \qquad A_2 = \{3, 4\},$$
$$B_1 = \{5, 6\}, \qquad B_2 = \{7, 8\}.$$

Next determine the individual Čech distances between each pair of subsets.

$$
\begin{aligned}
D_\rho(B_1, A_1) &= \inf\{\inf\{\rho(5, 1), \rho(5, 2)\}, \\
&\qquad \inf\{\rho(6, 1), \rho(6, 2)\}\}, \\
&= \inf\{\inf\{4, 3\}, \inf\{5, 4\}\}, \\
&= \inf\{3, 4\} = 3. \\
D_\rho(B_1, A_2) &= \inf\{\inf\{\rho(5, 3), \rho(5, 4)\}, \\
&\qquad \inf\{\rho(6, 3), \rho(6, 4)\}\}, \\
&= \inf\{\inf\{2, 1\}, \inf\{3, 2\}\}, \\
&= \inf\{1, 2\} = 1. \\
D_\rho(B_2, A_1) &= \inf\{\inf\{\rho(7, 1), \rho(7, 2)\}, \\
&\qquad \inf\{\rho(8, 1), \rho(8, 2)\}\}, \\
&= \inf\{\inf\{6, 5\}, \inf\{7, 6\}\}, \\
&= \inf\{5, 6\} = 5. \\
D_\rho(B_2, A_2) &= \inf\{\inf\{\rho(7, 3), \rho(7, 4)\}, \\
&\qquad \inf\{\rho(8, 3), \rho(8, 4)\}\}, \\
&= \inf\{\inf\{4, 3\}, \inf\{5, 4\}\}, \\
&= \inf\{3, 4\} = 3.
\end{aligned}
$$

Then determine the Čech distance between the collections in terms of the individual distances between the subsets in the collections.

$$
\begin{aligned}
D_\rho(\mathcal{B}, \mathcal{A}) &= \inf\{D_\rho(B_1, A_1), D_\rho(B_1, A_2), D_\rho(B_2, A_1), \\
&\qquad D_\rho(B_2, A_2)\} \\
&= \inf\{3, 1, 5, 3\} \\
&= 1
\end{aligned}
$$

Fig. 6 Two tolerance rough
sets zoomed ×1000

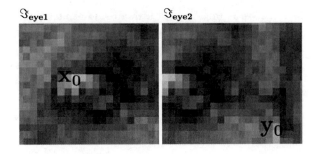

2.10 Sufficiently Near Tolerance Rough Sets

In keeping with recent work on near sets [31, 36–49], assume that the set Φ contains probe functions used in the description of members of a nonempty set X. For simplicity, assume each probe function $\phi : X \to [0, \infty]$ is a real-valued function used to extract feature values for objects $x \in X$. Also, recall that nonempty sets $A, B \subset X$ are considered near in proximity space theory [50, Sect. 1, p. 7] if, and only if, $D(A, B) = 0$. Since this is a somewhat unrealistic assumption[3] to make in natural science, engineering and the arts, the equality requirement for nearness of objects is relaxed. Instead, sets A and B are considered *sufficiently near* each other if, and only if, $D(A, B) < \varepsilon$ for $\varepsilon \in (0, \infty]$. The choice of a particular value of ε is application dependent and is typically determined by a domain expert.

Definition 2 (Sufficiently near sets)   Assume that nonempty subsets $A, B \subset X$ are tolerance rough sets relative to a cover on X defined by tolerance relation τ_ϕ. Sets $A, B \subset X$ are sufficient near if, and only if $D_{\rho_{\|\cdot\|}}(A, B) < \varepsilon$.

Definition 3 (Sufficiently near tolerance rough sets)   Assume $A, B \in \mathcal{P}X$ are tolerance rough sets relative to a cover on X defined by tolerance relation τ. Then A, B are sufficiently near if, and only if, $D_{\rho_{\|\cdot\|}}(A, B) < \varepsilon$ for $\varepsilon \in (0, \infty]$.

Example 7 (Sufficiently near tolerance rough sets)   From Example 2, recall that the boxed region in the zoomed image in Fig. 2 is a visual tolerance rough set, if we consider only pixel colour as a means of describing image pixels. Again, from Example 3, the boxed region in Fig. 3 is a visual tolerance rough set. That is, the boxed regions $\Im_{eye1}, \Im_{eye2}$ in Fig. 6 are visual tolerance rough sets, since there is least one tolerance class with pixels partly inside and partly outside these particular boxed regions of the Kodiak bear eye. Assume probe $\phi_{colour}(x)$ for $x \in \Im_{head}$ extracts the colour of pixel x. Let τ_ϕ be a tolerance relation defined by

$$\tau_{\phi_{colour}} = \{(x, y) \in \Im_{head} \times \Im_{head} : |\phi_{colour}(x) - \phi_{colour}(y)| < \varepsilon\}$$

---

[3]It is seldom possible to find distinct objects in the physical world that have identical descriptions. Hence, there is interest in discovering sets derived from the physical world and that are *sufficiently near* each other.

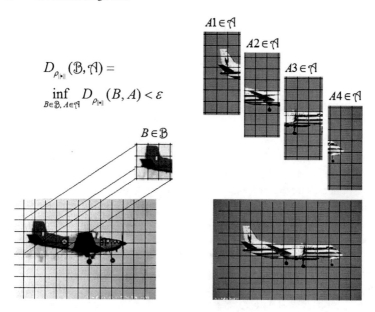

$$D_{\rho_{\|\cdot\|}}(\mathcal{B}, \mathcal{A}) =$$

$$\inf_{B \in \mathcal{B}, A \in \mathcal{A}} D_{\rho_{\|\cdot\|}}(B, A) < \varepsilon$$

Fig. 7 Sufficiently near collections of aircraft tolerance rough sets

for $\varepsilon \in (0, \infty]$. Notice, also, that the TRSs in Fig. 6 are examples of sufficiently near sets, since there are many instances of pixels in $\Im_{eye1}$ and $\Im_{eye2}$ with similar colours. In particular, it can be observed that for $x_0 \in \Im_{eye1}$ and $y_0 \in \Im_{eye2}$

$$\rho(\phi_{colour}(x_0), \phi_{colour}(y_0)) = |\phi_{colour}(x_0) - \phi_{colour}(y_0)| < \varepsilon.$$

For this reason, it safe to conclude that

$$D_{\rho_{\phi_{colour}}}(\Im_{eye1}, \Im_{eye2}) < \varepsilon.$$

Example 8 (Sample sufficiently near collections of TRSs) In this example, we consider only pixel gradient as the probe function used to described that parts of the aircraft in Fig. 7. Then pixels along the same unvarying edge (e.g., portion of aircraft tail section with an edge with unvarying angle such as the trailing edge or part of the top edge) will have the same gradient. Assume that the subsets $B \in \mathcal{B}$ and $A \in \mathcal{A}$ are tolerance rough sets (using an approach similar to that used in Example 3 in comparing zoomed pixels but this time with respect to pixel gradient taking into account the neighbours of each pixel). In the subimages in the aircraft in Fig. 7, notice that the tail sections in both aircraft are similar, i.e., $B \in \mathcal{B}$ and $A1 \in \mathcal{A}$ have edges on either side and tops of the tail sections that are very similar. In that case, it is reasonable to assume that

$$D_{\rho_{\|\cdot\|}}(\mathcal{B}, \mathcal{A}) < \varepsilon.$$

That is, from the images in Fig. 7, it is fairly apparent that the two collections of tolerance rough sets are sufficiently near, if we only consider pixel description in terms of pixel gradient. This is another way of saying that the Čech distance between the collections of TRSs is less than some $\varepsilon \in (0, \infty]$. Hence $\mathcal{A}$ and $\mathcal{B}$ are examples of near tolerance rough sets.

3 Associated Rough Sets

This section introduces associated rough sets inspired by the study of associated sets that started in 1922 [12] and elaborated in [13–16]. Instead of the traditional study of associated sets of a function, this chapter introduces the more general notion of associated sets of a set. Various types of associated sets of a set offer a means of defining rough sets in a variety of ways as well providing ways to characterise rough sets. That is, once we know that a set is rough, associated sets offer a means of conveying the meaning of the rough set derived from the knowledge of other sets that are, in some sense, *associated* with a particular rough set. Different rough sets will have different meanings, depending on which sets are associated with a particular rough set. In addition, an associated set of a rough set provides added knowledge about a rough set. In fact, since the *associated sets of a set* introduced in this section are each defined in terms of description-based Čech distance, the associated sets can be considered elements of a perceptual system that provide various perceptions of particular rough sets.

In addition to associated rough sets, this section also introduces associated near rough sets and the more general associated near sets. These two additional forms of associated sets are important because they provide us with a means of characterising rough sets in terms of other sets that are similar to a particular rough set. In effect, these two additional forms of associated sets offer us a means of gaining knowledge of rough sets in terms of other sets.

Definition 4 (Associated rough sets) Let Φ denote a set of functions representing features of objects. Assume that a nonempty set X is rough, i.e., the approximation boundary $Bnd_\Phi(X)$ is not empty. Let $\alpha \in (0, \infty]$. The associated nonempty sets of X are the sets of intersections

$$E^{\cap,\alpha}(X) = \{Y : |X \cap Y| > 0 \text{ and } |Bnd_\Phi(X \cap Y)| > \alpha\}, \quad \text{upper associated set,}$$

$$E_\alpha^\cap(X) = \{Y : |X \cap Y| > 0 \text{ and } 0 < |Bnd_\Phi(X \cap Y)| < \alpha\} \quad \text{lower associated set,}$$

or the associated nonempty sets of X are the sets of unions such that

$$E^{\cup,\alpha}(X) = \{Y : X \neq Y \text{ and } |Bnd_\Phi(X \cup Y)| > \alpha\}, \quad \text{upper associated set,}$$

$$E_\alpha^\cup(X) = \{Y : X \neq Y \text{ and } 0 < |Bnd_\Phi(X \cup Y)| < \alpha\} \quad \text{lower associated set.}$$

Remark 1 (About upper associated sets of a rough set from Definition 4) In each case, an upper associated set of a rough set has a bigger approximation boundary than the corresponding lower associated set of the same set. Then observe

Fig. 8 Hierarchy of
associated sets + dissimilar
sets

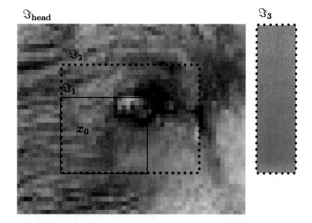

Upper.1 From $E^{\cap,\alpha}(X)$, we gain access to subsets of the rough set X with α-large
approximation boundaries. Notice that the rough set $X \cap Y$ is a subset of X.
When $X \cap Y \subset X$, it is then possible to work with a smaller rough set, i.e.,
a rough set smaller than X. This does not always happen, since a class
$x_{\sim_\Phi} \subset X$ is not a rough set. The gain from $E^{\cap,\alpha}(X)$ is a reduction in the
size of the rough set that is considered, i.e., a part of X that is also rough.

Upper.2 From $E^{\cup,\alpha}(X)$, we gain access to disjoint sets $X \cup Y$ with α-large approximation boundaries. This is an expansion of the rough set case. That is,
with $E^{\cup,\alpha}(X)$, the set X and an associated set Y are disjoint and both sets
are nonempty, then $X \cup Y$ is a rough set that is larger than X.

Example 9 (Intersection upper associated set) In Fig. 8, $E^{\cap,\alpha}(\Im_{head})$ is an intersection upper associated set. From Example 2, it is easy to verify that $\Im_1, \Im_2$ are rough
sets. Put $\alpha = |\frac{\Im_1}{2}|$. It is then easy to verify that $|Bnd_\Phi(\Im_1 \cap \Im_2)| > \alpha$ and $\{\Im_1, \Im_2\}$
constitute an intersection upper associated set of the set $\Im_{head}$.

Example 10 (Union upper associated set) In Fig. 8, $E^{\cup,\alpha}(\Im_{head})$ is a union upper
associated set. Again, put $\alpha = |\frac{\Im_1}{2}|$. It is then easy to verify that $|Bnd_\Phi(\Im_1 \cup \Im_2)| >$
α and $\{\Im_1, \Im_2\}$ also constitute a union upper associated set of the set $\Im_{head}$.

Remark 2 (About lower associated sets of a rough set from Definition 4) In each
case, a lower associated set of a rough set has a smaller approximation boundary
than the corresponding upper associated set of the same set. Then observe

Lower.1 From $E^{\cap}_\alpha(X)$, we gain access to subsets of the rough set X with α-small
approximation boundaries. Again, notice that the rough set $X \cap Y$ is a subset of X. When $X \cap Y \subset X$, it is then possible to work with a smaller rough
set, i.e., a rough set smaller than X. The gain from $E^{\cap,\alpha}(X)$ is a reduction
in the size of the rough set with an α-small approximation boundary.

Lower.2 From $E^{\cup}_\alpha(X)$, we gain access to disjoint sets $X \cup Y$ with α-small approximation boundaries. This is an expansion of the rough set case. That is,

with $E^{\cup,\alpha}(X)$, the set X and an associated set Y are disjoint and both sets are nonempty, then $X \cup Y$ is a rough set that is larger than X.

Example 11 (Intersection lower associated set) In Fig. 8, $E_\alpha^\cap(\Im_{head})$ is an intersection lower associated set. Observe that $\Im_1, \Im_2$ are rough sets. Put $\alpha = 2|\Im_{\mathbf{head}}|$. It is then easy to verify that $|Bnd_\Phi(\Im_1 \cap \Im_2)| < \alpha$ and $\{\Im_1, \Im_2\}$ is an intersection lower associated set of the set $\Im_{head}$.

Example 12 (Union lower associated set) In Fig. 8, $E_\alpha^\cup(\Im_{head})$ is a union lower associated set. Put $\alpha = 2|\Im_{\mathbf{head}}|$. It is then easy to verify that $|Bnd_\Phi(\Im_1 \cup \Im_2)| < \alpha$ and $\{\Im_1, \Im_2\}$ is an union lower associated set of the set $\Im_{head}$.

Proposition 1 *The associated sets of a rough set are rough.*

Proof Immediate from Definition 4 and the definition of a rough set.   □

It then possible to characterise rough sets in terms of associated near rough sets.

Definition 5 (Associated near rough sets) Let Φ denote a set of functions representing features of objects. Assume that a nonempty set X is rough, i.e., the approximation boundary $Bnd_\Phi(X)$ is not empty. Let $\varepsilon \in (0, \infty]$. The associated nonempty sets of X are near sets such that

$$E_\varepsilon(X) = \{Y : |Bnd_\Phi(Y)| > 0, \text{ and } D_{\|\cdot\|}(X, Y) < \varepsilon\}.$$

That is, $E_\varepsilon(X)$ is a set of all rough sets Y that are near X.

Example 13 (Associated near rough sets) Again, from Example 2, $\Im_{\mathbf{head}}$ is a rough set. Put $\varepsilon = |\Im_{\mathbf{head}}|$. It is then easy to verify that $E_\varepsilon(\Im_{\mathbf{head}}) = \{\Im_1, \Im_2\}$ is a set of all rough sets Y that are near $\Im_{head}$.

Definition 6 (Associated dissimilar rough sets) Let Φ denote a set of functions representing features of objects. Assume that a nonempty set X is rough, i.e., the approximation boundary $Bnd_\Phi(X)$ is not empty. Let $\varepsilon \in (0, \infty]$. The associated nonempty sets of X are dissimilar (apart) sets such that

$$E^\varepsilon(X) = \{Y : |Bnd_\Phi(Y)| > 0, \text{ and } D_{\|\cdot\|}(X, Y) > \varepsilon\}.$$

Proposition 2 *The associated near rough sets of a rough set are near.*

Proof Immediate from Definition 5 and Definition 3 (sufficiently near rough sets).   □

It also possible to characterise rough sets in terms of associated near sets that are not necessarily rough.

Definition 7 (Associated near sets) Let Φ denote a set of functions representing features of objects used to define $\| \cdot \|$ distances between descriptions of points. Let $\varepsilon \in (0, \infty]$. The associated sets of X are sets that are near X such that

$$E_\varepsilon(X) = \{Y : D_{\| \cdot \|}(X, Y) < \varepsilon\}.$$

This is a generalisation of Definition 5.

Example 14 (Associated near sets) In Fig. 8, $E_\varepsilon(\Im_{head})$ is an associated set of near sets, namely, $\{\Im_1, \Im_2\}$. To see this, put $\varepsilon = |\Im_{head}|$ and recall that the Čech distance returns the smallest distance between points in two nonempty sets.

Proposition 3 *The associated near sets of a set are near.*

Proof Let $\varepsilon \in (0, \infty]$. Immediate from Definition 7 and the fact that arbitrary nonempty sets X, Y are sufficiently near, provided $D_{\| \cdot \|}(X, Y) < \varepsilon$. □

Definition 8 (Associated dissimilar sets) Let Φ denote a set of functions representing features of objects used to define $\| \cdot \|$ distances between descriptions of points. Let $\varepsilon \in (0, \infty]$. The associated sets of X contain sets that are not near X (dissimilar) such that

$$E^\varepsilon(X) = \{Y : D_{\| \cdot \|}(X, Y) > \varepsilon\}.$$

Example 15 (Associated dissimilar sets) In Fig. 8, $E^\varepsilon(\Im_3)$ is an associated set of sets Y such that $\Im_3, Y$ are dissimilar, namely, $E^\varepsilon(\Im_3) = \{\Im_1, \Im_2, \Im_{head}\}$. To see this, put $\varepsilon = |\frac{\Im_{head}}{2}|$. The dissimilarity of the sets in the associated set $E^\varepsilon(\Im_3)$ relative to the set $\Im_3$ is due to the varying patterns in the pixel colours for $A \in \{\Im_1, \Im_2, \Im_{head}\}$ such as ■ that sharply contrast with the pixel colours such as ■ in $\Im_3$.

3.1 Strong Containment Property of Associated Rough Sets

In this section, we briefly consider the case where one set shares a property with another set and the one set is contained in the other set. Surprisingly, this is a common occurrence in a series of experiments in natural science or in engineering structures or even in the arts, especially the visual arts.

Definition 9 (Finite strong containment property [15]) Let p be a property defined for sets of real numbers with respect to sets containing them. A is p-contained in B (written $A \underset{p}{\subset} B$), provided A has the property p with respect to B. If $A \subset B$, then p is a finite strong containment property, provided

(p.1) If $A \subset B \subset F$ and p is defined for $A \subset F$, then $A \underset{p}{\subset} F$,
(p.2) If $A \underset{p}{\subset} B \underset{p}{\subset} F, A \underset{p}{\subset} F$,

(p.3) Assume $k \in [0, \infty)$. If for each natural $n \in \mathbb{N}$, $E_n \underset{p}{\subset} F_n$, then $\bigcup_{n=1}^{k} E_n \underset{p}{\subset}$ $\bigcup_{n=1}^{k} F_n$.

Example 16 (Strong containment of rough sets in a digital image) Property p denotes *sufficiently near*. The associated near sets relative to the rough sets in Fig. 8 provide an example of finite strong containment.

Proof (p.1) In Fig. 8, observe that

$$E^{\varepsilon}(\Im_1) \underset{p}{\subseteq} E^{\varepsilon}(\Im_2) \subset E^{\varepsilon}(\Im_{head}).$$

Further, observe that $\Im_1$, $\Im_2$, $\Im_{head}$ are rough sets, where $\Im_{head}$ is rough in relation to the classes covering the entire Kodiak bear in Fig. 1, where p is the property near shared by $\Im_1$ and $\Im_{head}$.

(p.2) $\Leftarrow$ (p.1).

(p.3) Observe that a digital image can be viewed as a set of real numbers, where each real number is a feature value extracted from an image pixel. Let $\Im_{head_n}$ denote a slightly different portion of the head in Fig. 1. For each $n \in \mathbb{N}$, $E_n^{\varepsilon}(\Im_n) \underset{p}{\subseteq} E^{\varepsilon}(\Im_{head_n})$, then $\bigcup_{n=1}^{k} E_n^{\varepsilon}(\Im_n) \underset{p}{\subseteq} \bigcup_{n=1}^{k} E^{\varepsilon}(\Im_{head_n})$. $\qquad\square$

4 Case Study: Image Analysis

This section offers a brief study of the similarities and dissimilarities of identification numbers displayed in different aircraft images. This is accomplished by bringing together what we have presented so far, namely, discovery of rough sets that consist of pixels found in a part of digital image zoomed $\times 1000$ and the use of the Čech distance between pairs of sets in determining the closeness or apartness image descriptions.

To accomplish this, we measure the distance between tolerance rough sets contained in subimages in a selection of 1074 aircraft images in the Caltech image database.[4] In computing distances between descriptions of pixels in pairs of images, two features are considered, namely, pixel greyscale intensity[5] and pixel gradient.[6]

---

[4]The Caltech image database contains large collections of images of front and rear views of automobiles, side view of motorcycles and aircraft, front view of faces, top view of leaves as well as 550 images of various scenes, gadgets, toys, offices, and Pasadena houses in 101 categories (available at http://www.vision.caltech.edu/html-files/archive.html).

[5]In an RGB colour space where individual pixel colours are a mixture of varying amounts of the R (red), green (G) and blue (B) primary colours. A pixel greyscale intensity i is computed using $i = \frac{R+G+B}{3}$.

[6]A common way to measure pixel gradient is to pick a pixel g in location (x, y) in a small $n \times n$ subimage in a greyscale image (usually, a 3×3 subimage). Then estimate the centre pixel gradient g_x in the x-direction and g_y in the y-direction and use

$$\alpha(x, y) = \tan^{-1}\left[\frac{g_y}{g_x}\right].$$

| 9 1: Aircraft 1 | 9.2: Aircraft 2 | 9.3: Aircraft 3 | 9.4: Aircraft 4 |

| 9.5: Aircraft 5 | 9.6: Aircraft 6 | 9.7: Aircraft 7 | 9.8: Aircraft 8 |

Fig. 9 Sample aircraft from the Caltech database

Fig. 10 Aircraft test id numbers extracted from Fig. 9

| 10.1: Tid 1 | 10.2: Tid 2 | 10.3: Tid 3 | 10.4: Tid 4 |

| 10.5: Tid 5 | 10.6: Tid 6 | 10.7: Tid 7 | 10.8: Tid 8 |

This case study is carried out in terms of sections of the aircraft in the eight (8) test images in Fig. 9. From the eight images in Fig. 9, we extract the aircraft sections containing id numbers[7] shown in Fig. 10. These images are used as *test* images for similarity comparisons. Observe that each of the eight images in Fig. 10 are rough sets. This can be verified by comparing the description of the pixels in each tail section with the pixels in the entire aircraft containing the tail section. That is, that are many classes contain pixels that are partly in and partly outside each tail section. In the effect, the approximations of the tail sections have nonempty boundaries.

In addition, we use a different set of aircraft images (ten images shown in Fig. 11) as *query* images. We then extract the aircraft sections containing id numbers shown

---

For a detailed explanation of how to determine g_x, g_y, see, e.g., [51, Sect. 3.6.4].

[7]The id letters *KGB* in Fig 9.4 have been whimsically inverted by the aircraft owner (see, also, Fig. 10.4).

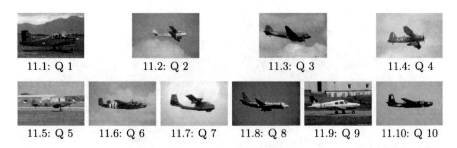

Fig. 11 Sample aircraft macro-query images

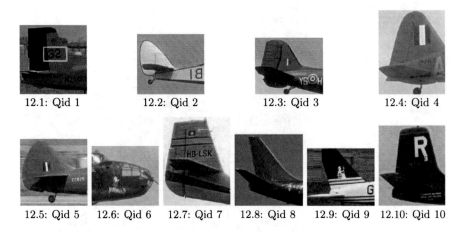

Fig. 12 Micro-query id images extracted from Fig. 11

in Fig. 12. This work leads to the discovery of associated sets that shed light on particular rough sets.

Table 2 gives the Čech distance measurements using the APm toolset.[8] From the Table, we can extract a number of associated sets. For conciseness, we consider only associated near sets. That is, for a set X, $E_\varepsilon(X)$ denotes an associated set, where each pair X, Y are sufficiently near each other.

Example 17 (Associated near rough sets) From Table 2, we obtain the following associated sets. For convenient reference in this example, the query images in the left hand column in Table 2 are denoted by $Q1, \ldots, Q10$ from Fig. 12 and the test images are denoted by $T1, \ldots, T8$ from Fig. 10. What follows is the enumeration of associated set of test images with each query image.

---

[8]APm is available at http://wren.ece.umanitoba.ca. *Caution*: In attempting to reproduce results shown in Table 2, the actual values will vary from the reported nearness measurements, depending on an image region that is selected.

Table 2 Čech distance measurements, $\varepsilon = 32$

$Q \backslash T_i$	T_1	T_2	T_3	T_4	T_5	T_6	T_7	T_8
	D(Q,T1)	D(Q,T2)	D(Q,T3)	D(Q,T4)	D(Q,T5)	D(Q,T6)	D(Q,T7)	D(Q,T8)
	0.0	2.92	1.53	122.07	2.99	4.43	20.06	24.47
	1.59	104.94	90.16	70.76	80.17	37.6	16.28	89.75
	61.51	103.13	86.01	7.6	15.40	3.75	7.72	113.97
	10.72	46.34	38.97	118.89	13.15	7.54	15.58	6.99
	19.94	119.67	58.46	73.59	3.12	7.14	28.54	93.03
	22.15	40.52	79.06	148.28	76.41	33.15	30.35	16.11
	27.39	67.76	51.35	85.26	0.27	1.76	18.91	71.99
	47.37	18.97	6.39	188.38	67.43	12.8	15.66	3.93
	98.55	137.48	116.05	63.95	95.02	21.49	9.81	103.28
	19.14	3.66	2.92	188.27	65.03	4.86	5.99	19.14

obs.1 Q1 = , and

$$E_\varepsilon(Q1) = \{T1, T2, T3, T5, T6, T7, T8\},$$

$$= \{ \text{}, \text{}, \text{}, \text{}, \text{}, \text{} \}.$$

obs.2 Q2 = , and

$$E_\varepsilon(Q2) = \{T1, T7\},$$

$$= \{ , \}.$$

obs.3 Q3 = , and

$$E_\varepsilon(Q3) = \{T4, T5, T6, T7\},$$

$$= \{\qquad,\qquad,\qquad,\qquad\}.$$

obs.4 $Q4 = $ , and

$$E_\varepsilon(Q4) = \{T1, T5, T6, T7, T8\},$$

$$= \{\qquad,\qquad,\qquad,\qquad,\qquad\}.$$

obs.5 $Q5 = $, and

$$E_\varepsilon(Q5) = \{T1, T5, T6, T7\},$$

$$= \{\qquad,\qquad,\qquad,\qquad\}.$$

obs.6 $Q6 = $, and

$$E_\varepsilon(Q6) = \{T1, T7, T8\},$$

$$= \{\qquad,\qquad,\qquad\}.$$

obs.7 $Q7 = $, and

$$E_\varepsilon(Q7) = \{T1, T5, T6, T7\},$$

$$= \{\qquad,\qquad,\qquad,\qquad\}.$$

obs.8 $Q8 = $, and

$$E_\varepsilon(Q8) = \{T2, T3, T6, T7, T8\},$$

$$= \{\qquad,\qquad,\qquad,\qquad,\qquad\}.$$

obs.9 $Q9 =$ 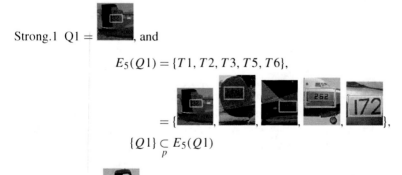, and

$$E_\varepsilon(Q9) = \{T6, T7\},$$

$$= \{ \quad , \quad \}.$$

obs.10 $Q10 =$, and

$$E_\varepsilon(Q10) = \{T2, T3, T6, T7, T8\},$$

$$= \{ \quad , \quad , \quad , \quad , \quad \}.$$

From Example 17, we can discover examples of strong containment.

Example 18 (Strong containment of a rough set in an associated set) Let X denote a nonempty rough set with features

$$\Phi = \{\text{pixel greylevel intensity, pixel gradient}\}$$

and let $E_\varepsilon(X)$ denote the associated near set. Then, property p is defined in the following way for this particular example.

$p \doteq$ *sufficiently near* explained in terms of nearness of members of set

$$\{X, Y : X \in \mathcal{P}(X), Y \in E_\varepsilon(X), D_{\rho_{\|\cdot\|}}(X, Y) < \varepsilon\}.$$

For this example, assume $\varepsilon = 5$. This leads to the following strongly contained sets extracted from Table 2 and Example 17. For the sake of brevity, we consider only the highlighted cases in Table 2.

Strong.1 $Q1 =$, and

$$E_5(Q1) = \{T1, T2, T3, T5, T6\},$$

$$= \{ \quad , \quad , \quad , \quad , \quad \},$$

$$\{Q1\} \underset{p}{\subset} E_5(Q1)$$

Strong.2 $Q10 =$, and

$$E_5(Q10) = \{T2, T3, T6\},$$

$$= \{ \quad , \quad , \quad \},$$

$$E_5(Q1) \cup E_5(Q10) = \{ \quad , \quad , \quad , \quad \},$$

$$F_5(Q1 \cup Q10) \doteqdot E_5(Q1) \cup E_5(Q10), \quad \text{then}$$

$$\{Q1\} \underset{p}{\subset} E_5(Q1) \subset F_5(Q1 \cup Q10)\}$$

In this case, the property p is a finite strong containment property relative to the set $Q1$ and the associated sets $E_5(Q1)$, $F_5(Q1 \cup Q10)$. From this observation, we gain additional knowledge about $Q1$ in terms of the images in the associated set $E_5(Q1)$.

Remark 3 (Patterns in associated sets) A number of benefits accrue from the discovery of associated sets of a set (see, e.g., [17]). Principal among these benefits is the extraction of patterns present in the comparisons between a particular set and the members in an associated set. For example, one can observe in $E_5(Q10)$ in Example 18, that the shape of the tail section in

$$Q10 =$$

calls attention to a similar shape pattern in each of the tail sections in the associated set (see, e.g., case Strong.2), if one considers the leading tail section edges. It can also be observed that parts of the id number in Q10 have configurations that are similar to the id numbers of each of the tail sections in the associated set. In addition, one can observe in the query image greylevel intensity patterns shared by the members of the lower associated set.

5 Concluding Remarks

This chapter introduces the study of the nearness of associated rough sets to particular sets. In each case, the illustrations of these structures is in terms of members of an associated set that are rough sets. The focus in this chapter has been on visual rough sets, since there are many applications of associated visual rough sets. We have given one such application, namely, image analysis. Future work will include the study of pattern recognition problems connected with associated sets whose members are compared descriptively as well as a study of additional types of associated sets and the finite strong containment one set in another set by virtue of a property shared by a pair of sets.

Acknowledgements Many thanks to S. Tiwari, S.A. Naimpally, M. Borkowski, A. Skowron and P. Wasilewski for their insights concerning a number of topics in this paper. This research has been supported by the Natural Sciences and Engineering Research Council of Canada (NSERC) research grants 185986 and 194376.

References

1. Pawlak, Z.: Classification of objects by means of attributes. Pol. Acad. Sci. **429** (1981)
2. Pawlak, Z.: Rough sets. Int. J. Comput. Inf. Sci. **11**, 341–356 (1982)
3. Pawlak, Z.: Information Systems. Theoretical Foundations. WNT, Warsaw (1983) (in Polish)
4. Pawlak, Z.: Rough Sets. Theoretical Aspects of Reasoning About Data. Kluwer Academic, Dordrecht (1991)
5. Pawlak, Z., Skowron, A.: Rudiments of rough sets. Inf. Sci. **177**, 3–27 (2007)
6. Pawlak, Z., Skowron, A.: Rough sets: some extensions. Inf. Sci. **177**, 28–40 (2007)
7. Pawlak, Z., Skowron, A.: Rough sets and Boolean reasoning. Inf. Sci. **177**, 41–73 (2007)
8. Peters, J.F.: Near sets. Special theory about nearness of objects. Fundam. Inform. **75**(1–4), 407–433 (2007)
9. Peters, J.F.: Near sets. General theory about nearness of objects. Appl. Math. Sci. **1**(53), 2609–2629 (2007)
10. Peters, J.F.: Near sets. Toward approximation space-based object recognition. In: Proc. 2nd Int. Conf. on Rough Sets and Knowledge Technology (RSKT 2007), Joint Rough Set Symposium (JRS 2007). Lecture Notes in Artificial Intelligence, vol. 4482, pp. 23–33. Springer, Heidelberg (2007)
11. Pawlak, Z., Peters, J.F.: Jak blisko. Systemy Wspomagania Decyzji **I**, 57 (2007)
12. Coble, A.B.: Associated sets of points. Trans. Am. Math. Soc. **24**(1), 1–20 (1922)
13. Zahorski, Z.: Sur la première dérivée. Trans. Am. Math. Soc. **69**, 1–54 (1950)
14. Bruckner, A.M.: On characterizing classes of functions in terms of associated sets. Can. Math. Bull. **10**(2), 227–231 (1967)
15. Agronsky, S.J.: A generalization of a theorem of Maximoff and applications. Trans. Am. Math. Soc. **273**(2), 767–779 (1982)
16. Petrakiev, I.: On self-associated sets of points in small projective spaces. Commun. Algebra **37**(2), 397–405 (2009)
17. Peters, J.F., Tiwari, S.: Associated near sets. Theory and application. Demo. Math. (2011), communicated
18. Marcus, S.: Tolerance rough sets, Cech topologies, learning processes. Bull. Pol. Acad. Sci. Ser. Sci. Tech. **42**(3)
19. Skowron, A., Stepaniuk, J.: Tolerance approximation spaces. Fundam. Inform. **27**, 245–253 (1996)
20. Ramanna, S., Meghdadi, A., Peters, J.F.: Nature-inspired framework for measuring visual image resemblance: a near rough set approach. Theor. Comput. Sci. **412**(42), 5926–5938 (2011). doi:10.1016/j.tcs.2011.05.044
21. Ramanna, S., Peters, J.F., Wu, W.Z.: Content-based image retrieval: perceptually near tolerance rough set approach. J. Zhejiang Ocean Univ. **29**(5), 62–471 (2010)
22. Ramanna, S.: Discovering image similarities: tolerance near set approach. In: Pal, S., Peters, J.F. (eds.) Rough Fuzzy Image Analysis. Foundations and Methodologies, pp. 12.1–12.15. CRC Press, Boca Raton (2010)
23. Ramanna, S.: Perceptually near Pawlak partitions. Trans. Rough Sets XII **6190**, 170–191 (2010)
24. Ramanna, S.: Near tolerance rough sets. Appl. Math. Sci. **5**(38), 1895–1902 (2011)
25. Dee, H.M., Velastin, S.A.: How close are we to solving the problem of automated visual surveillance? Mach. Vis. Appl. (2007). doi:10.1007/s00138-007-0077-z

26. Madduma, B., Ramanna, S.: Content-based image authentication framework with semi-fragile hybrid watermark scheme. In: International Conference on Man-Machine Interactions (ICMMI2011), pp. 239–247. Springer, Berlin (2011)

27. Atrey, P.K., Ibrahim, H., Hossain, M.A., Ramanna, S., Saddik, A.E.: Determining trust in media-rich websites using semantic similarity. Multimed. Tools Appl. **29**(5), 62–471 (2011). doi:10.1007/s11042-011-0798-x

28. Zhou, X., Zhou, X., Chen, L., Shu, Y., Bouguettaya, A., Taylor, J.A.: Adaptive subspace symbolization for content-based video detection. IEEE Trans. Knowl. Data Eng. **22**, 1372–1387 (2010)

29. Čech, E.: Topological Spaces. Wiley, New York (1966). Revised edn. by Z. Frolik and M. Katătov

30. Hausdorff, F.: Set Theory. AMS, Providence (1914)

31. Peters, J.F.: Sufficiently near sets of neighbourhoods. In: Rough Sets and Knowledge Technology (RSKT2011). LNCS, vol. 6954, pp. 17–24. Springer, Berlin (2011)

32. Peters, J.F., Borkowski, M.: ε-near collections. In: Rough Sets and Knowledge Technology (RSKT2011). LNCS, vol. 6954, pp. 533–542. Springer, Berlin (2011)

33. Sutherland, W.A.: Introduction to Metric & Topological Spaces, 2nd edn. Oxford University Press, Oxford (2009).

34. Beer, G.: Topologies on Closed and Closed Convex Sets. Kluwer Academic, Dordrecht (1993)

35. Henry, C.J., Ramanna, S.: Parallel computation in finding near neighbourhoods. In: Rough Sets and Knowledge Technology (RSKT2011), pp. 523–532. Springer, Berlin (2011)

36. Wolski, M.: Perception and classification. A note on near sets and rough sets. Fundam. Inform. **101**, 143–155 (2010). doi:10.3233/FI-2010-281

37. Peters, J.F., Wasilewski, P.: Foundations of near sets. Inf. Sci. **179**, 3091–3109 (2009)

38. Henry, C.J.: Near sets: theory and applications. Ph.D. dissertation, supervisor: J.F. Peters, Department of Electrical & Computer Engineering (2010)

39. Pal, S.K., Peters, J.F.: Rough Fuzzy Image Analysis. Foundations and Methodologies. Chapman & Hall/CRC Press Mathematical & Computational Imaging Sciences. CRC Press, Boca Raton (2010)

40. Peters, J.F.: Metric spaces for near sets. Appl. Math. Sci. **5**(2), 73–78 (2011)

41. Peters, J.F., Naimpally, S.A.: Approach spaces for near filters. Gen. Math. Notes **2**(1), 159–164 (2011)

42. Peters, J.F., Tiwari, S.: Approach merotopies and near filters. Gen. Math. Notes **3**(1), 1–15 (2011)

43. Hassanien, A.E., Abraham, A., Peters, J.F., Schaefer, G., Henry, C.: Rough sets and near sets in medical imaging: a review. IEEE Trans. Inf. Technol. Biomed. **13**(6), 955–968 (2009). doi:10.1109/TITB.2009.2017017

44. Peters, J.F., Puzio, L.: Image analysis with anisotropic wavelet-based nearness measures. Int. J. Comput. Intell. Syst. **2**(3), 168–183 (2009). doi:10.1016/j.ins.2009.04.018

45. Peters, J.F.: Tolerance near sets and image correspondence. Int. J. Bio-Inspired Comput. **1**(4), 239–245 (2009)

46. Peters, J.F.: Corrigenda and addenda: tolerance near sets and image correspondence. Int. J. Bio-Inspired Comput. **2**(5), 310–318 (2010)

47. Henry, C., Peters, J.F.: Image pattern recognition using approximation spaces and near sets. In: Proc. 11th Int. Conf. on Rough Sets, Fuzzy Sets, Data Mining and Granular Computing (RSFDGrC 2007), Joint Rough Set Symposium (JRS 2007). Lecture Notes in Artificial Intelligence, vol. 4482, pp. 475–482. Springer, Heidelberg (2007)

48. Henry, C., Peters, J.F.: Near set image in an objective image segmentation evaluation framework. In: GEOBIA 2008 Pixels, Objects, Intelligence. GEOgraphic Object Based Image Analysis for the 21st Century, University of Calgary, Alberta, pp. 1–6 (2008)

49. Peters, J.F.: Classification of objects by means of features. In: Proc. IEEE Symposium Series on Foundations of Computational Intelligence (IEEE SCCI 2007), Honolulu, Hawaii, pp. 1–8 (2007)

50. Naimpally, S.A.: Proximity Spaces. Cambridge University Press, Cambridge (1970)
51. Gonzales, R.C., Woods, R.E.: Digital Image Processing, 3rd edn. Prentice Hall, Upper Saddle River (2008)

Contributor's Biography

Haider Banka joined in the Department of Computer Science and Engineering, Indian School of Mines, Dhanbad an Assistant Professor in the year 2007. He has worked as a visiting Assistant Professor in the Center for Soft Computing Research, Indian Statistical Institute and was a visiting research scholar at the same unit for one year. He has also worked as a visiting Research Associate in the Department of Computer and Information Science (DISI), University of Genoa, Italy, for three months in the year of 2006. He was a Senior Research Fellow at Machine Intelligence Unit, Indian Statistical Institute, Kolkata, for 2 years from April 2004 to March 2006. Dr. H. Banka is a reviewer of many international journals and conferences including IEEE Transactions on Systems, Man, and Cybernetics: Part A, Part B, and Part C, Pattern Recognition, Information Sciences, International Journal of Pattern Recognition and Artificial Intelligence, Pattern Recognition Letters and many others. His area of interest includes soft computing, machine learning and bioinformatics.

Parag Bhalchandra received the B.Sc. (1998) and M.Sc. (2001) degrees in Computer Science from Dr. B.A.M. University, Aurangabad, MS, India and University Grants Commission's SET-NET qualifications in Computer Science in 2002. He has also completed M.Phil. in Computer Science from V.R.F. University, Salem, TN, India in 2009. He is currently a doctoral candidate and an Assistant Professor at the School of Computational Sciences, S.R.T.M. University, Nanded, MS, India. Prior to this, he worked as a Lecturer in the Department of Computer Science, Yogeshwari Mahavidyalaya, Ambajogai, MS, India from 2001–2009. His research interests include Algorithm Analysis, Data Mining, and Information and Communication Technology.

Cory J. Butz received the B.Sc., M.Sc., and Ph.D. degrees in computer science from the University of Regina, Saskatchewan, Canada in 1994, 1996 and 2000, respectively. He joined the School of Information Technology and Engineering at the University of Ottawa, Ontario, Canada as an Assistant Professor in 2000. In 2001, he joined the Computer Science Department at the University of Regina, Regina, Saskatchewan, Canada. He was promoted to Associate Professor in 2003 and to Professor in 2010. His research interests include uncertainty reasoning, database systems, information retrieval, and data mining.

G. Peters et al. (eds.), *Rough Sets: Selected Methods and Applications in Management and Engineering*, Advanced Information and Knowledge Processing,
DOI 10.1007/978-1-4471-2760-4, © Springer-Verlag London Limited 2012

Fernando A. Crespo graduated in Industrial and Mathematical Engineering from the University of Chile, Faculty of Physical and Mathematical Science, and he completed his Doctoral Degree in the Catholic University of Chile in Operational Research and Operations Management. He lived one year in the Colombian Caribbean working in the Universidad del Norte, Barranquilla. He is Associate Professor in the University of Valparaiso, Chile. He works and he was a founder of EURO Working Group to Development since 2004. His main research is focused in the areas of Operational Research, Data Mining, Applied Statistics, Operational Research for development and methodologies to make innovation in small and medium enterprises.

M. Gordon Hunter is a Professor Information Systems in the Faculty of Management, University of Lethbridge, Alberta, Canada. He has been appointed Visiting Professor, London South Bank University. He has held visiting positions at universities in Australia, England, Germany, Monaco, New Zealand, Poland, Turkey, and USA. In 2009 Gordon was a Fellow at the Munich University of Applied Sciences, Germany. During 2005 Gordon was an Erskine Fellow at the University of Canterbury, Christchurch, New Zealand. Gordon's research approach takes a qualitative perspective employing Personal Construct Theory and Narrative Inquiry to conduct in depth interviews. He applies qualitative techniques in interdisciplinary research such as small business, agricultural management, governance of intellectual assets, and cross-cultural investigations. His current research interests in the information systems (IS) area include the effective management of IS personnel; the role of Chief Information Officers; and the use of IS by small business.

Pawan Lingras is a Professor in the Department of Mathematics and Computing Science at Saint Mary's University, Halifax, Canada. His undergraduate education from Indian Institute of Technology, Bombay, India was followed by graduate studies at the University of Regina, Canada. He has authored more than 140 research papers in various international journals and conferences. He has also co-authored a textbook and co-edited a collection of research papers. His areas of interests include artificial intelligence, information retrieval, data mining, web intelligence, and intelligent transportation systems. He has served as the review committee chair, program committee member, and reviewer for various international conferences on artificial intelligence and data mining. He has also served as general workshop chair for IEEE conference on Data Mining (ICDM), and ACM/IEEE/WIC conference Web Intelligence, and Intelligent Agent Technologies (WI/IAT). He is an associate editor of Web Intelligence: An International Journal.

Sushmita Mitra is the Head and a full Professor at the Machine Intelligence Unit, Indian Statistical Institute, Kolkata. From 1992 to 1994 she was in the RWTH, Aachen, Germany as a DAAD Fellow. She was a Visiting Professor in the Computer Science Departments of the University of Alberta, Edmonton, Canada in 2004, 2007; Meiji University, Japan in 1999, 2004, 2005, 2007; and Aalborg University Esbjerg, Denmark in 2002, 2003. Dr. Mitra received the National Talent Search Scholarship (1978–1983) from NCERT, India, the University Gold Medal in 1988, the IEEE TNN Outstanding Paper Award in 1994 for her pioneering work in neuro-fuzzy computing, and the CIMPA-INRIA-UNESCO Fellowship in 1996. She is the author of the books "Neuro-Fuzzy Pattern Recognition: Methods in Soft Computing" and "Data Mining: Multimedia, Soft Computing, and Bioinformatics" published by John Wiley, and "Introduction to Machine Learning and Bioinformatics", Chapman & Hall/CRC Press, beside a host of other edited books. Dr. Mitra has guest edited special issues of several journals, is an Associate Editor of "IEEE/ACM Trans. on Computational Biology and Bioinformatics", "Neurocomputing", and is a Founding Associate Editor of "Wiley Interdisciplinary Reviews: Data Mining and Knowledge Discovery (WIRE DMKD)". She has more than 75 research publications in referred international journals. According to the Science Citation Index (SCI), two of her papers have been ranked 3rd and 15th in the list of Top-cited papers in Engineering Science from India during 1992–2001. Dr. Mitra is a Senior Member of IEEE, and Fellow of the Indian National Academy of Engineering and The National Academy of Sciences, India. She served in the capacity of Program Chair, Tutorial Chair, Plenary Speaker, and as member of programme committees of many international conferences. Her current research interests include data mining, pattern recognition, soft computing, image processing, and bioinformatics.

Georg Peters is a professor in the Department of Computer Sciences and Mathematics at Munich University of Applied Sciences. He received German diploma degrees ($\approx$ M.Sc.) in electrical engineering, industrial engineering and in business administration from RWTH Aachen University. He also obtained a Ph.D. in the field of intelligent data analysis from the same university. Prior to returning to academia Georg Peters worked as a consultant primarily in the telecommunications sector. He has published more than 50 papers in the fields of information systems and soft computing. Currently, his interests include rough approaches to dynamic clustering and applications of soft computing concepts, in particular rough sets, to workflow management. He has also served as reviewer and program committee member for several conferences in the field of soft computing.

James F. Peters, Ph.D., is a Full Professor in the Department of Electrical and Computer Engineering at the University of Manitoba and was a Postdoctoral Fellow, Syracuse University and researcher in the Rome AI Laboratory, Griffiss Air Force Base, New York (1991), Asst. Prof., University of Arkansas, 1991–1994, and Researcher in the Mission Sequencing and Deep Space Telecommunications Division, JPL/Caltech, Pasadena, California (1991–1994). In 1992, he verified the correctness of the command sequencing rules for the NASA TOPEX/Poseidon ocean-monitoring satellite and, in 1993–1994, he worked on a proof of correctness of an antenna controller for the NASA deep space network. His early work at the U of M included Petri net models of satellite subsystems and the design of robotic inspection systems for Manitoba Hydro transmission lines. He was Co-Editor (with E. Orlowska, G. Rosenberg, A. Skowron) of a book entitled New Frontiers in Scientific Discovery, Commemorating the Life and Work of Zdzislaw Pawlak, IOS Press, 2007, and Co-Editor (with S.K. Pal) of a book on rough-fuzzy image analysis published in 2010 by Chapman & Hall/CRC Press. He is the author of over 40 articles published in refereed journals during the past 5 years, including IJICC best journal article awards in 2008 and 2011 and JRS2007 best paper award. He is Co-Editor-in-Chief of the TRS journal, Associate Editor and Editorial Board member of a number of other journals. His main research interests are mereotopology, various forms of sets such as near sets, rough sets, and image analysis.

Sheela Ramanna is a Full Professor and Head of the Applied Computer Science Department at the University of Winnipeg. She received a Ph.D. in Computer Science from Kansas State University, USA and a B.E in Electrical Engineering and M.Tech in Computer Science and Engineering from Osmania University, Hyderabad, India. She is the Managing Editor for Springer Transactions on Rough Sets Journal (TRS). She serves on the Editorial Board of TRS, Journal of Intelligent Decision Technology (IOS Press), Int. Journal of Advanced Intelligent Paradigms (Inderscience), and Journal of Agents and Multi-Agent Systems. She served as Program Co-Chair for RSKT2011, RSCTC2010 and JRS2007. She is currently co-editing a Springer book on Emerging Paradigms in Machine Learning. Her paper on rough control co-authored with James F. Peters received the IFAC Best Paper Award in 1998. Her research interests include theory and applications of rough sets, near sets fuzzy sets, and perceptual systems with emphasis on image analysis.

Beata Sikora received the M.Sc. degree in applied mathematics from the University of Silesia in Katowice, Poland, in 1995, and Ph.D. degree in control engineering from Silesian University of Technology in Gliwice, Poland, in 2002. She is an assistant professor in the Silesian University of Technology, in the Institute of Mathematics. She is a member of the Polish Mathematical Society (PTM). Her scientific interest is controllability theory for linear dynamical systems, in particular the constrained controllability of dynamical systems with delays. Moreover, her current internet is data analysis, especially the analysis of data coming from monitoring systems, and machine learning methods application for natural hazards assessment. She is an author or coauthor of about 20 scientific papers and 3 university textbooks. She reviewed papers for international journals, e.g. International Journal of Robust and Nonlinear Control, Mathematics and Computers in Simulation.

Marek Sikora received the M.Sc. degree in applied mathematics from the University of Silesia in Katowice, Poland, in 1993, and Ph.D. degree in informatics from Silesian University of Technology in Gliwice, Poland, in 2002. He is an assistant professor in the Silesian University of Technology, in the Institute of Informatics, and in the Institute of Innovative Technologies EMAG in Katowice. He is a member of Scientific Council in the Institute of Innovative Technologies EMAG in Katowice. He is a member of the Polish Computer Society (PTI). His scientific interest is in rules induction and evaluation, machine learning, application of intelligent systems in industry, biology and medicine. He is an author or coauthor of more than 50 scientific papers. He reviewed papers for international journals, e.g. Applied Soft Computing, Information Sciences. He was a member of Program Committees for international conferences.

Dominik Ślęzak received his D.Sc. (habilitation) in 2011 from Institute of Computer Science, Polish Academy of Sciences, and his Ph.D. in Computer Science in 2002 from University of Warsaw, Poland. In 2005, he co-founded Infobright Inc., where he is currently working as chief scientist. He also is with Institute of Mathematics, University of Warsaw. He also used to be with University of Regina, SK, Canada, and Polish–Japanese Institute of Information Technology, Warsaw, Poland.

Dominik serves as an associate editor and editorial board member for a number of international scientific journals, including General Systems, Information Sciences, Intelligent Information Systems, Knowledge and Information Systems, and Transactions on Rough Sets. He is frequently chairing international scientific conferences, including the series of multi-conferences on Future Generation Information Technology. He has published over 100 papers for scientific books, journals, and conference proceedings. He has delivered invited lectures in Canada, China, Czech Republic, Egypt, Hungary, India, Japan, Korea, Malaysia, Poland, Russia, Singapore, UK, and US. His research interests include Rough Sets, Granular Computing, Data Mining, and Database Architectures. He is also an executive member of the International Rough Set Society.

Roger Tagg recently retired as a Senior Lecturer in Computer and Information Science at the University of South Australia in Adelaide. After graduating in Mathematics at Cambridge University in 1962, he worked for many years in Operational Research and Systems Analysis for organizations in the UK, Europe and Iran. He became a specialist in database management, and from 1980 worked as an independent consultant, advising on data-oriented development methodologies and information systems strategic planning. He moved into academia in 1994, initially at Massey University, New Zealand, where he led research projects into workflow and inter-organizational computing. More recently he has specialized on improving the individual's interface to his or her workload, involving the use of ontologies to categorize work requests that may arise from several different sources.

Richard Weber is an associate professor at the Department of Industrial Engineering of the University of Chile and academic director of the Ph.D. program on Engineering Systems. He obtained a German diploma ($\approx$ B.Sc. & M.Sc.) in mathematics as well as a master degree and a Ph.D., both in operations research, from RWTH Aachen University. From 1992 to 1998 he worked as data mining consultant for the company Management Intelligenter Technologien GmbH, Aachen. Richard Weber was visiting professor at the University of Osaka in 1992, the University of Tokyo in 2003, and the University of Alberta in 2006. His research interests include data mining, dynamic data mining, and computational intelligence. He serves on the editorial board of the journals "Intelligent Data Analysis" and "Computational Intelligence Research". He has also been a member of various program committees of international conferences. He is senior member of IEEE and member of ACM and INFORMS.

Sebastian Widz received the B.Sc. (2002) and M.Sc. (2004) degrees in Computer Science from Polish-Japanese Institute of Information Technology (PJIIT), Warsaw, Poland. In 2007 he co-founded XPLUS SA where he is currently working as Enterprise Resource Planning Software Technical Lead and Solution Architect. Prior to this he founded Infovision, company specializing in ERP and Business Intelligence implementations. He is currently a Ph.D. student at Polish Academy of Sciences at Systems Research Institute, Warsaw, Poland. He has published a number of papers in international conference proceedings. He is also reviewer for a number of international scientific journals. His research interests include Rough Sets, Genetic Algorithms, Decision Support and Data Mining applied in Business Environment.

Yiyu Yao is a professor of computer science in the Department of Computer Science, University of Regina, Regina, Saskatchewan, Canada. His research interests include information retrieval, rough sets, interval sets, granular computing, Web intelligence, data mining and fuzzy sets. He has published over 200 journal and conference papers. He is an area editor of International Journal of Approximate Reasoning, a member of the editorial boards of the Web Intelligence and Agent Systems journal, Transactions on Rough Sets, Journal of Intelligent Information Systems, Journal of Chongqing University of Posts and Telecommunication, The International Journal of Cognitive Informatics & Natural Intelligence (IJCiNi), International Journal of Software Science and Computational Intelligence (IJSSCI). He has served and is serving as a program co-chair of several international conferences. He is a member of ACM and IEEE.

Index

G. Peters et al. (eds.), *Rough Sets: Selected Methods and Applications in Management and Engineering*, Advanced Information and Knowledge Processing, DOI 10.1007/978-1-4471-2760-4, © Springer-Verlag London Limited 2012

Printed by Publishers' Graphics LLC USA

2012